W9-DCX-637

nutbread and nostalgia

favorite recipes from the junior league of south bend, indiana

the junior league of south bend, inc.
south bend, indiana
1979

PHOTO: BROWN BROTHERS

International Standard Book Number: 0-9607120-0-3

The purpose of The Junior League is exclusively educational and charitable and is: to promote voluntarism; to develop the potential of its members for voluntary participation in community affairs; and to demonstrate the effectiveness of trained volunteers. Proceeds from the sale of *Nutbread and Nostalgia* will be returned to the community through projects sponsored by The Junior League of South Bend.

If you wish to order additional copies, please use the order blanks in the back of the book or write to:

Nutbread and Nostalgia
The Junior League of South Bend, Inc.
P.O. Box 305
South Bend, Indiana 46624

Organizations and retail stores wishing to purchase *Nutbread and Nostalgia* may do so by writing to the above address for additional information.

Copyright © 1979 by The Junior League of South Bend, Inc., South Bend, Indiana. All rights reserved. No part of this publication may be reproduced, stored in a retrieval system, or transmitted, in any form or by any means, electronic, mechanical, photocopying, recording, or otherwise, without the prior written permission of The Junior League of South Bend, Inc. Printed in the United States of America by Petersen Printing Corporation, South Bend, Indiana.

First Printing: June 1979 — 5,000 copies
Second Printing: December 1979 — 4,000 copies
Third Printing: July 1980 — 10,000 copies
Fourth Printing: October 1982 — 10,000 copies
Fifth Printing: August 1985 — 10,000 copies

contents

dedication

To the communities in which our members live and to whom the proceeds from *Nutbread and Nostalgia* will be returned through League sponsored projects.

A very special thank you to an outstanding cookbook committee,
to all of the active and sustaining members, and to our families and friends
whose enthusiastic support, participation, and countless contributions made this book possible.

Dian Holdeman, chairman
Ruth Hubner and Nancy Peil, co-chairmen

introduction

Nutbread and Nostalgia is a collection of carefully chosen recipes, menus and photographs. We have combined treasures from the past with the conveniences of today. Old family recipes handed down from one generation to another are included along with modern day favorites.
The selections were made from hundreds of tested recipes.
We hope you will enjoy the photographs and sprinkling of nineteenth century manners and customs in addition to preparing and serving these dishes to your families and friends.

GROCERIES
MEATS
BRADFORD'S
BRADFORD'S
GROCERIES
MEATS.
IVORY SOAP
YEAST FOAM
IVORY SOAP

hors d'oeuvres and appetizers

"If this book should be the means of bringing into the household, happiness, peace and contentment; if the husband hereafter sits at the table with a smiling and satisfied countenance, and the wife feels less of care and anxiety, then the mission of this book will have been accomplished."

> "Get a husband what he likes,
> And save a thousand household strikes."

hot crab dip

This freezes beautifully!

2 cans (7½ oz. each) crabmeat, drained and flaked
¼ cup sauterne or dry sherry
2 tsp. prepared mustard
2 T. confectioners' sugar
3 pkgs. (8 oz. each) softened cream cheese
½ tsp. garlic salt
1 cup real mayonnaise
2 tsp. onion juice
½ tsp. seasoned salt

In a large saucepan, combine ingredients. Heat, stirring constantly. Serve in a chafing dish with garlic rounds.

Makes 4 cups

crab and artichoke canape

½ cup Russian dressing
¼ tsp. dry mustard
1 can (6½ oz.) crabmeat
2 cans (8½ oz. each) artichoke bottoms, drained
2 T. chopped parsley
lemon wedges

Combine Russian dressing with mustard. Fold in crabmeat gently. Thickly spread mixture onto artichoke bottoms. Brown under broiler. Sprinkle with parsley and serve with lemon wedges. These are easily made ahead of time and refrigerated. Broil at serving time.

Makes 12 canapes

minced clams with cheese on the half shell

2 cans (6½ oz. each) minced clams, drained
1 can (10½ oz.) white clam sauce
½ cup grated Cheddar cheese
⅔ cup Italian-seasoned breadcrumbs
grated Parmesan cheese
paprika
8 clam shells

In a medium bowl, combine clams, clam sauce and cheese. Add breadcrumbs. More or less may be needed, depending on consistency. Mixture should hold together like ground beef. Divide mixture among the 8 shells. Sprinkle generously with Parmesan cheese. Dust lightly with paprika. Place shells on baking sheet. Bake at 350° for 10 to 15 minutes or until hot and bubbly. Serve as a first course with lemon wedges on the side.

Note: If clam sauce is unavailable, substitute clam juice.

Serves 8

oriental shrimp toasts

Crisp-fried with a pungent dipping sauce.

1 can (4½ oz.) tiny shrimp
⅓ cup finely chopped green onions
½ cup drained bamboo shoots, finely chopped
1 clove garlic, minced
½ tsp. salt
1 egg, well beaten
2 T. cornstarch
8 slices white bread, crusts removed
peanut oil for frying

Hot Dipping Sauce:
½ cup soy sauce
1 clove garlic, minced
2 T. dry sherry
¼ tsp. ground ginger
2 T. thinly sliced green onions

In a medium bowl, combine shrimp, onions and bamboo shoots. Mash together until pasty. Add garlic, salt, egg and cornstarch. Mix thoroughly. Cut bread into triangles. Spread one side of each thickly and evenly with shrimp mixture. Set aside while preparing Dipping Sauce.

For Hot Dipping Sauce: In a saucepan, combine ingredients. Heat just to boiling point. Set aside and keep warm.

Heat oil (¾-inch deep) to 375°. Fry triangles, shrimp side down, until golden brown. Turn over and fry until bread side is browned. Drain on absorbent paper. Serve piping hot with Hot Dipping Sauce. The Shrimp Toasts may be frozen after frying, then reheated at 325° for 8 to 10 minutes.

Serves 8 to 10

colle-de-creve (paste of shrimp)

2½ cups water
2 tsp. lemon juice
2 tsp. salt
1 lb. frozen shrimp pieces, thawed
1 cup real mayonnaise
⅓ cup crumbled blue cheese
1 T. horseradish
juice of ½ lemon (1½T.)
1 tsp. Worcestershire sauce
2 drops Tabasco

In a large saucepan, bring water, lemon juice and salt to a boil. Add shrimp. Bring just to the boiling point. Remove from heat and drain. In a bowl, mix mayonnaise, blue cheese, horseradish, lemon juice, Worcestershire sauce and Tabasco. Stir in drained shrimp pieces *very gently*. Season with salt and pepper to taste. Serve with crackers.

Makes 3 cups

salmon party ball

1 can (1 lb.) salmon
1 pkg. (8 oz.) softened cream cheese
1 T. lemon juice
2 T. grated onion
1 tsp. prepared horseradish
¼ tsp. salt
¼ tsp. liquid smoke
½ cup chopped pecans
3 T. chopped fresh parsley

Drain salmon. Flake and remove skin and bones. Combine with cream cheese, lemon juice, grated onion, horseradish, salt and liquid smoke. Mix thoroughly. Cover and chill several hours. Combine pecans and parsley. Shape salmon mixture into a ball. Roll in pecan-parsley mixture. Chill. Serve with crackers.

Serves 8 to 10

hot shrimp sandwiches

1 can (4¼ oz.) small shrimp
1 tsp. lemon juice
1 pkg. (8 oz.) softened cream cheese
1 tsp. finely chopped onion
⅛ tsp. minced garlic
10 slices white bread, crusts removed, or 20 small dinner rolls, sliced in half

In a medium bowl, combine shrimp, lemon juice, cream cheese, onion and garlic. Mix until soft and creamy. Spread filling evenly on five of the bread slices or bottom half of the rolls. Press tops on gently. Cut bread into quarters. Place on cookie sheet. Bake at 350° for 8 to 10 minutes. Serve warm.

Makes 20 canapes

marinated artichokes with curry dip

3 cans (8½ oz. each) artichoke hearts, drained
¼ cup wine vinegar
¾ cup olive oil
minced garlic to taste
chopped parsley to taste

Curry Dip:
1 cup mayonnaise
1 cup sour cream
1 tsp. curry powder
2 T. lemon or lime juice

Cut artichokes in half and place in a bowl. Combine vinegar, olive oil, garlic and parsley. Pour over artichokes. Marinate for several hours in refrigerator, turning occasionally.

For Curry Dip: Combine ingredients and spoon into a serving bowl. Set on a platter and surround with drained, marinated artichoke hearts. Pass toothpicks for dipping.

Serves 8 to 10

asparagus-blue cheese roll-ups

15 slices white bread, crusts removed
½ lb. blue cheese, crumbled
1 pkg. (8 oz.) softened cream cheese
1 egg, beaten
1 T. real mayonnaise
1 can (15 oz.) asparagus spears
melted butter
caraway seeds

With a rolling pin, roll the bread slices flat. Beat together blue cheese, cream cheese, egg and mayonnaise. Spread on bread slices. Lay an asparagus spear on each and roll up jelly roll style. Cut each roll into 3 pieces, using a very sharp knife. Brush with melted butter and sprinkle with caraway seeds. Bake on an ungreased baking sheet at 350° for 15 minutes. Serve hot. These may be prepared early in the day, refrigerated, then baked at serving time.

Makes 45 roll-ups

asparagus vinaigrette

Especially nice served as a first course.

36-42 asparagus spears, trimmed
1 hard-cooked egg, sieved and divided
1 T. Dijon mustard
1 T. finely chopped shallots or green onions
salt and freshly ground black pepper to taste
½ cup vegetable oil
1 T. white wine vinegar
⅓ cup freshly chopped parsley
leaf lettuce

Simmer asparagus until just tender, being careful not to overcook. Drain and chill. In a small bowl, combine *half* of the sieved egg, mustard, shallots, salt and pepper. Slowly add vinegar and oil, stirring. Arrange a leaf of lettuce on each of six plates. Place asparagus spears on top. Spoon sauce over asparagus. Sprinkle with parsley and remaining sieved egg. May be served chilled or at room temperature.

Serves 6

guacamole dip

Versatile!

2 very ripe avocados, mashed
1 medium tomato, chopped
1 medium onion, chopped
6 slices bacon, fried crisp and crumbled
1 tsp. dried red pepper, crushed
2 tsp. lemon juice
1 tsp. salt

In a bowl, combine ingredients. Serve with corn chips or tortilla chips for dipping.

Variation: Guacamole also may be served over a tomato and lettuce salad. Or make a sandwich of Guacamole, sliced tomatoes, alfalfa sprouts, Monterey Jack cheese and lettuce on crusty dark bread.

Makes 2 cups

laura's marinated vegetables

Everyone will ask for the recipe!

2 medium red onions, thinly sliced
1 can (6 oz.) large, pitted black olives, drained
1 large head broccoli, cut into flowerets
1 head cauliflower, cut into flowerets
1 lb. fresh mushroom caps, cleaned

Marinade:
1⅓ cups vinegar
⅔ cup vegetable oil
3 T. lemon juice
½ cup sugar
2 tsp. oregano
1 tsp. salt
½ tsp. pepper
dash Tabasco

In a large bowl, combine ingredients for Marinade. Stir to dissolve the sugar. Add vegetables and stir gently to coat well with Marinade. Refrigerate for several hours, or overnight, stirring occasionally. At serving time, drain and arrange on a plate with the broccoli forming a "wreath" around the other vegetables. Serve with toothpicks.

Variation: You may substitute or add 1-pound fresh or frozen shrimp and cherry tomatoes. Add tomatoes at serving time. Serve as a luncheon salad.

Serves 8 to 10

spinach-filled mushrooms

A delicious hot hors d'oeuvre. Equally nice served as a side dish to a steak or standing rib roast.

16-20 large, fresh mushrooms
3 T. butter
1 cup finely chopped onion
1 pkg. (10 oz.) frozen chopped spinach, thawed
½ cup grated Swiss cheese
grated Parmesan cheese
salt and pepper to taste

Clean mushrooms. Remove stems and chop finely. In a large skillet, melt butter. Saute chopped mushroom stems and onion until tender but not brown. Drain spinach and squeeze dry. Add to mushroom-onion mixture. Stir to mix thoroughly. Add Swiss cheese, stirring lightly. Remove from heat. Fill mushroom caps with mixture. Sprinkle with Parmesan cheese. Place in a buttered, shallow baking dish. Bake at 300° for 15 to 20 minutes. Serve warm.

Serves 8 to 10

spanakopeta

In Greek, Spinach Triangles. These can be stored in the freezer and taken out as needed.

4 pkgs. (10 oz. each) frozen chopped spinach
1 pkg. (8 oz.) softened cream cheese
1 lb. feta cheese
1 small onion, finely chopped
4 eggs, lightly beaten
3 T. olive oil
1 tsp. salt
pepper
1 tsp. dill weed (optional)
2 lbs. filo dough (see Note)
1 lb. melted butter

Thaw spinach; drain and squeeze dry with paper towels. Chop very fine. In a bowl, combine cream cheese, feta cheese and onion; stir in spinach. Add eggs, olive oil, salt and pepper. Add dill, if desired. Blend thoroughly. (Spinach mixture can be done in the food processor.) To make triangles, use one sheet of the filo dough, short end toward you. Brush butter on with a pastry brush, preferably a feather one. Fold in half and brush with butter again. Cut folded sheet into 3-inch wide, even strips. (Keep remaining dough covered with wax paper and a damp cloth to prevent drying.) Place 1 teaspoon of spinach mixture at end of each strip and fold one corner over to make a triangle. Fold dough from side to side in the shape of a triangle until you reach end of strip. Place on ungreased baking sheet. Repeat. Bake at 350° for 20 minutes. Serve hot. Spanakopetas can be frozen up to two months. Place unbaked triangles in plastic container, separating layers with wax paper; cover and freeze. When ready to serve, place frozen triangles on ungreased baking sheet and bake, allowing additional baking time.

Note: Filo (or phyllo) dough can be found in specialty food stores and some bakeries. If frozen, dough must be thawed for several hours before unwrapping. Strudel dough may be substituted.

Makes 200

cheesy mushrooms on rye

1 pkg. (8 oz.) softened cream cheese
2 egg yolks
1½ tsp. grated onion
seasoned salt
1 oz. blue cheese, crumbled
18 party rye slices
½ lb. fresh mushrooms, cleaned and sliced
paprika

Combine cream cheese, egg yolks, onion, salt and blue cheese. Place a mushroom slice on each rye slice. Spread cheese mixture on top. Sprinkle with paprika. Broil until lightly brown and bubbly. Serve immediately.

Makes 18 canapes

spicy beef dip

Men love this!

1 lb. ground beef
½ cup chopped onion
1 clove garlic, minced
1 can (8 oz.) tomato sauce
¼ cup ketchup
¾ tsp. oregano
1 tsp. sugar
1 pkg. (8 oz.) softened cream cheese
⅓ cup Parmesan cheese

In a large skillet, cook ground beef, onion and garlic until beef is lightly browned and onion is tender. Spoon off excess fat. Stir in tomato sauce, ketchup, oregano and sugar. Cover and simmer for 10 minutes. Remove from heat. Stir in cream cheese and Parmesan cheese until melted. Serve immediately with tortilla chips.

Makes 3 cups

dried beef dip

Serve hot or cold, depending on the season.

1 pkg. (4 oz.) dried beef, cut into thin slices
2 pkgs. (8 oz. each) softened cream cheese
1 cup sour cream
4 T. minced onion
4 T. milk
1 cup pecan pieces
4 T. butter

In a large bowl, combine dried beef, cream cheese, sour cream, onion and milk. In a skillet, saute pecans in butter until lightly browned. Stir pecans and butter into cream cheese mixture. Cover and refrigerate several hours before serving. Serve with crackers. The dip may also be baked at 350° for 20 minutes and served hot.

Makes 3 cups

meatballs in sour cream sauce

1½ lbs. ground beef
1 small onion, minced
¼ tsp. each: oregano, thyme, pepper
½ tsp. celery salt
1 tsp. salt
1 egg
2 T. butter
flour
2½ cups water, divided
3 beef bouillon cubes
1 T. soy sauce
3 T. flour
½ cup sour cream

In a large mixing bowl, combine beef, onion, seasonings and egg. Blend well. Form into balls using 1 teaspoon as measure. Melt butter in large skillet. Roll meatballs in flour and brown on all sides in skillet. Remove. In same skillet, add 2 cups of the water, bouillon cubes and soy sauce. Bring to boil. Meanwhile, blend flour with remaining ½ cup water. Add to boiling bouillon mixture, stirring constantly. Lower heat. When sauce is thickened, add meatballs. Simmer 15 minutes. Remove from heat and stir in sour cream. Serve immediately.

Makes 3 dozen

pork balls in oriental barbecue sauce

Pork Balls:
2 lbs. ground pork sausage
1 egg, slightly beaten
2 T. grated lemon peel
1 tsp. nutmeg
⅛ tsp. ground cloves
½ cup breadcrumbs
dash cayenne pepper

Oriental Barbecue Sauce:
⅔ cup brown sugar
2 T. lemon juice
2 T. cider vinegar
2 tsp. soy sauce
¼ tsp. dry mustard
⅛ tsp. ginger
⅓ cup water
1 T. cornstarch

For Pork Balls: In a large mixing bowl, thoroughly mix all ingredients. Shape into ¾-inch balls. Place on wire rack in shallow roasting pan. Bake at 350° for 20 minutes, or until juices are clear.

For Oriental Barbecue Sauce: In small saucepan, combine all ingredients. Bring to a boil. Reduce heat and simmer 2 to 3 minutes until sauce thickens. Pour over Pork Balls in chafing dish. Serve warm with toothpicks. The baked Pork Balls may be frozen and reheated at 350° for 20 to 25 minutes. Sauce may be prepared a day ahead.

Serves 10 to 12

water chestnut-bacon wrap

Serve in a chafing dish and they will stay warm and tasty!

1½ 8 oz.-cans water chestnuts
1 lb. lean bacon strips, cut into thirds
½ cup ketchup
6 T. brown sugar
2 T. vinegar
2 T. prepared mustard

Cut whole water chestnuts in half, no smaller than a marble. Wrap ⅓ slice of bacon around each chestnut half and fasten with a toothpick. Place on rack in broiler pan. Bake at 350° for 30 minutes, or until bacon is cooked. Remove and place in a shallow casserole. In a small bowl, combine ketchup, brown sugar, vinegar and mustard. Pour mixture over bacon-wrapped chestnuts. Return to 350° oven and bake 30 minutes. Sauce should be thick but not browned.

Serves 8 to 12

bacon and onion canape

4 slices dry white bread, crusts removed, or 16 party rye slices
2 T. softened butter
1 medium onion, thinly sliced
4 slices bacon, fried crisp and crumbled
½ cup real mayonnaise
1 T. grated Parmesan cheese
Dijon mustard, to taste (optional)

Cut trimmed bread slices into squares or circles. Spread with softened butter. Place a slice of onion on each. Top with crumbled bacon. Combine mayonnaise, Parmesan cheese and mustard. Spread carefully over bacon to edges. Broil until brown and bubbly. Serve immediately.

Variation: Shaved ham and thin slivers of Muenster cheese may be substituted for the bacon.

Makes 16 canapes

caviar mousse

Delicious, and easy to prepare!

1 envelope unflavored gelatin
1 cup water, divided
1 cup small curd cottage cheese
½ cup sour cream
½ cup real mayonnaise
3 T. chopped chives
2 tsp. lemon juice
1 jar (3½ oz.) small, pink lumpfish caviar
1 hard-cooked egg, sieved

Soften gelatin in ⅓ cup of the cold water. Boil remaining ⅔ cup water and add to gelatin. In a blender, mix gelatin mixture, cottage cheese, sour cream and mayonnaise. By hand, stir in chives, lemon juice and caviar. Pour into a lightly oiled 4-cup mold. Chill until firm, about 2 to 4 hours. Unmold and garnish with sieved egg. Serve with crackers.

Variation: Substitute ½ cup finely chopped shrimp or crabmeat.

Serves 8 to 10

scotch eggs

A tradition in English pubs.

1 lb. ground pork sausage
1 T. chopped mixed herbs
salt and pepper to taste
8 small hard-cooked eggs, peeled and dried
flour
1 egg, well beaten
1 cup dry white breadcrumbs
vegetable oil for frying

Mix sausage with herbs, salt and pepper in a bowl. Divide into 8 equal portions. On a dampened board, pat meat into rounds. Place an egg on each. Fold sausage around eggs, covering completely and evenly. Roll each in flour. Brush with egg and coat well with breadcrumbs. Fry at 350° in deep fat until russet-brown. Cool slightly before cutting in half to serve. Good either hot or cold for brunch or as a snack or appetizer.

Serves 8

molded egg and caviar spread

4 hard-cooked eggs, finely chopped
¼ cup chopped onion
1 tsp. Dijon mustard
2 T. finely chopped parsley
1 tsp. lemon juice
6 T. melted butter
1 jar (3½ oz.) caviar
1 cup sour cream
parsley sprigs

In a small bowl, combine eggs, onion, mustard, parsley, lemon juice and butter. Line a small mold or plate with plastic wrap; press mixture into mold or, with hands, form into mound on plate. Cover and refrigerate until set, 3 to 4 hours. Place on serving plate; spread with caviar. Top with thin layer of sour cream. Garnish with parsley. Serve with favorite crackers or toasted bread strips and lemon wedges. May be refrigerated for up to two days before adding caviar and sour cream. Should sit at room temperature 30 minutes before serving.

Serves 12

camembert mousse

An almond-coated mousse, delicious served with Carr's water biscuits.

1 wheel (8 oz.) Camembert cheese
1 cup softened butter
6 T. dry vermouth
3-4 dashes Tabasco
toasted slivered almonds

Trim crust from cheese. Cut into small cubes. Let stand at room temperature for several hours until softened. With electric mixer, beat butter. Gradually add cheese, beating until light and fluffy. Add vermouth *very slowly,* drop by drop, while beating at medium-high speed. Add Tabasco. Line a 3-cup mold with plastic-wrap. Turn mousse mixture into mold, pressing down with back of a spoon. Cover and refrigerate overnight. At serving time, remove from mold. Remove plastic-wrap. Press almonds around top and sides.

Serves 8 to 10

trilby

A popular, delicious cheese and egg spread.

1 lb. mild Cheddar cheese, crumbled by hand
2 medium onions, minced or 4-6 scallions with green part, finely chopped
6 hard-cooked eggs, chopped
2 sprigs parsley, chopped
salt to taste
pepper to taste
dash paprika
1 cup or more mayonnaise
parsley for garnish

In a large bowl, combine all ingredients except mayonnaise. Mix well. Add mayonnaise. Mash together to form a cohesive ball. Add more mayonnaise if necessary. Divide into 2 balls. Chill. Garnish with parsley. Serve with crackers or party-size bread slices.

Variation: Trilby makes a delicious sandwich spread.

Makes 2 cheese balls

jane goris' french boursin

This mellow herb-seasoned cheese with cracked pepper is even better than store bought Boursin!

1 pkg. (8 oz.) softened cream cheese
¼ cup butter *(not margarine)*
½ tsp. beau monde seasoning
1 medium clove garlic, minced
1 tsp. water
1 tsp. minced parsley
¼ tsp. red wine vinegar
¼ tsp. Worcestershire sauce
pinch of: sage, savory, rosemary, thyme
cracked black pepper

With an electric mixer, beat cream cheese and butter together until light and fluffy. Scrape down sides of bowl frequently. Add remaining ingredients and beat well. Refrigerate for several hours to mellow. To serve, shape into a ball and roll in pepper. Allow to reach room temperature before serving. Serve with crackers.

Variation: For an extra treat, spread over broiled steak. Return to broiler until bubbly.

Serves 10

curried onion-cheese bake

A tasty first course appetizer.

1⅔ cups coarsely crumbled, salted soda crackers
¾ cup melted butter, divided
¾ tsp. curry powder
1 large onion, minced
½ cup grated Cheddar cheese
2 cups scalded milk, cooled
1 egg, lightly beaten
⅓ tsp. salt
dash cayenne pepper
3 T. freshly-grated Parmesan cheese
paprika

In a bowl, combine crackers, ½ cup plus 1 tablespoon of the butter, and curry powder. Spread one-half of mixture in bottom of lightly buttered 8-inch square pan. In a small skillet, saute onion in remaining 3 tablespoons of butter until tender. Spread onions over crackers. Sprinkle with grated cheese. Combine milk, egg, salt and cayenne pepper; mix well. Pour over cheese. Sprinkle remaining cracker mixture over milk. Top with Parmesan cheese and paprika. Bake at 375° for 20 to 25 minutes or until set. Cut into squares. Serve hot on individual plates.

Serves 6 to 8

cocktail cornucopias

An excellent idea for all types of fillings!

20 slices thin-sliced white bread
½-¾ cup real mayonnaise

Filling:
3 T. real mayonnaise
1 can (4½ oz.) deviled ham
2 hard-cooked eggs, finely chopped
½ T. prepared mustard
paprika

Cut each slice of bread with a round cookie cutter. Flatten circles with rolling pin. Spread both sides with mayonnaise. Roll each circle to form a cornucopia. Fasten with toothpick. Bake on an ungreased cookie sheet at 350° for 12 to 15 minutes or until lightly browned. Cool. Remove toothpicks. For Filling: Combine ham, mayonnaise, chopped egg and mustard. Chill. Fill cornucopias and sprinkle with paprika.

Makes 20 canapes

liptauer cheese

A rich-flavored Hungarian spread to serve with thin slices of buttered pumpernickle bread.

1 cup softened butter
1 pkg. (8 oz.) softened cream cheese
1 T. finely chopped green pepper
1 T. chopped onion
2 tsp. chopped capers
¼ tsp. dry mustard
⅛ tsp. black pepper

With an electric mixer, beat butter and cream cheese until light and fluffy. Add remaining ingredients and continue beating for several minutes. The taste improves with blending. Refrigerate or freeze. Allow spread to reach room temperature before serving.

Serves 6 to 8

cheddar cheese and olive canape

½ lb. Cheddar cheese, shredded (2 cups)
1 jar (4 oz.) pimento, drained and sliced
1 can (7 oz.) pitted black olives, drained and sliced thinly
1 small onion, grated
¼ cup mayonnaise
pepper to taste
1 loaf party rye bread

Combine ingredients. Spread on party rye bread slices. Bake at 350° for 10 minutes.

Makes about 30 appetizers

mexicali dip

1 can (10 oz.) condensed bean soup
1 pkg. (6 oz.) garlic cheese, cut in small pieces
1 cup sour cream
2 green onions with tops, chopped
dash Tabasco
dash Worcestershire sauce

In a medium saucepan over low heat, warm the soup. Add the cheese and stir until melted. Remove from heat. Add sour cream, onions, Tabasco and Worcestershire sauce. Serve immediately with tortilla chips for dipping.

Serves 8 to 10

beverages

"Much of life's pleasure would be taken from very young men if they couldn't whistle. . . .
You *may* whistle when you are in the country,
or anywhere else if no one is disturbed by it, that is if you are alone.
Of course you would not whistle in the presence of others."

rum eye-opener

2 oz. freshly squeezed orange juice
½-1 oz. lime juice
1-2 tsp. granulated sugar
2 oz. white rum
ice cubes
tonic or soda water

Place orange juice, lime juice and sugar in a tall glass. Stir to dissolve sugar. Add the rum, ice cubes and enough tonic or soda water to fill glass.

Serves 1

kir

The popular French aperitif with the flavor of blackcurrant.

3 bottles Pinot Chardonnay or dry white wine
1 small bottle creme de cassis

Fill a large crystal pitcher with the wine. Slowly add the creme de cassis until the color is similar to a light rose wine. More may be added to suit individual taste for sweetness. Pour into individual wine glasses. Serve with nuts, a selection of cheeses and plain crackers.

Note: The wine and creme de cassis may be combined in individual wine glasses when serving a smaller number of people.

Serves 12

banana-orange freeze

Very refreshing on a hot summer day.

2 ripe bananas, sliced
1 tsp. lemon juice
½ cup orange juice
½ cup milk
2 cups orange sherbet

Combine all ingredients in a blender. Blend until smooth. Pour into glasses. Serve with straws.

Serves 2 to 3

lime wine cooler

½ cup lime juice
¼ cup sugar
3 cups Rhine wine
crushed ice
lime juice
confectioners' sugar
4 lime wedges
mint sprigs

Combine first 4 ingredients. Chill for 1 hour or longer. Before serving, frost glasses with rims dipped into lime juice and powdered sugar. Pour chilled beverage into frosted glasses. Garnish with lime wedge and mint sprig.

Serves 4

perfect sangria

A Spanish wine punch—perfect with a summer meal.

½ cup superfine sugar
1 cup cold water
1 lime, thinly sliced
1 orange, thinly sliced
ice cubes
1 bottle red wine

Stir the sugar and water together in a small pan over moderate heat, stirring constantly. When syrup just begins to boil, remove from heat. Add the lime and orange slices. Let sit at room temperature at least 4 hours. Just before serving, fill a tall crystal pitcher with ice cubes. Add the marinated fruit and one-half the syrup. Fill the pitcher with wine and stir well. Serve in pre-chilled glasses. Keep the remaining syrup for refills.

Makes 6 to 8 drinks

mint julep

2 sprigs fresh mint
1 tsp. confectioners' sugar
1 T. club soda or 7-up
shaved ice
1 jigger (1½ oz.) bourbon
club soda or 7-up
sprigs fresh mint

Place 2 sprigs of mint into a tall, 12-ounce glass. Add sugar and club soda or 7-up. Muddle. Fill glass with ice. Pour in bourbon. Work a long-handle spoon up and down in glass until outside of glass is frosted. Top with a splash of club soda or 7-up. Decorate with a sprig of mint.

Serves 1

raspberry delicious

A drink to serve for dessert.

1 quart raspberry sherbet
⅓ cup raspberry flavored brandy
¼ cup pecan pieces
sprig of mint

Place sherbet and brandy in a blender. Blend at low speed until thoroughly mixed. Stir in nuts. Serve in brandy glasses. Garnish with mint.

Serves 3 to 4

strawberry spritzer

1 pkg. (10 oz.) frozen strawberries, thawed
1 bottle white wine, chilled
14 oz. soda water, chilled
fresh strawberries for garnish

Place undrained strawberries in electric blender. Cover and blend until smooth. In a large glass pitcher, combine blended strawberries with wine and soda water. Pour into wine glasses and garnish each with a fresh strawberry.

Makes 12 (4 oz.) servings

hot mulled cider

1 tsp. whole allspice
1 tsp. whole cloves
¼ tsp. salt
dash nutmeg
1 (3-inch) cinnamon stick
½ cup brown sugar
2 quarts apple cider
orange wedges for garnish
cinnamon sticks

Tie all the spices in a cheesecloth bag. Place brown sugar, spice bag and cider in a large kettle. Slowly bring to a boil; cover and simmer for 20 minutes. Before serving, remove spice bag. (Or, place all the spices in the basket of a large party-size coffee pot. Add the brown sugar and cider and perk through normal cycle.) Serve in mugs with an orange wedge and cinnamon stick muddler in each. Can be mulled ahead and reheated at serving time.

Serves 10

peach daiquiri

1 can (6 oz.) frozen lemonade, slightly thawed
6 oz. vodka
1 cup frozen sliced peaches, slightly thawed
8 ice cubes

Combine all ingredients. Blend in blender.

Serves 8

dutch punch

2 (3-inch) cinnamon sticks, broken.
1 tsp. whole cloves
1 medium orange, sliced
1 medium lemon, sliced
1 cup sugar
2 fifths dry red wine
1 cup water
orange slices for garnish

Tie cinnamon and cloves in cheesecloth. Combine with orange, lemon, sugar and 1 bottle of the wine in a 3-quart pan. Bring to boil. Simmer 30 minutes, covered. Remove spices and fruit. Add remaining wine. Heat, but do not boil. Ladle into a heat-proof bowl. Garnish with orange slices. Serve warm.

Makes 7 cups

goombay smash

2 oz. apricot brandy
2 oz. light rum
2 oz. Pina Collada mix
1 egg
3 cups pineapple juice

Place all ingredients in an electric blender. (Add pineapple juice within 3-inches of top.) Blend and pour into ice-filled glasses. Serve immediately with a straw.

Serves 4

winter warmer

8 tsp. sugar
4 orange slices
24 whole cloves
4 cinnamon sticks
4 cups hot orange-pekoe tea
rum or orange brandy (optional)

Place 2 teaspoons sugar and an orange slice studded with 6 cloves in each cup or mug. Put in a cinnamon stick. Fill with freshly brewed tea. Add rum or orange brandy, if desired.

Serves 4

wassail

1 box whole cloves
6 oranges
1 gallon apple cider (without preservatives)
1½ cups lemon juice
10 (2-inch) cinnamon sticks
2 cups vodka
¼ cup brandy

Insert cloves ¼-inch apart in oranges. Bake, uncovered, in a shallow pan at 350° for 30 minutes. Meanwhile, heat the cider in a large kettle until bubbles form around edges. Remove from heat. Add lemon juice, cinnamon sticks and oranges. Cover and heat over very low heat for 30 minutes. Remove from heat. Add vodka and brandy, mixing well. Pour into a punch bowl and serve warm.

Makes 36 (4 oz.) servings

mocha milk punch

1 quart coffee ice cream
1 cup milk
½ cup bourbon
¼ cup light rum
¼ cup creme de cocao

In a blender, combine *half* the ice cream, the milk, bourbon, rum and creme de cocao. Cover and blend until smooth. Pour into six glasses. Top with scoop of remaining ice cream. Garnish with chocolate, if desired.

Serves 6

harry's heavenly hangover

1½ oz. milk
2 oz. kahlua
1½ oz. creme de cocao
1½ pints vanilla ice cream

In an electric blender, blend all the ingredients at high speed. Serve in champagne glasses.

Serves 4

brunch and luncheon dishes

"In every house, great or small, the Dining Room should be
as bright, cheerful and cosey as possible,
and at the table the mistress should wear her brightest smile."

HISTORICAL ROOM OF THE NAPPANEE PUBLIC LIBRARY

feather-weight pancakes with brown sugar syrup

Pancakes:
1 egg, beaten
1 cup (scant) milk
1 T. vanilla
2 T. vegetable oil
1¼ cups sifted flour
3½ tsp. baking powder
1 T. granulated sugar
2 T. confectioners' sugar
½ tsp. salt

Brown Sugar Syrup:
½ cup brown sugar
½ cup granulated sugar
1 cup water
2 drops maple flavoring

For Pancakes: In a large bowl, combine egg, milk, vanilla and oil. Set aside. Mix remaining dry ingredients. Add dry ingredients to milk mixture. Stir lightly. Batter will be a little lumpy. Cook on hot, lightly greased griddle until both sides are golden brown. Turn only once. Serve with melted butter and Brown Sugar Syrup or your own favorite syrup. For Brown Sugar Syrup: In small saucepan, combine syrup ingredients. Boil for 5 to 10 minutes. Serve warm.

Makes approximately 12 3-inch pancakes.

old bonneyville mill buckwheats

For a hearty, old-fashioned Sunday breakfast.

1 cup buckwheat flour (stone ground is best)
1 tsp. baking powder
1 tsp. baking soda
⅛ tsp. salt
1 cup buttermilk
1 egg, beaten
maple syrup
lemon juice

Stir together the dry ingredients in a large bowl. Make a well in the center. Pour in the buttermilk and egg. Stir until blended but still somewhat lumpy. Let sit for 10 minutes. Stir gently a few seconds. Spoon batter onto a hot buttered griddle. When the bubbles pop and the edges begin to look dry, flip over. Cook quickly on the second side. Serve immediately with warm maple syrup and a few drops of lemon juice sprinkled on top.

Serves 2 to 4

puffy dutch pancake

Children love to watch it puff up! It's never the same!

½ cup butter
½ cup flour
3 eggs
½ cup milk
nutmeg
1½ T. lemon juice (approximately ½ lemon)
confectioners' sugar

In a 10-inch iron skillet or a 9-inch pie pan, melt butter. While butter melts, mix flour, eggs and milk in a blender. Pour over melted butter. *Do not stir.* Sprinkle with nutmeg. Bake at 425° *in preheated oven* for 20 minutes. Sprinkle lemon juice and confectioners' sugar over top. Serve immediately.

Serves 4 to 6

honey oatmeal pancakes

2 eggs, beaten
2 cups buttermilk, divided
½ cup oil
1½ cups flour
½ cup rolled oats
¼ cup wheat germ
1 tsp. salt
1 tsp. baking soda
2 T. honey

In a large bowl, combine eggs, 1 cup of the buttermilk, oil and dry ingredients. Beat until smooth. Add honey and remaining buttermilk. Cook on both sides on lightly greased skillet.

Makes 14 to 20 pancakes

sausage-and-egg bake with dill

Everyone's favorite—sausage and eggs—sparked with dill.

7 slices bread, broken into small pieces
½ tsp. dill seed, divided
1 T. minced onion, divided
1 cup diced, cooked sausage or ham
½ tsp. salt
½ tsp. pepper
3 cups milk
8 eggs, slightly beaten

In a buttered 13 x 9 x 2-inch casserole, place bread. Sprinkle with half of the dill and onion. Put meat on top. Sprinkle with remaining dill and onion. In a separate bowl, mix salt, pepper, milk and eggs. Pour mixture over bread and meat. Cover casserole. Refrigerate overnight. Bake, uncovered, at 350° for 30 to 40 minutes until set.

Serves 8

bacon and cheese puff pie

An easy breakfast, brunch, luncheon or supper dish.

14 slices bacon
1 can (8 oz.) refrigerated crescent rolls
2 medium tomatoes, sliced
5-6 slices American process cheese
3 eggs, separated
¾ cup sour cream
½ cup flour
½ tsp. each: salt, pepper, paprika

Fry bacon; drain and crumble. Unroll dough; form crust in a 9-inch pan. Sprinkle bacon over crust. Top with tomato slices. Place cheese slices over all. In a mixing bowl, beat egg whites until stiff. In a separate bowl, combine egg yolks, sour cream, flour and seasonings; blend thoroughly. Gently fold in egg whites. Pour mixture over cheese layer. Sprinkle with additional paprika. Bake at 350° for 35 to 40 minutes or until inserted knife comes out clean.

Variation: Hot peppers can be added to tomato-bacon mixture. Additional herbs such as basil, oregano or parsley may be used according to taste.

Serves 6

creamed eggs in chive-biscuit ring

Biscuit Ring:
¼ cup chopped chives
½ cup melted butter
2 pkgs. (8 oz. each) refrigerated biscuits

Creamed Eggs:
¼ cup melted butter
¼ cup flour
2 cups milk
½ tsp. salt
2 T. prepared mustard
6 hard-cooked eggs, shelled and quartered

For Biscuit Ring: In small bowl, mix chives with melted butter. Separate biscuits. Dip biscuit rounds into butter-chive mixture. Stand biscuits upright in ungreased 8-inch ring mold. Bake at 375° for 20 minutes. Turn out. Fill center with hot creamed eggs. Serve immediately.

For Creamed Eggs: In medium saucepan, add flour to melted butter. Blend until smooth. Add milk gradually. Cook until thick, stirring occasionally. Add salt and mustard. Gently fold in eggs. Continue heating for a few minutes. The cream sauce may be made in advance. However, be sure to allow time to heat through before adding eggs.

Serves 4 to 6

party scrambled eggs

A great way to please so many.

½ cup butter
3 dozen eggs, slightly beaten
1½ lbs. shaved ham
2 cans (10½ oz. each) condensed cream of mushroom soup
2 cans (8 oz. each) mushroom pieces and stems, drained
1 can (13 oz.) evaporated milk
½ lb. (2 cups) grated sharp cheese

In large skillet, melt butter; add eggs. Scramble until barely congealed. Sprinkle ham into bottom of 2 buttered 13 x 9 x 2-inch casseroles. Pour eggs over ham. In a separate bowl, mix remaining ingredients. Pour over eggs. Bake at 350° for 30 minutes. Keeps in refrigerator 2 days before baking. It can be reheated slowly. Microcook 3 minutes to reheat.

Serves 20

amish country scrapple

Even better than bacon or sausage for Sunday breakfast!

1½ cups yellow cornmeal
1 cup water
1 lb. bulk pork sausage
½ tsp. dried sage
½ tsp. salt
1 T. chopped parsley
1 can (10¾ oz.) condensed chicken broth
2 cups water
butter

In a medium bowl, blend together cornmeal and water. Set aside. In a large saucepan, combine pork sausage, sage, salt, parsley and chicken broth. Gradually stir in water, separating sausage into fine pieces. Bring to boil. Slowly add cornmeal mixture while stirring constantly with a whisk. Reduce heat. Simmer gently, uncovered, for 15 minutes. Turn into a 9 x 5 x 3-inch loaf pan. Cool. Refrigerate, covered, until ready to use. To serve, cut into quarter-inch slices. Saute in butter in a skillet until golden brown on both sides. Freezes well.

Serves 8

crabmeat quiche

An intriguing combination of ingredients makes this gourmet fare.

½ cup real mayonnaise
2 T. flour
2 eggs, beaten
½ cup milk
2 pkgs. (6 oz. each) crabmeat
8 oz. shredded Swiss cheese
¼ cup diced green pepper
¼ cup chopped green onion
1 can (8 oz.) mushrooms, drained
4 slices bacon, crumbled
1 unbaked 8-inch pastry shell

Mix mayonnaise, flour, eggs and milk. Add crabmeat, Swiss cheese, pepper, onion, mushrooms and bacon. Spread in pastry shell. Bake at 350° for 40 to 50 minutes until golden. Let stand 10 minutes to settle before cutting. Serve immediately.

Serves 6

tuna quiche

1 can (7 oz.) tuna in water, drained
8 or 9-inch pastry shell, baked at 450° for 5 minutes
½ cup chopped onion
1½ cups grated Swiss cheese
2 eggs, beaten
1 cup evaporated milk
1 tsp. lemon juice
1 tsp. garlic salt
1 tsp. chopped chives
⅛ tsp. pepper

Sprinkle tuna in bottom of slightly pre-cooked pastry shell. Layer onion and cheese on top of tuna. Beat remaining ingredients. Pour over tuna and cheese. Bake at 450° for 15 minutes. Reduce heat to 350°. Bake 12 minutes more.

Variation: Canned shrimp may be substituted for tuna.

Serves 6

tomato quiche

New variation of a classic.

1 unbaked 9-inch pastry shell
2 medium tomatoes
1½ cups milk
2 cups shredded Swiss cheese
½ cup chopped onion
1¼ tsp. salt
¼ tsp. pepper
4 eggs, lightly beaten

Dice one tomato; slice the other. Set both aside. Refrigerate pastry shell 10 minutes. Then bake at 450° about 8 minutes or until golden. Remove from oven. Reduce heat to 325°. Stir milk, cheese, onion, salt, pepper and diced tomato into beaten eggs. Pour into pastry shell. Bake at 325° for 30 minutes. Top with sliced tomato. Bake about 25 minutes more until a knife inserted in center comes out clean. Let stand at room temperature 10 minutes before cutting.

Serves 6

basic crepe batter

Just the starting point for creativity.

3 eggs, beaten
1 cup milk
1 T. melted butter
1 cup flour
½ tsp. salt
½ cup vegetable oil for frying crepes
For Sweet Crepe Batter; add 1 T. sugar and ½ tsp. flavoring

Put eggs, milk, melted butter, flour and salt in an electric blender. Cover and blend at top speed for 30 seconds. Stop and scrape down sides of blender jar. Beat at top speed 10 to 15 seconds more. Batter should have consistency of heavy cream. Cover and set aside in refrigerator for 1 hour before cooking. Heat 6-inch crepe pan over moderately high heat. Dip pastry brush in oil, *coating pan extremely well.* When pan is quite hot, pour about 2 tablespoons of the batter in the pan, holding pan away from heat. Immediately tip the pan in all directions to cover entire surface of pan with a very thin film of batter. If too much batter is in pan, quickly pour it back into bowl or use to patch up any holes. *Work quickly!* Set pan over heat. Cook one side about 1 minute. Can peek to see if bottom side is lightly browned. Cook on one side. Invert onto a linen towel, wax paper or plate. The unbrowned side of a crepe is the filling side. Repeat process until all batter is used. Crepes should be as thin as possible. If batter seems too thick, beat in a few teaspoonfuls of water. Crepes can be stacked between layers of wax paper, covered and frozen.

Makes 14 to 16 crepes

ham crepes with mustard sauce

8 8-inch crepes or 16 smaller ones.

Filling:
1 lb. ground ham
1 cup sour cream
2 eggs, beaten
½ tsp. onion powder
2 tsp. Worcestershire sauce
salt
white pepper
¼ cup chopped black olives (optional)

Mustard Sauce:
2 egg yolks
½ tsp. salt
dash white pepper
2 tsp. vinegar
1 cup vegetable oil
1½ tsp. lemon juice
2 T. prepared mustard
1½ T. honey

For Filling: Mix ground ham and remaining ingredients together. Spread evenly on each crepe. Roll up and place filled crepes side by side in a greased, shallow rectangular baking dish. Bake at 375° for 10 to 12 minutes. Serve with Mustard Sauce. Filled crepes may be frozen, defrosted and then baked.

For Mustard Sauce: Place egg yolks in blender. Beat lightly. Add salt, pepper and vinegar. Blend thoroughly. Pour oil in *very slowly* while beating continually at medium speed. Add lemon juice, mustard and honey. Mix well.

Makes 8 8-inch crepes

chicken crepes veronique

The grapes make this tantalizing.

16 6-inch warm crepes
⅓ cup butter
½ lb. fresh mushrooms, sliced
1 T. grated onion
3 T. cornstarch
1 tsp. salt
¼ tsp. white pepper
½ cup half-and-half cream
1 cup whipping cream
3 T. dry sherry
2 cups diced, cooked chicken
1½ cups seedless grapes
grape clusters for garnish

In a heavy pan, melt butter. Saute mushrooms and onion. Blend in cornstarch, salt and pepper. Add creams and sherry. Cook over low heat, stirring until thickened. Add chicken; heat to boiling, stirring constantly. Stir in grapes. Remove from heat. Place 2 to 3 tablespoons of mixture on each crepe; roll up. Place crepes in individual serving dishes. Allow two per serving. Garnish with a small cluster of grapes. Serve immediately.

Serves 8

sausage-filled crepes

16 crepes
1 lb. bulk sausage
¼ cup chopped onions
½ cup shredded American process cheese
1 pkg. (3 oz.) cream cheese
¼ tsp. marjoram

Sauce:
½ cup sour cream
¼ cup softened butter

In a medium skillet, cook sausage and onion. Drain off fat. Add remaining ingredients. Blend together. Place 2 tablespoons sausage filling in center of each crepe. Roll up. Place in a greased 12 x 8 x 2-inch baking dish. Cover. Chill several hours. Bake, uncovered, at 375° for 35 minutes.

For Sauce: While crepes are baking, blend sour cream and butter. Spoon sauce over crepes. Bake, uncovered, an additional 5 minutes. Filled crepes may be frozen, defrosted and baked. Do not freeze sauce.

Makes 16 crepes

crepes with shrimp and water chestnuts

14 to 16 5-inch crepes

2 scallions, diced
¼ cup butter, divided
1 lb. shrimp, cooked, peeled and cut into thirds
¼ lb. fresh mushrooms, finely chopped
1 T. chopped parsley
1 can (4 oz.) water chestnuts, chopped
2 T. flour
1 cup milk
2 T. whipping cream
2 T. white wine
½ tsp. thyme
salt and pepper to taste
dash paprika
Parmesan cheese
parsley sprigs

In a saucepan, saute scallions in 2 tablespoons of the butter. Add shrimp; cook and gently stir until well coated with butter. Stir in mushrooms and parsley; cook 2 minutes. Add water chestnuts. Set aside. In a separate saucepan, melt remaining 2 tablespoons of butter over low heat. Blend in flour. Add milk gradually, stirring constantly. Cook until well blended. Stir in cream, wine and seasonings. Add shrimp mixture to cream sauce. Heat only until well mixed. Cool. Fill crepes with 2 to 3 tablespoons filling. Roll up and place seam-side down into a large buttered baking dish or into two smaller baking dishes. Bake, covered, at 400° for 10 to 15 minutes. To serve, sprinkle lightly with grated Parmesan cheese. Garnish with parsley. Serve immediately. Can be prepared in advance, covered and refrigerated until baking time.

Makes 14 to 16 5-inch crepes

fresh mushroom crepes

Serve as an appetizer, vegetable or side dish.

6-8 warm crepes
½ lb. fresh mushrooms, sliced
2 T. butter
1 beef bouillon cube, crumbled
2 T. dry white wine
¼ tsp. salt
¼ tsp. seasoned salt
½ cup sour cream
1 T. minced chives

In a medium skillet, saute mushrooms in butter. Dissolve bouillon in wine. Add wine mixture and salts to mushrooms. Cook over medium heat until bubbly. Stir in sour cream and chives. Heat but do not boil. Fill crepes with the mixture. Serve immediately.

Makes 6 to 8 crepes

zucchini crepes

Crepes:
1 cup sifted flour
1 tsp. salt
¾ tsp. each: baking powder, garlic powder, pepper
5 eggs, beaten
⅔ cup milk
2 cups finely grated zucchini
olive oil
chopped parsley
butter

Filling:
2 cups sour cream
2 cups grated Parmesan cheese

For Crepes: Into a large bowl, sift flour, salt, baking powder, garlic powder and pepper. Add milk to beaten eggs. Beat until blended. Add egg mixture to dry ingredients. Blend. Add grated zucchini. Blend. Lightly grease a 6-inch skillet with olive oil. Pour 2 tablespoons of batter into the skillet. Cook until golden brown, turning once. Keep cooked crepes warm or reheat in a microwave just before serving.

For Filling: Combine sour cream and cheese. Fill crepes with 2 tablespoons of the filling. Roll up. Garnish with additional cheese and chopped parsley. Serve warm.

Makes approximately 24 crepes

chicken souffle

Prepare one day. Bake and serve the following day for a tasty supper.

6-8 slices firm white bread, crusts removed
3-4 cups cooked chicken, cut into bite-size pieces
2 T. real mayonnaise
2 tsp. lemon juice
6-8 thin slices Cheddar cheese
4 eggs, beaten
2 cups milk
¼ tsp. salt
1 can (10½ oz.) condensed cream of mushroom soup
1 can (10½ oz.) condensed cream of celery soup
1 jar (2 oz.) pimentos, chopped
1 can (8 oz.) water chestnuts, sliced
¼ cup dry breadcrumbs
1½ T. butter

Line a buttered 13 x 9 x 2-inch casserole with bread. In a separate bowl, mix chicken with mayonnaise and lemon juice. Cover bread with chicken mixture. Cover with cheese slices. Add milk and salt to beaten eggs. Pour over cheese and chicken. Mix soups, pimentos, and water chestnuts. Spread over top of casserole. Sprinkle with dry breadcrumbs. Dot with butter. Cover with foil. Refrigerate overnight. Bake covered at 350° for 1 hour. Uncover; bake 20 to 30 minutes more.

Serves 10 to 12

ham and cheese souffle with mushroom sauce

Souffle:
12 slices white bread, crusts removed
30 slices American cheese
2½ lbs. ham, cubed
12 hard-cooked eggs
3½ cups milk
4 eggs, beaten
1 T. salt
1 tsp. pepper
1 tsp. paprika
1½ tsp. dry mustard
1 T. grated onion

Mushroom Sauce:
2 cans (10¾ oz. each) condensed golden mushroom soup
2 jars (4 oz. each) button mushrooms, drained
1½ cups white wine

For Souffle: Butter sides and bottoms of 2 13 x 9 x 2-inch ovenproof casseroles. Cut 10 slices of bread into quarters. Lay on bottom of casseroles. Layer with cheese slices, then ham. Slice 10 of the eggs. Place egg slices on top of ham. Crumble the 2 reserved bread slices. Chop the 2 remaining eggs. Sprinkle breadcrumbs and chopped eggs over tops of casseroles. In a medium bowl, mix together the remaining ingredients. Pour over casseroles. Bake at 350° for 1 hour. Serve with Mushroom Sauce. Souffle may be made a day ahead, baked for 30 minutes and refrigerated. Finish baking before serving.

For Mushroom Sauce: In a medium saucepan, combine all ingredients. Bring to slow boil. Simmer 10 minutes. Serve with Souffle.

Serves 12

salmon asparagus pie

Lovely to serve—richly colored and delicious.

1 pkg. (10 oz.) frozen asparagus spears, cooked according to pkg. directions, or fresh asparagus
¼ cup onion
2 T. butter
3 eggs, slightly beaten
½ cup milk
2 T. minced parsley
½ tsp. salt
¼ tsp. basil
1 can (1 lb.) salmon, flaked
1 unbaked 9-inch pastry shell

In a small skillet, saute onion in butter. In medium bowl, combine eggs, milk, seasonings and cooked onion. Fold in flaked salmon. Drain asparagus well. Set aside 6 asparagus spears. Arrange remaining asparagus in pastry shell. Pour salmon mixture in shell. Arrange 6 asparagus spears on top. Bake at 425° for 35 to 40 minutes or until set.

Serves 4 to 6

soups and sandwiches

"Ladies should be seated first, beginning with the mother, or the lady who presides at table.
Sit erect without being stiff; not too close nor too far away from the table,
and carry the food to the mouth; don't carry the mouth to the food."

san fernando salad soup

A great cold soup that has to be made a day ahead.

1 clove garlic, mashed
1 T. sugar
1½ tsp. salt
1 can (46 oz.) V-8 juice
¼ cup olive oil
2 T. lemon juice
1 tsp. Worcestershire sauce
2 cups finely diced tomatoes
1½ cups finely diced cucumber
1 cup shredded carrots
1 cup thinly sliced celery
¼ cup thinly sliced green onions
4 cups croutons
oregano (optional)

In a large mixing bowl, combine first 7 ingredients. Mix with a hand-mixer and beat until olive oil is well blended with other ingredients. Blender can be used, if desired. Cover; chill while preparing vegetables. (The liquid part can be saved in the refrigerator for several days.) Stir in vegetables; chill for 24 hours. Serve with croutons and a sprinkling of oregano, if desired.

Serves 8

mediterranean summer soup

A recipe from the sunny coast of France using ingredients typical of the area.

1 cup chopped onion
3 T. olive oil
1½ lbs. tomatoes, peeled, seeded and chopped
2 cloves garlic, mashed
5 cups chicken stock
5 cups water
¼ cup rice (short-grain, if possible)
6 sprigs parsley
1 T. sugar
pinch saffron (optional)
salt and pepper
1 bay leaf
½ tsp. thyme
4 fennel seeds
minced parsley for garnish

In a large skillet, saute onions lightly in olive oil. Add tomatoes and garlic. Simmer on medium heat for 5 minutes. Transfer to a large soup kettle. Add next 7 ingredients. Combine the bay leaf, thyme and fennel seeds; tie in cheesecloth or place in metal tea ball. Add to soup. Simmer for 30 minutes to 1 hour. When ready to serve, add minced parsley for garnish. Keeps well in glass jars in refrigerator for several days.

Serves 6

vichyssoise

A delicious soup from which two additional soups can be made.

¼ cup butter
1½ cups chopped onions or leeks
3½ cups rich chicken broth, divided
4 cups diced potatoes
½ tsp. each: salt, garlic salt, celery salt
2 cups half-and-half cream
white pepper
finely chopped chives

In a soup kettle, saute onions or leeks in butter until soft, but not brown. Add 1 cup of the broth; simmer, covered, for 10 minutes. Add remaining broth, potatoes and salts. Cover and cook over low heat until potatoes are soft, 15 to 20 minutes. Cool. Pour mixture into blender in small batches; blend until smooth. Stir in cream. Season with pepper and additional salt, if needed. Mix well. Refrigerate for several hours or overnight. Serve cold and garnish with chives.

Note: Thickness of soup depends on use of rich broth and cream.

Makes 3 quarts

vichyssoise and avocado soup

Rich and refreshing.

1 quart Vichyssoise, divided (see index)
2-3 ripe avocados, peeled and diced
1 cup half-and-half cream
1 cup sour cream
1-2 T. lemon juice
salt
⅛ tsp. white pepper
dash Tabasco
lemon wedges

In a blender, combine half of the Vichyssoise with the avocados. Blend until smooth. In a mixing bowl, add blended mixture to remaining Vichyssoise. Stir in creams, lemon juice and seasonings. Serve cold with lemon wedges.

Serves 6 to 8

zucchini soup

Delicious summer soup—make it ahead!

2 T. butter
2 cups finely chopped green onions
3 cups diced zucchini
2 quarts chicken broth, simmered with celery leaves, bay leaves and parsley
2 cups half-and-half cream
salt and pepper
dill weed

In a large soup kettle, melt butter. Add onions; simmer until tender but not brown. Add zucchini and chicken broth. Cook until zucchini is soft. Let cool. Place mixture in a blender, 1 to 2 cups at a time. Blend thoroughly. Return soup stock to kettle; add cream. Heat slowly. Add seasonings to taste. Serve hot or cold. Most people prefer the soup cold. When served cold, sprinkle with dill. Soup keeps 4 to 5 days in refrigerator. Flavor is best if made a few days before serving. Summer squash may be substituted for zucchini.

Serves 6 to 8

cold cucumber-watercress soup

Simply sublime.

½ cup butter
1 medium onion, chopped
3 medium cucumbers, unpeeled, seeded and diced
1 medium potato, peeled and diced
3 bunches watercress, chopped
3 cups chicken broth
½ tsp. dry mustard
1 tsp. salt
½ tsp. white pepper
2 cups half-and-half cream
1 cup whipping cream

In a large saucepan, melt butter. Add onion; saute until tender. Add remaining ingredients *except* the creams. Simmer for 1 hour. Puree in food mill or blender. Refrigerate several hours. Stir in creams. If desired, soup may be garnished with thinly sliced radishes and chopped fresh chives.

Variation: A pinch or two of dill or curry powder may be added, if desired.

Serves 8

borscht

¼ cup butter
1 clove garlic, minced
1 cup finely chopped onion
3 carrots, peeled and diced
1 potato, peeled and diced
½ cup diced celery
2 lbs. chuck roast, cubed and boned
¼ lb. Polish sausage, sliced
1 can (1 lb. 12 oz.) tomatoes, undrained
2 cans (1 lb. each) beets (4 cups), pureed, undrained
1 lb. red cabbage, coarsely shredded
4-5 cups beef broth
⅓ cup red wine vinegar
2 T. chopped parsley
1 tsp. MSG
1 tsp. caraway seed
2 tsp. salt
pepper
1 T. sugar
1 bay leaf
dash Tabasco
sour cream
dill

In a 10-quart kettle, melt butter. Add garlic and onions. Cook, stirring frequently, until soft but not brown, about 3 minutes. Add carrots, potato and celery. Coat with butter. Simmer about 3 minutes. Add remaining ingredients *except* the sour cream and dill. Bring soup to boil. Reduce heat and simmer for 1½ hours. Stir occasionally, skimming surface as needed. Continue cooking, partially covered, for 30 minutes over very low heat. Turn off heat. Cover and cool on top of stove for 2 to 3 hours. Reheat before serving. Serve hot with sour cream sprinkled with dill.

Note: Soup may be strained and served without meat and vegetables. Can be prepared in advance and frozen or stored in refrigerator. Vegetables may become mushy if frozen.

Serves 10 to 12

broccoli soup

Or, if you prefer, Cauliflower Soup!

3 large pieces fresh broccoli
½ cup chopped onion
2½ cups water
1 T. instant chicken bouillon
2 cups half-and-half cream
¼ tsp. curry powder
salt and white pepper to taste
sour cream
chopped chives
thinly sliced radish

In a large saucepan, place broccoli, onion, water and instant chicken bouillon. Bring to a boil; simmer until broccoli is tender but still bright green. Puree in a blender in two batches for 30 seconds. Return to saucepan. When ready to serve, add the cream, curry powder, salt and pepper to taste. Heat through but *do not boil*. Ladle into hot bowls and garnish with sour cream, chopped chives and thinly sliced radish.

Variation: Substitute ½ head fresh cauliflower for the broccoli.

Serves 6

cream of leek and carrot soup

Excellent with crusty French bread and a crisp salad after a day of cross-country skiing.

¼ cup butter
2 cups chopped leeks
2 cups diced carrots
¼ cup chopped celery
½ cup chopped onion
1½ cups chicken broth
1 tsp. Maggi sauce
¼ tsp. garlic salt
dash Tabasco
1-1½ cups cream
salt and pepper
parsley

In a 2-quart saucepan, cook vegetables in butter until soft. Add chicken broth and seasonings; simmer for 5 minutes. Pour mixture into blender in small batches; blend until smooth. Add cream to desired consistency. Serve warm or cold with parsley for garnish.

Serves 4 to 6

czechoslovakian cabbage soup

A hearty meal in itself. Well worth the effort.

2 lbs. beef bones
1 cup chopped onion
3 carrots, pared and coarsely chopped
2 cloves garlic
1 bay leaf
2 lbs. beef shortribs
1 tsp. thyme
½ tsp. paprika
8 cups water
8 cups shredded cabbage
2 cans (16 oz. each) tomatoes
2 T. salt
½ tsp. Tabasco sauce
¼ cup chopped parsley
3 T. lemon juice
3 T. sugar
1 jar (14 oz.) sauerkraut
sour cream

In a roasting pan, place beef bones, onion, carrots, garlic and bay leaf. Top with shortribs; sprinkle with thyme and paprika. Bake, uncovered, at 450° for 20 minutes, or until meat is browned. Transfer meat and vegetables to a large soup kettle. Add water, cabbage, tomatoes, salt and Tabasco sauce. Bring to a boil. Cover and simmer for 1½ hours. Skim off fat. Add parsley, lemon juice, sugar and sauerkraut. Cook, uncovered, 1 hour. Remove bones and shortribs from kettle. Remove meat from bones. Cut into cubes and return to kettle. Simmer 5 additional minutes. Serve with sour cream. Perfect with crusty French bread and a tossed salad.

Serves 10 to 12

carrot soup

2 slices bacon, diced
¼ cup chopped onion
1 clove garlic, crushed
2 cans (13¾ oz. each) condensed chicken broth
2 cups chopped carrots
1 cup diced potatoes
1 tomato, peeled and chopped
1 tsp. salt
dash white pepper
sour cream
dill

In a large saucepan, sauté bacon, onion and garlic until bacon is crisp. Stir in remaining ingredients *except* the sour cream. Heat to boiling. Reduce heat. Simmer, uncovered, until vegetables are tender, about 20 minutes. Pour mixture into blender. Blend at high speed until smooth. Garnish with sour cream and sprinkle with dill.

Serves 4

fresh mushroom soup

A quick and easy creamy soup.

1 lb. fresh mushrooms, chopped
1 small onion, chopped
5 T. butter
5 T. flour
3 cups chicken broth
½ tsp. salt
pepper to taste
1 cup half-and-half cream

In a large saucepan, saute onions in butter for 3 minutes. Add mushrooms and saute 5 minutes longer. Sprinkle flour gradually over mushrooms and onions. Stir well. Add chicken broth, stirring constantly, until mixture comes to a boil. Add salt and pepper. Reduce heat; simmer for 30 minutes. Stir in cream just before serving.

Serves 4 to 6

french onion soup

Enhanced with Cognac.

2 lbs. white or Bermuda onions, peeled and sliced (about 6 cups)
½ cup plus 2 T. butter
¼ cup olive oil, divided
½ tsp. salt
½ tsp. sugar
3 T. flour
6 cans (13¾ oz. each) beef broth or consomme
1 tsp. dried garlic chips
1 bay leaf
8 slices very stale French bread
¾ cup grated Parmesan cheese, divided
4 slices Swiss cheese, sliced into strips
¼ cup Cognac (optional)

Melt ½ cup butter and 2 tablespoons olive oil in a Dutch oven; add onions. Cover and simmer for about 25 minutes, or until onions are transparent. Add salt and sugar; cook another 25 minutes until golden brown. Stir frequently so onions do not burn. Sprinkle onions with flour. Simmer and stir until flour is absorbed. Add broth, garlic chips and bay leaf. Simmer 40 minutes. Pour into 8 oven proof bowls. Place bread on a cookie sheet. Mix the remaining 2 tablespoons butter and 2 tablespoons olive oil; spread on the bread. Sprinkle ¼ cup of the grated cheese on the bread. Broil until cheese melts. Place slice of bread on top of each bowl. Sprinkle remaining grated cheese on top of bread. Criss-cross each bowl with strips of Swiss cheese. Add about 1 teaspoon of Cognac to each bowl, if desired. Bake at 350° for 20 minutes. Bowls of soup may be made ahead to point of baking. Refrigerate. When ready to serve, bake 30 minutes.

Note: To make stale French bread, lay bread on a flat surface for several days, turning occasionally, or dry out in a 325° oven for 30 minutes.

Serves 8

dutch pea soup

A hearty soup, best on a cold evening.

1 lb. dried peas
1 16-inch piece smoked sausage, cut into bite-size pieces
3 quarts water
1 cup chopped celery
1 cup chopped onion
3 potatoes, cubed
2 carrots, sliced
salt and pepper

Soak peas overnight in cold water. Drain. Cook meat and peas in 3 quarts water on low heat 2½ to 3 hours. Add the next 4 ingredients and seasonings. Simmer another 1½ to 2 hours. Soup should be very thick when finished.

Serves 8 to 10

onion-tomato soup

A delicious soup to serve after skiing, skating or sledding.

½ lb. crisply fried bacon, crumbled and divided
1 T. bacon drippings
3 T. butter
8 cups chopped onions
1 can (28 oz.) tomatoes
1 tsp. salt
2 tsp. garlic salt
2 tsp. Maggi sauce
1 tsp. dry mustard
dash white pepper
dash Tabasco
¼ cup flour
½ cup sauterne
2½ cups beef broth
2½ cups beef consomme
2 eggs, well beaten
¼ cup dry red wine
croutons
sour cream

In a heavy 4½-quart pan, saute onions in the butter and bacon drippings until onions are soft. Stir in next 7 ingredients. Mix the flour with the sauterne to make a paste. Add to tomato-onion mixture. Stir until mixture begins to thicken. Gradually stir in broth, consomme and *one half* of the the bacon. Simmer, covered, over low heat for 1 hour. Add wine and ¼ cup of the hot soup to the eggs. Stir well; add to soup. Do not reheat soup after the eggs have been added or the soup will curdle. Pour into individual bowls. Garnish with remaining bacon, croutons or sour cream. Serve with grilled ham and Swiss cheese on rye, or with a green salad and herb bread. Soup can be made ahead and frozen before adding the eggs and wine.

Serves 4 to 6

vegetable soup with dumplings

Very filling—a meal in itself. The flavor is best if made a day ahead.

Soup:
1 3-lb. beef arm roast or other soup meat
2 quarts water
1 can (49 oz.) tomato juice
8 potatoes, peeled and coarsely chopped
8 carrots, peeled and coarsely chopped
1 onion, chopped
2 stalks celery, chopped
½ cup dried beans
¼ cup dried peas
¼ cup dried lentils
2 T. salt
1 tsp. pepper
2 tsp. parsley flakes
2 cans (16 oz. each) mixed vegetables or leftovers

Dumplings:
1 dozen eggs
1 tsp. salt
3-4 cups flour

For Soup: In a 10-quart soup kettle, simmer meat in water over medium heat for 2 hours. Skim off fat. Remove fat and bones from meat. Add tomato juice, vegetables and remaining ingredients except mixed vegetables and Dumplings. Cook 4 to 5 hours over low heat. During last 30 minutes, add mixed vegetables. Add Dumplings 15 minutes before serving.

For Dumplings: Beat eggs until well mixed. Add flour until mixture is sticky and stringy and falls from a spoon. Drop dough by tablespoon into *boiling* soup. Cover soup tightly for 10 minutes. Dumplings will double in size. Serve immediately.

Serves 14 to 16

chicken velvet soup

A masterpiece—buttery and smooth.

2 whole chicken breasts, cooked, boned and cubed
¾ cup butter
¾ cup flour
1 cup milk, warmed
6 cups chicken stock, divided
1 cup whipping cream, warmed
½ tsp. salt
dash pepper

In a 3-quart saucepan, melt butter and blend in flour. Gradually add the warm milk, 2 cups of the chicken stock and warm cream, stirring constantly. When well blended, simmer for at least 20 minutes. Add chicken, the remaining chicken stock and seasonings. Do not boil. Serve hot.

Serves 6

chicken and corn soup

A tasty, interesting combination!

¼ cup butter
½ cup chopped onion
1 carrot, diced
1 stalk celery, diced
1¼ cups chicken broth, divided
2 cups (1 lb. can) creamed corn
1 cup milk or cream
½ tsp. poultry seasoning
⅛ tsp. mace
dash Tabasco
salt and pepper
1 cup diced, cooked chicken

In a 2-quart pan, melt butter and saute onion until soft. Add carrot, celery and ¼ cup of the chicken broth. Cover and cook until vegetables are tender. Add remaining ingredients *except chicken* and simmer, covered, for 20 minutes, stirring occasionally. Remove from heat. Blend in small batches in a blender at medium speed for 30 seconds. Return to cooking pan. Add chicken; heat just to boiling. Serve hot. Can be prepared ahead. Add additional poultry seasoning and mace, if more seasoning is preferred.

Serves 4 to 6

chicken-noodle-vegetable soup

6 cups rich chicken broth
½ cup chopped onion
½ cup diced celery
½ cup diced carrots
¼ cup chopped parsley
1 tsp. MSG
½ tsp. garlic salt
½ tsp. tarragon
dash Tabasco
salt and pepper
½ cup fine noodles
2 cups diced, cooked chicken
½ cup frozen peas

Combine all ingredients *except peas* in a 4-quart kettle. Bring to a boil. Reduce heat; cover and simmer slowly for 40 minutes. Add peas during last five minutes; cook until tender. Serve hot. Garnish with additional chopped parsley. To prepare ahead, follow same procedure adding peas before reheating.

Serves 4 to 6

cream of spinach soup

Serve hot or cold, depending on the season.

¼ cup butter
¾ cup onion
2 pkgs. (10 oz. each) frozen spinach, thawed
½ tsp. salt
¼ tsp. pepper
⅛ tsp. nutmeg
3 T. flour
6 cups chicken broth
2 egg yolks
½ cup whipping cream
sour cream

In a large saucepan, melt butter and saute onion until tender. Add spinach. Cover and cook over low heat until spinach is tender. Stir in seasonings. Add flour gradually, stirring until well blended and smooth. Add chicken stock. Simmer, uncovered, 7 minutes, stirring until thick. Place soup in a blender, 2 cups at a time. Blend for 30 seconds. Return soup to a clean saucepan. (At this point, soup can be frozen.) Blend egg yolks with cream. Add cream mixture to soup, stirring constantly. Heat soup thoroughly but *do not boil*. Serve in soup bowls. Garnish with sour cream. Can be served cold, if desired.

Serves 8

new england clam chowder

3 slices bacon, cut into small strips
½ cup chopped onion
¼ cup minced celery (optional)
4 medium potatoes, peeled and cubed
2 carrots, thinly sliced
2 cans (6½ oz. each) minced clams, undrained
1 bottle (8 oz.) clam juice
2 cups water
2-3 T. flour
2 cups whipping cream
salt and cayenne pepper

In a large saucepan, fry bacon over medium heat until brown. Add onions and celery; cook until transparent. Add the next 5 ingredients. Simmer until vegetables are soft, about 25 to 30 minutes. In a tight fitting container, add cream to flour; shake until blended. Add slowly to soup mixture in pan. Cook to thicken but *do not boil*. Season with the salt and pepper. May be prepared in advance to point of adding flour and cream which must be done at the last minute.

Serves 4 to 6

crab and shrimp gumbo

An excellent main-dish soup for a cold winter night or after a sporting event.

1 lb. bacon
2 onions, chopped
2 garlic cloves, chopped
2 cans (16 oz. each) stewed tomatoes
6½ cups consomme
1 carrot, diced
4 green onions, chopped
1½ lbs. shrimp
1 lb. crabmeat
½ tsp. pepper
½ tsp. saffron
1 tsp. salt
1 lb. frozen okra
4-6 T. flour
1 cup water
3 T. chopped parsley
2 cups prepared instant rice

In a large skillet, fry bacon until crisp. Remove from skillet. Crumble and save for garnish. Saute onions and garlic in the bacon drippings. Drain excess fat from onions and garlic; place in a large soup kettle. Add tomatoes and consomme; cover and boil. Add carrots and green onions. Simmer for 30 minutes. Add seafood and seasonings. Reheat to simmering and add okra. Simmer another 30 minutes. Combine flour with water and add to soup. Simmer on medium heat until soup thickens. Add parsley just before serving. Place gumbo in individual bowls. Garnish with bacon and rice. Serve with a green salad and hot muffins.

Serves 6

ground beef and vegetable soup

A meal in itself.

½ cup butter
1 cup flour
2 quarts water
1½-2 lbs. ground beef
1 cup coarsely chopped onions
1 cup sliced carrots
1 cup sliced celery
2 cups frozen mixed vegetables
1 can (15 oz.) tomatoes
1 tsp. MSG
2 T. instant beef bouillon (granulated)
1 tsp. freshly ground pepper

In a large soup kettle, melt butter. Whip in flour to make a smooth paste. Stir in water. Heat until bubbly and free of lumps. Continue heating until mixture comes to a boil; reduce heat to simmer. In a large skillet, brown ground beef. Drain off fat; add meat to soup liquid in kettle. Add onions, carrots and celery. Simmer for 20 minutes. Add remaining ingredients to soup. Simmer another 10 to 20 minutes or until vegetables are tender. This soup freezes well.

Makes 1 gallon

beef-vegetable soup with braunschweiger balls

Braunschweiger Balls:
½ lb. Braunschweiger, mashed
½ cup fine, dry breadcrumbs
1 egg, slightly beaten
3 T. chopped, fresh parsley
½ tsp. salt
⅛ tsp. garlic powder
¼ tsp. ground marjoram

Soup:
2 lbs. beef brisket
1 beef soup bone
2 quarts water
2½ tsp. salt
few grains pepper
1 cup coarsely chopped onion
1 cup coarsely chopped green pepper
2 medium carrots, cut into 1½-inch pieces
1 cup diced celery
1 cup diced, peeled potatoes
1 can (16 oz.) tomatoes
½ lb. zucchini, sliced

For Braunschweiger Balls: Mix all ingredients together in a bowl. Chill for 1½ to 2 hours in refrigerator. Shape mixture into 1¼-inch balls. Makes about 25 balls.

For Soup: Place meat, bone, water, salt and pepper in a soup kettle. Cover. Bring to a boil over moderately high heat. Skim off any foam that forms on soup surface. Reduce heat to low. Simmer for 2 hours, or until meat is fork-tender. Remove soup from heat. Cool quickly. Chill in refrigerator several hours or overnight to allow fat to harden. Remove and discard fat from soup surface. Add all the vegetables except zucchini. Simmer over low heat for 1 hour. Remove from heat. Remove bone and meat from stock. Discard bone. Trim fat from meat. Cut meat into 1-inch cubes. Add meat and zucchini to soup. Bring to boil over moderately high heat. Reduce heat to low. Simmer for 5 minutes. Add Braunschweiger Balls. Cover and simmer *very gently* another 10 minutes. Serve immediately.

Serves 8 to 10

sausage-tomato soup

This recipe is adapted from one that appeared originally in a summer issue of *Vogue*.

4 strips bacon, diced
1 medium onion, peeled and diced
6 ripe tomatoes, peeled, seeded and diced
½ tsp. sugar
1½ lbs. sweet Italian sausage, casing removed
8 cups beef stock or broth
1 cup uncooked rice
1½ cups grated Parmesan cheese
4 T. butter
2 T. parsley
salt and freshly ground pepper
grated Parmesan cheese

Saute bacon and onion in a large soup kettle until onion is lightly browned. Add tomatoes and sprinkle with sugar. Simmer mixture for 10 minutes, or until tomatoes are soft. In a large skillet, brown sausage until cooked thoroughly, about 10 minutes. Drain off excess fat. Add sausage and beef stock to soup kettle. Cook until mixture comes to a rolling boil, then add rice. Simmer, covered, over medium heat until rice is tender. Add additonal stock or water, if needed. Remove from heat. Stir in cheese, butter and parsley. Season with salt and pepper. Serve hot. Garnish with extra Parmesan cheese.

Note: Substitute canned stewed tomatoes, if ripe fresh ones are not available.

Serves 10

cheesy potato soup

1 quart Vichyssoise (see index)
1 cup grated Cheddar cheese
salt
dash cayenne pepper
10 slices bacon, crisply fried and crumbled

In a 2-quart saucepan, cook Vichyssoise and cheese over low heat until cheese is melted. Do not boil. Add seasonings. Serve hot. Garnish with crumbled bacon. Soup is thinner when warm.

Serves 6 to 8

baked open-face crabmeat sandwich

An hors d'oeuvre or light supper sandwich.

6 Holland rusks or bread rounds
butter
1 pkg. (8 oz.) softened cream cheese
1 can or pkg. (6 oz.) crabmeat
1 T. Worcestershire sauce
1½ T. lemon juice
2 small green onions, finely chopped
1 T. chopped black olives
12 fresh mushroom caps
½ cup mayonnaise
½ cup grated sharp Cheddar cheese

Butter one side of rusks or bread rounds. Combine cream cheese, crabmeat, Worcestershire sauce, lemon juice, onions and olives; blend well. Pile on buttered-side of rusks or bread rounds. Place 2 mushrooms on each sandwich. Combine and mix mayonnaise and cheese. Spread on top of each sandwich. Place on baking sheet; bake at 350° for 15 to 20 minutes, or until warm and lightly browned.

Makes 6 sandwiches

chicken or crab souffle sandwiches

Glamorous sandwiches!

⅔ cup real mayonnaise
¼ cup shredded Cheddar cheese
2 T. diced green pepper
⅛ tsp. Worcestershire sauce
2 egg whites
4 slices toast, buttered
1 large tomato, sliced
1 avocado, sliced
4 slices cooked chicken breast or 6 oz. crabmeat, drained

In a small bowl, combine mayonnaise, cheese, green pepper and Worcestershire sauce. Beat egg whites until stiff but not dry. Carefully fold mayonnaise mixture into egg whites. Set aside. Place tomato slices then avocado on toast. Place on broiler pan; broil 2 to 3 minutes. Remove from broiler. Place chicken or crabmeat on toast. Top with egg white mixture, allowing it to drip down sides. Broil 2 minutes more until brown.

Serves 4

shrimp salad sandwich

The coconut and almonds give this shrimp salad a different twist.

1 lb. small shrimp, cooked and drained
⅓ cup shredded coconut
½ cup diced celery
⅔ cup real mayonnaise
1 tsp. lemon juice
½ tsp. salt
1 cup slivered, toasted almonds
12 slices whole wheat bread

In a medium bowl, mix all ingredients *except* almonds and bread. Refrigerate for several hours or overnight. When ready to serve, stir almonds into shrimp mixture. Spread salad between slices of whole wheat bread.

Makes 6 sandwiches

everyone's favorite barbecue

Plan on serving seconds with this tasty recipe.

Meat:
1 medium onion, halved
1½ lbs. lean beef, cubed
½ lb. lean pork, cubed

Barbecue Sauce:
1 bottle (26 oz.) ketchup
1 green pepper, chopped
2 T. each: dry mustard, white vinegar, sugar
1 tsp. salt
2 T. whole pickling spice, tied in clean cloth bag

For Meat: Place onion halves, beef and pork in large pot. Cover with a generous amount of water. Boil approximately 2½ hours until tender. Tear cooked meat apart. Set aside.

For Sauce: Simmer ketchup, green pepper, dry mustard, vinegar, sugar, salt and pickling spice in large saucepan for 30 minutes. Add meat to sauce. Simmer an additional 20 minutes. Remove pickling spice bag. Serve on warm rolls or buns.

Liquid from boiled meat may be used as stock in other recipes. Barbecue may be made several days ahead. Freezes well.

Serves 10 to 12

stroganoff steak sandwich

Perfect with a frosty stein of beer.

⅔ cups beer
⅓ cup vegetable oil
1 tsp. salt
1 clove garlic, slivered
1 tsp. MSG
½ tsp. coarsely ground pepper
1 2-2½ lb. flank steak
2 T. butter
½ tsp. each: salt, paprika
4 cups sliced onions
¼ cup sliced mushrooms (optional)
12 oz. sour cream
½-1 tsp. horseradish
12 slices French bread

Combine beer, oil, salt, garlic, MSG and pepper in a pan large enough for the steak. Add meat and marinate, covered, overnight. Turn occasionally. Drain meat. Grill or broil meat for 5 to 7 minutes on each side for medium rare. In a medium saucepan, melt butter with paprika and salt. Add onions (and mushrooms); cook until onions are barely tender. In another saucepan, gradually warm sour cream and horseradish. Toast French bread just lightly. Slice meat diagonally in very thin strips. Place meat over toast. Cover with onions and then sour cream. Sprinkle with paprika. If you plan to use just one flank steak weighing about 1½ pounds, do not cut the ingredients for the marinade in half.

Makes 12 sandwiches

sandwich beef brisket

A delicious "make-ahead" for week-end entertaining.

1 bottle (8 oz.) Italian salad dressing
1 cup Concord grape wine
1 3-lb. beef brisket

Mix salad dressing and wine in a container large enough for brisket; add brisket. Cover and refrigerate 24 hours. Roast, uncovered, turning once, in marinade at 275° for 4 hours, or until tender.

Makes 12 to 15 sandwiches or serves 4 to 6 for dinner.

bright's burgers

Great for tailgate picnics before the game.

1½ lbs. ground beef
1 medium onion, finely chopped
½ green pepper, finely chopped
1 celery stalk, finely chopped
½ tsp. salt
1 can (10¾ oz.) condensed tomato soup
1 T. prepared mustard
5 T. green tomato relish or 2-3 T. pickle relish
15-20 slices American cheese (1 per bun)
15-20 *small* hamburger buns

In a large skillet, saute ground beef, onion, green pepper and celery. Drain excess fat. Add salt, soup, mustard and relish; stir well. Spoon onto buns; top with cheese slice. Replace top of bun. Place buns on cookie sheet. Heat at 350° until cheese melts. Serve hot. To freeze, wrap individually in foil. Reheat.

Makes 15 to 20 small sandwiches

tuna muffins

With very little effort, tuna becomes elegant.

2 cans (7 oz. each) tuna in water, drained
1 pkg. (8 oz.) softened cream cheese
2 T. sherry
3 English muffins, split and lightly toasted
6 slices Colby cheese

Mix tuna with cream cheese and sherry. Heap on muffin halves. Top with Colby cheese. Bake at 350° for 10 minutes or until cheese melts.

Makes 6 sandwiches

BECHERER'S.
BAKERY & CONFECTIONERY.

breads

"Attention to neatness is doubly important in bread-making.
Be sure the hair is neatly combed and put up,
(which ought to be done before the dress is put on every morning).
A neat calico apron with bib, and sleeves of dress well-tucked up and fastened
so they will not come down, add much to the comfort
of this the most important task of the kitchen queen."

coffee panettonne

While baking, this Italian breakfast or tea bread has the delightful aroma of roasting coffee beans.

1 pkg. dry yeast
¼ cup warm water
1 cup strong, warm coffee
2 T. butter
2 tsp. salt
2 T. sugar
¼ tsp. baking soda
1 tsp. vanilla
3½-4 cups flour
⅓ cup raisins
⅓ cup mixed, diced, candied fruit
⅓ cup chopped walnuts
Glaze (See Carrot Coffee Cake)
diced candied fruit for garnish

In a large mixing bowl, dissolve yeast in warm water. Add warm coffee, butter, salt, sugar, baking soda and vanilla. Stir until sugar dissolves. Stir in enough flour to make a dough barely stiff enough to knead. Knead 7 to 10 minutes, kneading in the fruits and nuts at the end. Place dough in a greased bowl; cover with a moist towel. Let rise in a warm place (85°) until doubled in bulk. Punch down. Knead a few times to remove remaining bubbles. Divide dough in half. Form into 2 balls and place in 2 well-greased 1-pound coffee cans. Cover and let rise in a warm place until dough nearly reaches the rim. Bake at 375° for 30 to 40 minutes or until loaves sound hollow when tapped. Frost with Glaze and sprinkle additional fruits on top.

Makes 2 loaves.

carrot coffee cake

Nice for Christmas gifts.

2 cups sifted flour
2 tsp. each: baking powder, baking soda, cinnamon
1 tsp. salt
2 cups sugar
½ cup vegetable oil
3 cups grated, fresh carrots
4 unbeaten eggs
½ cup chopped nuts
½ cup dark or golden raisins (optional)
2 T. rum or sherry (optional)

Glaze:
1⅓ cups sifted confectioners' sugar
2 T. milk
¼ tsp. vanilla or other flavoring
dash of salt

For Cake: Sift flour once and measure. Add baking powder, baking soda, cinnamon and salt to measured flour. Sift together twice. Set aside. In a large bowl, combine sugar and oil; beat well. Add carrots and blend. Add eggs one at a time, blending thoroughly after each addition. Add dry ingredients and nuts; stir well. Add optional ingredients, if desired. Blend. Bake in a greased 10-inch bundt or tube pan at 350° for 45 minutes. Cool 10 minutes. Remove from pan. Combine ingredients for Glaze and mix until well blended. Spread over cake and serve.

Serves 12 to 15

rhubarb coffee cake

You can substitute 6 cups sliced apples for the rhubarb.

2 cups flour
1 T. baking powder
pinch salt
¼ cup butter or margarine
1 cup sugar
1 egg, beaten
milk, enough to make 1 cup when added to egg
2 cups diced rhubarb (¼-inch dice)

Topping:
1 cup flour
1 cup sugar
½ cup butter

Sift dry ingredients together into a large bowl. Cut in butter with pastry blender until crumbly. Add sugar. Mix well. Put egg in measuring cup; add enough milk to make 1 cup liquid. Add mixture to dry ingredients and stir lightly with a fork. Spread in a 9 x 13-inch greased pan. Layer with rhubarb. Cover with Topping. Bake at 350° for 1 hour. The top should be lightly browned. If not, brown under broiler for a few seconds.

For Topping: Stir flour and sugar together in a medium bowl. With a fork blend in butter until mixture is crumbly.

Serves 12 to 14

currant-pecan crown

Currant-Pecan Filling:
1 cup melted butter
1 cup brown sugar
1½ cups currants
2 cups ground pecans
1 recipe Brown Sugar Yeast Dough (see index)
1 egg white
1 tsp. water
2 T. granulated sugar

For Currant-Pecan Filling: In a small mixing bowl, combine melted butter, brown sugar, currants and pecans. Mix well and set aside.

For Brown Sugar Yeast Dough: Prepare as directed for Cinnamon-Raisin Loaf. Divide dough in half. Roll out one-half on lightly floured surface into a 8 x 16-inch rectangle. Spread one-half of currant mixture to within 1 inch of edges. Roll as for a jelly roll, starting with long side. Place on greased baking sheet, seam-side down. Shape into a ring, pinching and sealing ends together with small amount of water. With sharp scissors cut at ½-inch intervals around ring, deep enough that sections can overlap each other at an angle without becoming disconnected at bottom. Each section may need twisting to lie evenly. Repeat procedure with remaining dough and filling. In a small bowl, beat egg white lightly with water until foamy. Brush surface of rings with egg white mixture. Sprinkle each top with 1 tablespoon of the sugar. Bake at 375° for 30 minutes or until golden brown. (Dough does not need to rise before baking.)

Makes 2 rings

cinnamon-raisin loaf

Makes two delicious loaves.

Brown Sugar Yeast Dough:
2 pkgs. dry yeast
¼ cup warm water
1 cup scalded milk
½ cup brown sugar
1 tsp. salt
½ cup softened butter
5-5½ cups flour
2 eggs, beaten

Cinnamon-Raisin Filling:
½ cup melted butter
1 cup raisins
1 cup sugar
2 tsp. dark corn syrup
2 tsp. cinnamon

Confectioners' Sugar Frosting:
1 cup confectioners' sugar
1 T. milk
½ tsp. vanilla

For Brown Sugar Yeast Dough: Soften yeast in warm water; set aside. In a large bowl, combine scalded milk, sugar, salt and butter. Stir well. Add 2 cups of the flour and beat well. Stir in yeast mixture and eggs. Gradually add remaining 3 to 3½ cups flour. Knead 8 to 10 minutes, or until dough is smooth and elastic and no longer sticks to fingers. Form into a ball. Place in a greased bowl; cover and let rise until doubled, about 2 hours. Meanwhile, combine ingredients for Cinnamon-Raisin Filling in a mixing bowl. Set aside. After dough has doubled, punch down and shape into 2 balls. Allow dough to rest 10 minutes. Roll out on a lightly floured surface into a 9-inch square. Spread with half the Cinnamon-Raisin Filling. Roll up to form a loaf, pinching seam to seal. Place into a greased 9 x 5-inch loaf pan, seam side down. Repeat process with second ball. Let rise until doubled, about 1 hour. Bake at 375° for 40 to 45 minutes. Cool. Combine ingredients for Confectioner's Sugar Frosting. Beat until smooth. Drizzle over top of loaves.

Makes 2 loaves

danish puff

Crust:
½ cup butter
1 cup flour
⅛ tsp. salt
2 T. water

Filling:
½ cup butter or margarine
1 cup water
1½ tsp. almond extract
1 cup flour
3 eggs

Glaze Topping:
1 cup confectioners' sugar
2-3 T. milk or cream
1 tsp. almond extract
dash salt
¼ cup slivered almonds

For Crust: Cut butter into flour and salt. Sprinkle water over dough and mix with fork. Roll into a ball and divide in half. Pat dough with hands into two 4 x 12-inch strips. Place strips at least 3 inches apart on an ungreased baking sheet.

For Filling: In a large pan, bring water and butter to boil. After butter melts, add almond extract and remove from heat. Stir in flour quickly to keep it from lumping. When smooth and thick, add eggs one at a time, beating until smooth after each addition. Divide in half and spread over each pastry strip. Bake at 350° for 45 to 60 minutes. When puffs are cool, drizzle glaze over top. Sprinkle with slivered almonds. May be prepared in advance and frozen, unbaked. Then, thaw overnight in refrigerator and bake.

For Glaze Topping: In small bowl, combine glaze ingredients, except slivered almonds.

Makes 9 to 12 slices

sherri's blueberry coffee cake

Perfect for a neighborhood coffee klatsch.

2 cups flour
¾ cup sugar
½ tsp. baking powder
½ tsp. salt
1 cup butter or margarine
2 eggs, beaten
½ cup orange juice
1 tsp. almond extract
1-2 cups blueberries, divided

Glaze:
½ cup powdered sugar
⅓ cup milk

Sift dry ingredients together. Cut in butter or margarine. Add eggs, orange juice and almond extract. Spread half of the blueberries in bottom of a 9 x 9-inch greased pan. Top with batter. Spread remaining blueberries over top and mix. Bake at 350° for 40 to 45 minutes. Mix Glaze ingredients and spread on top of cake.

Serves 12 to 15

sour cream coffee cake

Make ahead and freeze.

¾ cup butter or margarine
1 cup sugar
2 eggs
1 cup sour cream
½ tsp. vanilla
2 cups sifted flour
1 tsp. baking powder
¼ tsp. salt
½ cup brown sugar
1 T. cinnamon
1 cup chopped pecans

Glaze:
½ cup confectioners' sugar
2 tsp. hot milk
¼ tsp. vanilla

In a large bowl, cream butter, gradually adding sugar. Beat until light and fluffy. Beat in eggs one at a time; fold in sour cream and vanilla. Fold in flour, baking powder and salt. In separate bowl, combine brown sugar, cinnamon and pecans. Pour one-third of the batter into a greased and floured tube pan. Sprinkle with one-third sugar mixture; repeat procedure twice. Bake at 350° for 1 hour. Cool and remove from pan. Combine Glaze ingredients and drizzle on cake.

Serves 12

pecan brunch cakes

Excellent with salads and luncheon dishes.

¾ cup flour
½ tsp. baking powder
½ tsp. baking soda
¼ tsp. salt
3 eggs, lightly beaten
1¼ cups brown sugar
½ tsp. vanilla
1½ cups chopped pecans

Brown Sugar Frosting:
2 T. each: butter, brown sugar, milk
⅔-¾ cup confectioners' sugar

Sift flour, baking powder, soda, and salt. In a mixing bowl, mix the eggs, sugar and vanilla. Stir in sifted ingredients and pecans. Mix well. Bake in greased medium-size muffin tins or paper baking cups at 325° for 20 minutes. Cool in tins for a few minutes before removing. Serve with or without frosting. Frost cakes in a criss-cross design. Very little frosting is needed as cakes are very rich.

For Brown Sugar Frosting: Melt butter and brown sugar in a small saucepan. Cool. Beat in milk and sugar alternately to spreading consistency.

Makes 18

pecan sticky buns

2 pkgs. dry yeast
½ cup lukewarm water
½ cup sugar
2 tsp. salt
½ cup butter or margarine
¾ cup milk, scalded
1 egg
4 cups flour, divided

Topping:
1 cup melted butter or margarine
2½ cups brown sugar, divided
1½ cups chopped pecans, divided

In a large warm bowl, dissolve yeast in water. In a separate bowl, stir together sugar, salt, butter or margarine and scalded milk until butter is melted. Cool until lukewarm. Stir milk mixture into yeast. Add egg and 2 cups of the flour. Beat until smooth. Stir in remaining flour to make a stiff dough. Place in an oiled bowl. Cover tightly and refrigerate at least 2 hours or up to 3 days.

For Topping: Stir together melted butter, 1½ cups of the brown sugar and 1 cup of the pecans. Spoon mixture into 2 greased muffin pans. Combine remaining 1 cup of brown sugar and ½ cup of pecans. Set aside.

To assemble: Divide dough in half. On a lightly floured board, roll each half into a 12-inch square. Sprinkle with reserved sugar mixture. Roll up lengthwise as for a jelly roll. Cut into 1-inch slices and place in prepared pans. Cover and let rise in a warm place until doubled, about 1 hour. Bake at 350° for 20 to 25 minutes.

Makes 2 dozen

blintz roll-ups

Sweet, good and different!

7 slices white bread, crusts removed
4 oz. whipped cream cheese
raisins (optional)
6 T. butter, melted
cinnamon-and-sugar mixture
1 cup sour cream

With a rolling pin, roll bread slices flat. Spread with cream cheese. Sprinkle 2 or 3 raisins on each. Roll up jelly roll style. Cut in half. Roll in melted butter, then in cinnamon-and-sugar mixture. Bake at 350° for 10 minutes. Pass with a bowl of sour cream for dipping. Rolls may be frozen before baking.

Makes 14 roll-ups

quicky-sticky rolls

Shhh! Everyone will think they're homemade.

1 pkg. (8 oz.) refrigerator crescent rolls
2-3 T. softened butter
¼ cup brown sugar
½ cup finely chopped pecans

Unroll dough and separate into 8 triangles. Spread generously with softened butter. Sprinkle with sugar and pecans. Roll up and bake according to package directions.

Note: For mini-size rolls, cut triangles in half before rolling.

Makes 8 rolls

cinnamon rolls

They will melt in your mouth!

1 pkg. dry yeast
¼ cup water
1 cup milk, scalded
¼ cup sugar
¼ cup butter or margarine
1 tsp. salt
3½ cups sifted flour, divided
1 egg

Filling Mixture:
½ cup sugar
¼ cup melted butter
1½ tsp. cinnamon

Dissolve yeast in warm water. Set aside. In a saucepan, combine milk, sugar, butter and salt. Heat until butter is melted. Cool to lukewarm. Add 1 cup of the flour and beat well. Beat in yeast and egg. Gradually add enough remaining flour to make soft dough. Cover and let rise in warm place, approximately 1½ to 2 hours. On a lightly floured board, roll the dough into two 16 x 8-inch rectangles.

For Filling Mixture: Combine sugar, butter and cinnamon. Spread on dough. Roll up beginning with long side and cut into 1-inch slices. Place into 3 or 4 greased 8-inch round pans. Let rise for 30 to 45 minutes. Bake at 350° for 20 to 25 minutes. Can be frozen. Thaw and allow to rise before baking.

Makes 32 rolls

melt-in-your-mouth biscuits

Like grandma used to make!

1 cup sifted flour
2 tsp. baking powder
½ tsp. salt
3 T. butter or margarine
½ cup milk

In a large bowl, combine dry ingredients. Cut in butter or margarine. Slowly add milk. Mix well, but gently. On a floured surface, gently pat out dough. Knead lightly once or twice. Press with heel of hand to ½-inch thickness. Cut into 2-inch circles. Place on greased baking sheet so that circles touch. Bake at 425° for 12 minutes or until golden brown. Serve immediately.

Note: If used for shortcake, add 2 T. sugar. This recipe doubles easily.

Makes 6 biscuits

old-fashioned biscuits

Delicious served with fresh strawberries over them as an old-fashioned shortcake!

2 cups sifted flour
1 T. baking powder
1 tsp. salt
1 T. sugar (optional)
6 T. shortening, butter or margarine
1 egg, slightly beaten
½ cup milk, approximately

Sift together dry ingredients. Cut in shortening finely with a pastry blender. Put egg into a measuring cup. Pour milk in cup on top of egg until you have ⅔ to ¾ cup of liquid. Stir liquid into dry ingredients to make a soft dough. Form into ball and place on lightly floured board. Knead lightly about 30 seconds. Roll or pat out about ½ to ¼-inch thick. Cut out with round cutter in the desired size. Place on ungreased baking sheet. Bake at 450° for 10 to 12 minutes until golden brown. Serve hot.

Makes 20 biscuits

orange popovers with honey butter

Sensational served with fruit salad for a special luncheon!

4 eggs
2 cups milk
2 cups flour
1 tsp. salt
grated peel of 1 orange

Honey Butter:
1 T. honey
½ cup softened butter

In small bowl, beat eggs and milk until smooth. In another bowl, stir flour with salt; make a well in the center and pour egg mixture into it. Add orange peel. Beat with wire whisk until well blended, but no longer. Pour batter into hot popover pans sprayed with vegetable cooking-spray. Fill about two-thirds full. Bake on lowest rack at 450° for 20 minutes. Reduce heat to 350° and bake an additional 15 to 20 minutes or until brown and crusty. *Do not open oven door during baking.* Remove from oven and insert sharp knife to release steam. While popovers bake, beat honey and butter until light and fluffy. Serve popovers hot from the oven with Honey Butter.

Makes 10 popovers

date bran muffins

Batter may be refrigerated up to three weeks and used as needed.

2 cups bran-buds cereal
1 cup all-bran cereal
1 cup boiling water
1 cup shortening
1½ cups sugar
2 eggs
2½ cups flour
1½ tsp. salt
2½ tsp. baking soda
2 cups buttermilk
1 cup chopped walnuts or pecans
1 pkg. (8 oz.) diced dates

In a large bowl, combine the two cereals. Add boiling water and shortening. Stir until shortening melts. Cool. Add remaining ingredients. Mix gently. Bake in greased or paper-lined muffin pan for 30 to 40 minutes at 375°. Do not cover tightly while stored in refrigerator.

Makes 3 dozen

brown-and-serve whole wheat bread and rolls

Homemade bread and rolls out of the freezer anytime!

6-7 cups all-purpose flour
4 pkgs. dry yeast
⅔ cup nonfat dry milk powder
½ cup firmly packed brown sugar
2 tsp. salt
2 T. butter or margarine
4 cups warm water (115°-120°)
4½ cups whole wheat flour

In large mixing bowl, completely stir together 4 cups of the flour and next 4 ingredients. Stir butter with warm water until melted. Add to flour mixture. Beat at low speed for 30 seconds, scraping bowl constantly. Beat 3 minutes at high speed. By hand, stir in whole wheat flour and enough of the remaining all-purpose flour to make a moderately stiff dough. Turn dough onto a lightly floured board. Knead until smooth and elastic, 10 to 12 minutes. Place in a greased bowl, turning to grease surface. Cover and let rise in a warm place until doubled. Punch dough down and divide in half. Divide each half into 5 parts. Cover and let rest 10 minutes. Shape each part into a loaf and place in greased 4½ x 2½ x 1½-inch loaf pans. Shape remaining dough into 24 rolls. Cover loaves and rolls. Let rise in a warm place until doubled. Bake loaves at 350° for 20 to 25 minutes. Bake rolls at 325° for 12 to 15 minutes. *Do not brown.* Cool on racks. Wrap and freeze. When ready to use, unwrap slightly. Thaw at room temperature 10 to 15 minutes. Unwrap completely. Place on baking sheet. Bake at 450° until golden brown, about 5 to 10 minutes.

Makes 10 mini-loaves and 2 dozen rolls, or 4 dozen rolls.

oatmeal-raisin muffins

A delicious, flaky muffin.

1 cup quick-cooking oatmeal
1 cup buttermilk
½ cup raisins
½ cup water
½ cup brown sugar
½ cup melted butter
1 large or 2 small eggs
1 cup flour
½ tsp. salt
1 rounded tsp. baking powder
1 rounded tsp. baking soda

In large bowl, soak oatmeal in buttermilk for 1 hour. In small saucepan, simmer raisins in water until plump and water has evaporated. Add remaining ingredients to oatmeal mixture and mix well. Stir in raisins. Line muffin pan with paper baking cups and fill two-thirds full. Bake at 400° for 15 to 20 minutes.

Makes 12 muffins

home-baked crescent rolls

Be sure to allow several per person. Easily frozen for convenience.

1 cup milk
¾ cup butter
¼ cup sugar
1½ tsp. salt
1 pkg. dry yeast
¼ cup warm water
4 cups unbleached flour, divided
2 eggs
oil
melted butter

In a small saucepan, heat together milk, butter, sugar and salt until butter is completely melted. Cool slightly. In a large bowl, dissolve yeast in warm water. Beat in warm milk mixture. Add 2 cups of the flour and beat slowly for 2 minutes. Beat in eggs. Slowly add 1 cup flour and beat again for 2 minutes. With a wooden spoon, beat in ¾ cup flour. On a floured board, knead dough until smooth and elastic, about 10 minutes. Oil a large bowl and turn dough into it. Brush top with oil and cover with plastic wrap. Set in warm place and let rise until doubled. Punch down dough and knead 2 to 3 times. At this point, the dough can rest for an hour, if necessary. Divide dough into 4 equal portions. Roll each part into a circle on a lightly floured board. Brush with melted butter. Cut into 8 pie-shaped wedges. Roll each wedge, wide end to narrow, and form into crescent. Place on greased baking sheets leaving enough room for dough to triple in size. Brush with melted butter and let rise until tripled, about 1 hour. Bake at 400° about 10 to 12 minutes. Remove to racks to cool. Place in plastic bags and freeze, if desired. To reheat after freezing, bake at 350° about 15 minutes, partially covered with foil.

Makes 32 rolls

herb crescent rolls

½ recipe Home-Baked Crescent Rolls (see above)

Herb Butter:
½ cup softened butter or margarine
¼ cup grated Parmesan cheese
4 tsp. chopped parsley or 1 tsp. parsley flakes
1 tsp. oregano
¼ tsp. garlic powder

Prepare ½ Home-Baked Crescent Roll recipe. For Herb Butter, combine butter with seasonings. Blend well. Spread each pie-shaped wedge with 1 teaspoon Herb Butter instead of brushing with melted butter. Roll up crescents and bake as directed.

Makes Herb Butter for 16 rolls

swedish rye bread or rolls

2 pkgs. dry yeast
1½ cups lukewarm potato water (water in which potatos have been boiled)
2-3 T. sugar
¼-⅓ cup molasses
2 T. shortening
1 T. each: salt, caraway seeds, grated orange peel
1 cup scalded milk
3 cups rye flour
3½ cups sifted white flour
melted butter

In a large, warm mixing bowl, dissolve yeast in lukewarm potato water (110°-115°). In another bowl, stir together sugar, molasses, shortening, seasonings and milk until shortening melts. Cool mixture to lukewarm. Add to dissolved yeast in large bowl. Stir in rye flour with a wooden spoon. Gradually add enough white flour until dough handles easily. Knead for 10 minutes on a floured board, adding additional flour if necessary to prevent sticking. Turn dough into an oiled bowl. Cover with a damp towel and let rise in a warm place until doubled, about 1 hour. Punch down. Let rise again, about 30 minutes. Punch down. Divide dough in half and shape into 2 large loaves. Place in greased loaf pans. (If oval loaves are desired, shape and place on a cookie sheet that has been greased and sprinkled with cornmeal.) Let rise until sides reach top of pans and tops are well rounded, about 1 hour. Brush tops with melted butter. Bake at 375° for 30 to 35 minutes.

Variation: Individual hard rolls may be made, if desired. After second rising, shape dough into 2-inch balls. Place 3-inches apart on a greased cookie sheet sprinkled with cornmeal. With a razor blade, slit the top of each. Brush with butter and sprinkle with caraway seeds, if desired. Let rise until doubled. Place a large pan of boiling water on bottom of oven. Bake rolls at 450° for 20 minutes. The steam makes the rolls nice and crusty.

Makes 2 loaves or about 1½ dozen rolls

ann's herb bread

The butter oozes . . .Yum!

1 loaf unsliced butter crust bread
1 cup softened butter
¼ tsp. each: salt, paprika, savory
½ tsp. thyme
dash pepper
dash garlic salt (optional)

Trim crusts off bread. Slice into 2-inch thick slices. In a small bowl, combine butter and seasonings. Blend well. Spread butter on both sides of each slice and around entire outside surface except bottom. Wrap in foil. Refrigerate overnight. *Roll foil down* and bake at 325° for 25 minutes.

Serves 4 to 6

christmas bread

This Norwegian sweet bread is full of the good things that smell of Christmas.

1 pkg. dry yeast
⅓ cup lukewarm water
1 cup scalded milk
½ cup sugar
½ cup butter
1½ tsp. salt
1 tsp. ground cardamom
5-6 cups flour
2 eggs
1 cup raisins
½ cup chopped mixed candied fruits
Glaze (See Carrot Coffee Cake)

Dissolve yeast in warm water and set aside. In a large bowl, combine milk, sugar, butter, salt and cardamom. Stir until butter is melted. Stir in 2 cups of the flour. Add eggs and beat well. Stir in yeast mixture, raisins and fruit. Add enough flour to make a soft dough. Turn out onto a floured board and knead until smooth and elastic. Place dough in a greased bowl. Cover and let rise until doubled. Punch down. Divide dough in half and let rest for 10 minutes. To braid, divide each half into thirds. Roll into strands 15 inches long. Place 3 strands close together on a greased cookie sheet. Starting in the middle, braid loosely toward each end. Seal ends. Cover and let rise until doubled. Bake at 350° for 25 to 30 minutes. When cool, drizzle Glaze over the tops.

Makes 2 large braids

french bread

2¼ cups lukewarm water
2 pkgs. dry yeast
2 T. sugar
1 T. salt
3 T. vegetable oil
6-7 cups flour
cornmeal
vegetable oil
1 egg white
1 T. cold water

In a large warm bowl, stir yeast into warm water. Let stand 5 minutes. Add sugar, salt and oil. Stir in 2 cups of the flour and beat with mixer until smooth. Add 1 cup of the flour. Beat with spoon 100 strokes until smooth. Work in more flour until dough is firm but still slightly sticky. Knead 8 to 10 minutes. Place in a bowl. Cover with plastic wrap and let rise in a warm place for 20 minutes. Punch down. Divide dough in half. On a lightly floured board, roll into two 10 x 15-inch rectangles. Roll lengthwise, tightly sealing edges by pinching together. Grease cookie sheet and sprinkle with cornmeal. Place loaves on sheet and brush with oil. Place plastic wrap loosely over bread and refrigerate 2 to 24 hours. One hour before serving, take out and let stand 20 minutes. Puncture any air bubbles with toothpick. Make 4 cuts on each loaf diagonally with a sharp razor blade. Bake at 450° for 25 minutes. Brush with egg white mixed with cold water. Bake 5 minutes more.

Note: Follow directions for Herb French Bread (see index) to make one plain loaf and one herb loaf.

Makes 2 loaves

herb french bread

½ recipe French Bread (see index).

Herb Filling:
1 cup chopped fresh parsley or ½ cup parsley flakes
½ cup chopped green onions
2 T. butter
¾ tsp. salt
dash pepper
1½ tsp. oregano
1 egg, beaten

Follow directions for French Bread. After dough is rolled into 10 x 15-inch rectangle, smooth Herb Filling on top and roll up as directed. Proceed with French Bread directions.

For Herb Filling: Saute parsley and onion in butter until wilted but not browned. Remove from heat; cool. Add seasonings and egg. Brush on dough as directed. Recipe can be doubled easily.

Filling for 1 loaf

dilly french bread

6 T. softened butter
2 tsp. lemon juice
½ tsp. dill weed
8 slices French bread

Mix together softened butter, lemon juice and dill weed. Broil one side of French bread until light brown. Turn over and spread mixture on unbroiled side. Broil until light brown around the edges.

Makes 8 slices

french bread pizza

1 loaf French bread
3 tomatoes, seeded, peeled and finely chopped
¼-½ cup olive oil
3 cloves of garlic, minced
pinch of oregano and basil
salt and pepper
1 pkg. (8 oz.) shredded mozzarella cheese

Cut bread in half lengthwise. Combine tomatoes, oil, garlic and spices. Spread on top of bread. Sprinkle cheese over tomato mixture and place on cookie sheet. Bake at 350° for 10 to 15 minutes or until bubbly. Delicious reheated.

Serves 6

french cheddar loaf

Warms up any main dish.

1 pkg. (10 oz.) brown-and-serve French rolls or 2 loaves brown-and-serve French bread
1 jar (10 oz.) sharp Cheddar cheese spread
garlic salt
2 T. melted butter
⅓ cup caraway or sesame seeds

Make deep diagonal slashes in rolls or loaves, cutting almost to bottom crust. Spread cheese between slices. Sprinkle with garlic salt. Brush tops with melted butter and sprinkle with seeds. Bake at 425° for 12 to 15 minutes until golden brown.

Serves 6

oatmeal bread

Makes wonderful toast!

2 pkgs. yeast
½ cup lukewarm water
¾ cup boiling water
1 cup quick-cooking oatmeal
½ cup mild molasses
½ cup shortening
1 T. salt
6 cups flour
2 beaten eggs

In a small bowl, soften yeast in ½ cup lukewarm water. In large bowl, combine boiling water, oatmeal, molasses, shortening and salt. Stir until shortening is melted. Cool to lukewarm; add 2 cups flour. Mix well. Add eggs and yeast mixture. Beat well. Add enough flour to make a soft dough. Knead on floured board, adding flour as needed to keep dough from getting sticky. Place in well-greased bowl. Cover with greased wax paper. Let rise in warm place until doubled in bulk, about 1 hour. Punch down and let rise again, about 45 minutes. Shape into 2 loaves; place each in a well-greased 9 x 5-inch loaf pan. Let rise until doubled in bulk, 45 minutes to 1 hour. Bake at 375° for 40 to 50 minutes (350° in glass pans).

Makes 2 loaves

apple crumb bread

More like a moist, sweet cake.

½ cup shortening
1 cup sugar
2 eggs
1 tsp. baking soda
2 T. milk soured with 1 T. vinegar
1 tsp. vanilla
2 cups chopped apples
2 cups flour
¼ tsp. salt

Topping:
2 T. each: butter, flour and sugar
1 tsp. cinnamon

Cream together shortening and sugar in a mixing bowl. Add remaining bread ingredients, mixing well after each addition. Pour into a greased 5 x 9-inch loaf pan. Combine Topping ingredients and mix until crumbly. Sprinkle Topping over bread batter. Bake at 350° for 1 hour.

Makes 1 loaf

fresh apple nutbread

1 cup vegetable oil
2 cups sugar
1 tsp. vanilla
3 eggs
3 cups flour
1 tsp. baking soda
1 tsp. cinnamon
3 cups peeled and diced apples
1 cup chopped pecans

In a large bowl, mix oil, sugar and vanilla. Add eggs and mix well. Sift together dry ingredients; add to oil mixture along with apples and nuts. Blend until dry ingredients are just moistened. Pour into 4 greased and floured small loaf pans. Bake at 300° for 1 hour and 15 minutes. While bread is still hot, wrap in foil to keep moist.

Note: If two 5 x 9-inch loaves are preferred, bake for 1½ hours.

Makes 4 small or 2 large loaves

banana-pecan bread

A moist, cake-like bread.

1 cup softened butter
2 cups sugar
4 eggs
4 cups flour
2 tsp. baking soda
½ tsp. salt
7 medium bananas, mashed
1 cup finely chopped pecans
1 T. shredded coconut

In a large mixing bowl, cream butter and sugar until light and fluffy. Add eggs one at a time, beating well after each addition. Combine flour, soda and salt. Gradually add flour mixture alternately with bananas to creamed mixture. Mix thoroughly. With a wooden spoon, stir in pecans and coconut until evenly distributed. Grease and flour three 9 x 5-inch loaf pans. Bake at 300° for 1 hour or until done.

Makes 3 loaves

tea toasts

6 slices Fresh Apple Nutbread, cut in half
¼ cup softened butter
¼ cup light brown sugar

Place nut bread on a cookie sheet. Cream together the butter and brown sugar. Spread evenly on nut bread. Bake at 400° for 5 to 6 minutes or until lightly browned and bubbly. Serve immediately with afternoon tea.

Makes 1 dozen toasts

three grain peanut butter bread

1 cup flour, stirred to aerate before measuring
½ cup quick oats
½ cup yellow cornmeal
½ cup nonfat dry milk
½ cup sugar
3 tsp. baking powder
1 tsp. salt
⅔ cups creamy peanut butter
1 egg
1½ cups whole milk

Combine flour, oats, cornmeal, dry milk, sugar, baking powder and salt. Cut in peanut butter until mixture consists of small particles. Beat egg and milk together and pour into flour mixture. Stir well. Pour into a greased 9 x 5 x 3-inch loaf pan. Bake at 325° for 1 hour and 10 minutes. Remove from pan after 10 minutes.

Makes 1 loaf

whole wheat zucchini bread

3 eggs
2 cups sugar
1 cup vegetable oil
1 T. vanilla
2 cups coarsely grated zucchini
2 cups sifted whole wheat flour
2 tsp. baking soda
1 tsp. salt
1 tsp. baking powder
1 T. cinnamon
1 cup chopped nuts (optional)

Beat eggs until frothy. Add sugar, oil and vanilla. Beat mixture until lemon colored. Stir in remaining ingredients. Pour into 2 greased and floured 8 x 5-inch loaf pans. Bake at 350° for 1 hour or until done. Cool in pans 10 minutes. Then invert on racks.

Makes 2 loaves

pumpkin bread

3 cups flour
2 cups sugar
2 tsp. baking soda
1 tsp. each: ground cloves, cinnamon, nutmeg, salt
½ tsp. baking powder
1 can (16 oz.) pumpkin
3 eggs, slightly beaten
⅔ cup vegetable oil

Mix the first 8 ingredients together. Add pumpkin, oil and eggs and mix well. Pour into 2 greased 9 x 5-inch loaf pans. Bake at 350° for 60 minutes. Cool 10 minutes. Then remove from pans. Refrigerate or freeze for later use.

Makes 2 loaves

tippecanoe tea bread

An old-fashioned nut bread with the added zest of orange.

2 cups sifted flour
1 cup sifted whole wheat flour
½ cup sugar
4 tsp. baking powder
½ tsp. salt
1 egg, lightly beaten
½ cup orange marmalade
1¼ cups milk
½ tsp. vanilla
zest of 1 orange (or grated rind)
2 T. melted butter
1 cup chopped pecans

Sift together into a large bowl the flour, sugar, baking powder and salt. In a medium bowl, beat together remaining ingredients except pecans. Pour over dry ingredients; add pecans. Stir very gently until dry ingredients are just moist. Turn into a greased 9 x 5 x 3-inch loaf pan. Let stand for 20 minutes. Bake at 350° for 50 to 60 minutes or until tester comes out clean. Remove from pan and cool on wire rack. Nut bread always slices easier the next day, if you can wait that long!

Makes 1 loaf

zucchini-pineapple bread

Two fine loaves! One for family, one for friends!

3 eggs
1 cup vegetable oil
2 cups sugar
2 tsp. vanilla
2 cups shredded, unpeeled zucchini
1 can (8¼ oz.) crushed pineapple, well drained
3 cups flour
2 tsp. baking soda
¼ tsp. baking powder
2 tsp. cinnamon
1 tsp. nutmeg
1 tsp. salt
1 cup chopped dates
1 cup chopped pecans

Beat eggs, oil, sugar and vanilla until thick. Stir in remaining ingredients and mix well. Pour into 2 greased 9 x 5-inch loaf pans. Bake at 350° for about 1 hour.

Makes 2 loaves

salads and salad dressings

"Plant the seed of herbs in little boxes on the window sill, or in a sunny spot in the yard.
Gather and dry them as follows: parsley and tarragon in June and July,
just before flowering; mint in June and July; thyme, marjoram and savory in July and August;
basil and sage in August and September. All herbs should be gathered in the sunshine."

HISTORICAL ROOM OF THE NAPPANEE PUBLIC LIBRARY

special salad

The Salad Seasoning can be kept refrigerated in a jar to make numerous *special* salads!

Dressing:
¼ cup lemon juice
½ cup olive oil
1 egg, beaten

Salad Seasoning:
2¼ tsp. salt
1 tsp. each: dry mustard, sugar, MSG
2 tsp. oregano
½ tsp. garlic powder
3 tsp. freshly ground pepper
2 cups (approximately ½ lb.) freshly grated Romano cheese

mixed salad greens
garlic croutons
bacon, fried crisp and crumbled
1 T. Salad Seasoning per person

For Dressing: In a small bowl, mix together ingredients. Refrigerate until serving time. Makes about 1 cup dressing.

For Salad Seasoning: In a large jar, combine ingredients. Cover and store, refrigerated, until ready to use. Makes 20 servings.

To assemble salad: In a large bowl, combine salad greens, croutons, crumbled bacon and 1 tablespoon Salad Seasoning for each serving. Toss with dressing to taste and serve.

Serves 4 to 6

oriental spinach salad

Dressing:
1 cup vegetable oil
¾ cup sugar
⅓ cup ketchup
¼ cup vinegar
1 tsp. Worcestershire sauce
1 T. chopped onion (or less, to taste)
¼ tsp. salt

Salad:
1 lb. fresh spinach, washed and drained
1 can (16 oz.) bean sprouts, drained, or 2 cups fresh bean sprouts
1 can (8 oz.) water chestnuts, drained and thinly sliced
2 hard-cooked eggs, sliced
8 slices bacon, fried crisp and crumbled

For Dressing: Combine all ingredients in a blender. Blend well and refrigerate. To assemble salad: In a large bowl, combine salad ingredients. Pour desired amount of dressing over all. Toss well. Refrigerate remaining dressing for future use.

Serves 6 to 8

make-ahead spinach salad

1 pkg. (10 oz.) frozen peas
½ lb. fresh spinach
½ head of lettuce
6 green onions, chopped
3 hard-cooked eggs, chopped
⅓ cup real mayonnaise
⅓ cup yogurt
1 tsp. salt
1 tsp. dried parsley
½ tsp. each: onion powder, garlic powder, thyme

In a small saucepan, place frozen peas in enough boiling water to cover. Stir for 1 minute. Remove from heat, drain and cool. Tear spinach and lettuce; toss in a salad bowl. Place peas, onions and eggs in layers on top. Mix remaining ingredients and cover (or frost) the salad. Chill. Toss before serving.

Serves 6

super salad with sprouts

Nice accompanied by an omelet for a light supper.

½ head of lettuce
1 bunch leaf lettuce
¼ lb. fresh spinach
1 small head cauliflower, broken into flowerets
8 large fresh mushrooms, sliced
½ can (6 oz.) pitted black olives, sliced
½ cup Monterey Jack cheese, cut into julienne strips
½ cup longhorn cheese, cut into julienne strips
2 cups alfalfa sprouts
¾ cup oil and vinegar dressing

Tear greens into bite-size pieces. Put all ingredients into a large salad bowl. Toss and serve.

Makes 3 luncheon salads or 6 side-dish salads

greek salad

2 heads Boston lettuce
4-6 tomatoes, cut in wedges, or whole cherry tomatoes
1 large red onion, thinly sliced
½ cup grated feta cheese
1 bottle (8 oz.) red wine vinegar and oil dressing
2 tsp. crushed oregano
freshly ground black pepper
12 pitted black olives

In a large bowl, toss together lettuce, tomatoes, onion and cheese. Pour enough dressing over salad to coat well. Add oregano and pepper. Toss lightly. Garnish with black olives. Serve with moussaka.

Serves 6 to 8

mushrooms vinaigrette

4½ T. Dijon mustard
4½ T. red wine vinegar
½ tsp. each: salt, oregano, tarragon
¼ tsp. pepper
¾ cup olive oil
1 lb. fresh mushrooms, thinly sliced
leaf or bibb lettuce
chopped parsley

In a small bowl, combine first 6 ingredients. Gradually add olive oil, blending quickly and thoroughly with a whisk. (This may also be done in a blender.) Refrigerate dressing until serving time. Pour desired amount of dressing over sliced mushrooms. Toss gently. Serve in a bowl lined with lettuce. Sprinkle with parsley. Refrigerate remaining dressing for future use.

Serves 4 to 6

cucumber salad finlandia

This will keep nicely for several days in the refrigerator.

3-4 large cucumbers, pared
½ cup granulated sugar
½ tsp. white pepper
1 tsp. salt
½ cup white wine vinegar
dill weed

Slice cucumbers very thin. Place in a large bowl. Sprinkle with sugar, pepper and salt. Stir all together. Pour vinegar over cucumbers. Stir again. Cover with lid or foil and refrigerate overnight. Serve in small bowls. Garnish with dill.

Serves 8

cucumber ring mold

2 pkgs. (3 oz. each) lime gelatin
2 cups boiling water
2 tsp. vinegar
2 T. horseradish
2 tsp. grated onion
1 large cucumber, grated
1 cup real mayonnaise

In a bowl, mix together gelatin, water and vinegar; cool. Add horseradish, onion and cucumber. Put mixture into a blender. Add mayonnaise and blend thoroughly. Pour into a ring mold. Chill until firm. Unmold on a serving dish and garnish with salad greens.

Serves 8

summer slaw

Best if stored in refrigerator at least 36 hours before serving.

2 quarts finely shredded cabbage (about 2 lb. head)
2 medium green peppers, finely chopped
1 jar (4 oz.) pimento, finely chopped
3 medium onions, finely chopped
1 pint vinegar
1½ cups sugar
1½ tsp. salt
½ tsp. mustard seed
½ tsp. tumeric

Combine cabbage, green pepper, pimento and onion in a large bowl to make the slaw. Pack slaw in a glass half-gallon jar or stone crock. In a large saucepan, combine vinegar, sugar, salt, mustard seed and tumeric. Bring to a boil for 2 to 3 minutes, stirring constantly. Pour hot mixture over the slaw. Store in refrigerator.

Serves 14 to 16

chinese slaw

Vegetables with an Oriental flair.

1 can (16 oz.) French-style green beans, drained
1 can (16 oz.) English peas, drained
1 can (16 oz.) Chinese vegetables, drained
1 can (8 oz.) water chestnuts, drained and sliced
1½ cups diced celery
1 large onion, diced
1 can (2 oz.) chopped pimento
1 can (4 oz.) mushrooms, drained
1 cup vinegar
1 cup sugar
salt and pepper

Put all the vegetables into a large bowl. In a small saucepan, heat vinegar and sugar, bringing it just to a boil. Pour hot mixture over vegetables. Season to taste with salt and pepper. Toss gently. Cover and refrigerate 24 hours. Drain and serve.

Variation: Substitute frozen vegetables, cooked until crisp-tender.

Serves 8 to 10

piquant beet salad

1 can (16 oz.) diced or julienne beets
3 T. tarragon vinegar
1 pkg. (3 oz.) lemon gelatin
1 tsp. salt
2 T. grated onion
3 T. horseradish
¾ cup diced celery
1 cup sour cream

Drain juice from beets, adding enough water to make 1½ cups liquid. Pour into a small saucepan. Add vinegar and bring to a boil. Stir in gelatin, salt, onion and horseradish. Chill until partially set. Stir in beets and celery. Pour mixture into a lightly oiled ring mold. Chill until firm. Unmold and serve with sour cream.

Serves 10

bean salad extraordinaire

A delicious combination of layered vegetables to marinate overnight.

1 can (16 oz.) green beans, drained
1 can (16 oz.) wax beans, drained
1 can (8 oz.) artichoke hearts, drained and cut in eighths
½ lb. fresh mushrooms, sliced
2-3 fresh tomatoes, cut in wedges
1 pkg. Italian salad dressing mix
salad seasoning

In a large bowl, alternate layers of beans, artichokes, mushrooms and tomatoes. Sprinkle liberally with salad seasoning. Prepare Italian salad dressing as directed on the package.Pour over the layered vegetables. Cover and let stand in refrigerator at least 8 hours before serving. Stir occasionally.

Serves 6 to 8

broccoli and cauliflower salad

1 head broccoli, separated into flowerets
1 head cauliflower, separated into flowerets
1 bunch green onions, thinly sliced
½ cup mayonnaise
¼ cup sugar
⅓ cup vinegar
⅓ cup vegetable oil
½ tsp. salt
⅛ tsp. black pepper
pimento or bacon, fried crisp and crumbled, for garnish

Soak broccoli and cauliflower in a large bowl of cold, salted water for 10 to 15 minutes. Drain. Slice flowerets thinly, about ⅛ to ¼-inch thick. Combine with green onions. In a small bowl, mix mayonnaise, sugar, vinegar and oil. Beat well. Season with salt and pepper. (A bit of mustard or horseradish may be added for more flavor.) Toss vegetables with dressing, using a wooden spoon. Cover and refrigerate for 24 hours or overnight. Serve on a platter lined with lettuce leaves. Garnish with pimento or bacon.

Variation: Artichoke hearts and sliced water chestnuts may be combined with salad ingredients.

Serves 12

beet and romaine lettuce salad

1 can (1 lb.) julienne beets (2 cups), drained
½ cup French dressing
1 T. horseradish
½ cup diced celery
¼ cup chopped green onions and tops
3 slices bacon, crisply fried and crumbled
2 hard-cooked eggs, finely chopped
6-8 crisp romaine lettuce leaves

Mix French dressing with horseradish in a small bowl. Add drained beets to dressing; cover. Refrigerate and marinate 4 to 6 hours. Combine celery, onions, bacon and eggs; toss gently. To serve, spoon beets equally onto lettuce leaves. Sprinkle beets with bacon-egg mixture. Arrange on platter in petal design with small bowl of French dressing in the center or serve on individual plates.

Serves 6 to 8

broccoli ring mold

2 pkgs. (10 oz. each) frozen broccoli
1½ T. unflavored gelatin
1 can (10½ oz.) beef consomme
2 hard-cooked eggs, sliced
1 cup mayonnaise
2 T. lemon juice
1 tsp. Tabasco
1-2 T. Worcestershire sauce
1 pkg. (4 oz.) softened cream cheese

Cook broccoli according to package directions until tender-crisp; drain. Cool. Set aside a few broccoli buds. Place remaining broccoli in an electric blender. Set aside. In a small saucepan, combine gelatin and consomme. Heat until gelatin is dissolved. Cool. Arrange egg slices and broccoli buds, flower-side down, in bottom of an oiled 6-cup ring mold. Spoon about ½ cup cooled consomme over egg slices and broccoli. Refrigerate until set. Pour remaining consomme into blender with broccoli. Add remaining ingredients to blender. Puree until smooth. Pour over the jelled consomme in mold. Refrigerate until firm. Unmold and garnish with sliced cherry tomatoes and sprigs of parsley.

Serves 6 to 8

epicurian vegetable salad

Dressing:
1 cup vegetable oil
½ cup white wine vinegar
2 tsp. sugar
1 tsp. salt
½ tsp. paprika

Salad:
½ cup sliced, stuffed olives
1 small head cauliflower, separated into flowerets
½ Bermuda onion, thinly sliced
½ cup crumbled Roquefort or blue cheese
mixed salad greens

For Dressing: Put all ingredients in a jar and shake well. Refrigerate. To assemble salad: Marinate olives, cauliflower and onion in dressing for 1 hour, or longer. At serving time, toss cheese with greens in a large bowl. Add marinated vegetables. (You may wish to drain off some of the dressing.) Toss lightly.

Serves 8

mandarin orange and avocado salad

The oranges and avocado are a perfect pairing.

Dressing:
½ cup vegetable oil
¼ cup vinegar
½ cup sugar
2 tsp. minced onion
½ tsp. salt
dash paprika

8-10 cups bibb and leaf lettuce, torn into pieces
1 can (11 oz.) mandarin oranges, drained
1 avocado, peeled, sliced and tossed lightly in lemon juice
1 can (3 oz.) French-fried onion rings

For Dressing: 6 hours or more before serving, put all ingredients into a blender. Blend well and refrigerate. Just before serving, blend again.

To assemble salad: In a large salad bowl, combine lettuce, mandarin oranges, avocado slices and onion rings. Toss lightly with dressing and serve. This is especially nice with chicken.

Serves 8 to 10

marinated vegetables

Attractive for a summer party.

1 cup vegetable oil
¾ cup wine vinegar
¼ cup chopped parsley
1 clove garlic, minced
½ tsp. each: onion powder, dill weed, salt
¼ tsp. pepper
2 lbs. potatoes, cooked until tender, peeled and sliced
1 lb. carrots, cut in strips and cooked
2 lbs. cooked broccoli spears or 3 pkgs. (10 oz. each) frozen broccoli, cooked
romaine lettuce

In a bowl, combine first 8 ingredients. Place each vegetable in a separate container. Pour ⅓ of the marinade over each vegetable. Toss gently. Cover and refrigerate at least 2 hours or overnight. To serve, drain vegetables and arrange attractively on a lettuce-lined platter.

Serves 8

pea salad

A combination of crisp vegetables with a colorful garnish.

1 cup mayonnaise
1 T. sugar
1 tsp. salt
⅛ tsp. pepper
1 pkg. (10 oz.) frozen peas, thawed
½ cup chopped green onions
½ cup chopped celery
¼ cup chopped green pepper
lettuce
3 hard-cooked eggs, sliced
1 cup cherry tomatoes
6 slices bacon, fried crisp and crumbled

In a bowl, combine mayonnaise, sugar, salt and pepper. Toss with peas, green onions, celery and green pepper. Refrigerate, covered, several hours. At serving time, line salad bowl with lettuce, torn into bite-size pieces. Arrange mixture in the center. Garnish with sliced eggs, tomatoes and crumbled bacon.

Serves 6

melon balls with minted rum-lime sauce

May also be served as a light summer dessert with crisp cookies.

⅔ cup mint jelly
¼ cup water
½ tsp. grated lime peel
6 T. lime juice
¼ cup light rum
2 quarts mixed melon balls
fresh mint

Combine jelly and water in small saucepan; bring to boil. Reduce heat and simmer until jelly has dissolved. Add lime peel; cool to room temperature. Stir in lime juice and rum. Pour over melon balls. Chill, covered, for 4 hours. Gently stir 2 or 3 times to allow sauce to marinate all of the fruit. Serve garnished with fresh mint.

Serves 6 to 8

frozen island salad

So easy, children will love to make it, too.

1 pkg. (3 oz.) softened cream cheese
1 cup pineapple yogurt
¼ cup sugar
1 can (8¾ oz.) crushed pineapple, drained
chopped pecans
slices of banana, strawberries and oranges

Thoroughly blend cream cheese and yogurt. Stir in sugar and pineapple. Blend well. Line a muffin pan with 6 paper baking cups. Spoon mixture into cups. Cover and freeze. At serving time, remove paper cups from salad. Place salads on lettuce leaves. Sprinkle with chopped pecans. Garnish with slices of fresh fruit. Allow to stand 10 minutes before serving.

Serves 6

frozen fruit salad

2 pkgs. (3 oz. each) cream cheese
2 T. sugar
2 T. mayonnaise
1 can (13¼ oz.) crushed pineapple
1 can (16 oz.) cranberry sauce
1 carton (4½ oz.) frozen dessert topping, thawed

In large mixing bowl, blend cheese, sugar and mayonnaise with an electric mixer. Beat until smooth and fluffy. Beat in pineapple with juice and cranberry sauce. Fold in topping. Turn into a 9 x 9 x 2-inch pan or 10 to 12 individual molds. Cover with foil or plastic wrap; freeze. Remove from freezer 10 to 15 minutes before serving. Cut into squares.

Serves 10 to 12

24-hour salad

Rich in taste and color!

1 can (16 oz.) Royal Anne cherries, drained
1 can (20 oz.) diced pineapple, drained
1 can (16 oz.) mandarin oranges, drained
2 cups miniature marshmallows
¼ lb. almonds, sliced, buttered and toasted
2 eggs, beaten until light and fluffy
2 T. sugar
¼ cup cream
juice of 1 small lemon
1 cup whipping cream, whipped

Combine cherries, pineapple and oranges in a mixing bowl. Add marshmallows and almonds. Set aside. Beat eggs; add sugar, cream and lemon juice. Cook in double boiler until thick, stirring constantly. Cool. Fold in whipped cream. Fold fruits, marshmallows and almonds into cool mixture. Pour into 9 x 13 x 2-inch glass dish. Refrigerate 24 hours. Sprinkle with additional toasted almonds, if desired.

Serves 12

grapefruit shells

6 grapefruit
1 pkg. (6 oz.) lemon gelatin
3 pkgs. (3 oz. each) cream cheese
½ cup mayonnaise

Cut 4 of the grapefruit in half. Remove fruit and juice; reserve. Clean inside of shell, removing white membrane. Reserve shells. Reserve fruit and juice of 2 remaining grapefruit; discard shells. Use all juice, adding boiling water to make 3 cups liquid. Add gelatin and stir until dissolved. Shred all grapefruit meat. Cream mayonnaise and cream cheese together. Add one-third of gelatin mixture to cheese mixture. Pour remaining two-thirds of gelatin over shredded grapefruit meat. Fill shells with grapefruit-gelatin mixture. Chill until set. Add cream cheese mixture. Chill until set. Pour remaining grapefruit-gelatin mixture on top of cheese layer. Chill until set. To serve, cut shells in half; serve on lettuce. Top with mayonnaise.

Serves 6 to 8

marinated fruit

Delicious for brunch . . . as an appetizer with wooden picks or as a fruit salad.

3 cups cantaloupe and/or honeydew melon balls
1 can (13½ oz.) pineapple chunks, drained
1 can (11 oz.) mandarin oranges, drained
1 cup strawberries, hulled
1 can (6 oz.) frozen grapefruit juice or frozen lemonade
¼ cup orange marmalade
2 T. orange liqueur (optional)

Combine fruits in bowl. Combine grapefruit juice (or lemonade), marmalade and orange liqueur. Pour over fruits; stir gently. Chill at least 2 hours before serving.

Makes 6 cups

apricot delight

Serve as a salad or dessert.

1 pkg. (6 oz.) apricot gelatin
1 can (20 oz.) crushed pineapple, juice drained and reserved
2 large bananas, thinly sliced
1 cup miniature marshmallows

Topping:
½ cup pineapple juice, reserved from crushed pineapple
½ cup sugar
1 egg, slightly beaten
2 T. butter
2 T. flour
1 pkg. (3 oz.) cream cheese
2 cups dessert topping

Prepare gelatin according to package directions. Pour into a 13 x 9 x 2-inch glass dish. Add pineapple, bananas and marshmallows. Chill until set. For Topping: Cook reserved pineapple juice, sugar, egg, butter and flour in a heavy saucepan. Stir constantly until thick. While hot, add cream cheese; stir to melt. Cool. Fold in whipped topping. Pour over chilled apricot-gelatin layer. Chill. Serve on a bed of lettuce with bran muffins or nut bread for a spring or summer luncheon.

Serves 12

cranberry-raspberry salad

2 cups boiling water
1 pkg. (6 oz.) raspberry gelatin
1 can (16 oz.) jellied cranberry sauce
2 pkgs. (10 oz. each) frozen raspberries, thawed and drained
1 cup chopped pecans

Add boiling water to raspberry gelatin. Stir until dissolved. Melt cranberry sauce over low heat. Add to gelatin, stirring well. Add raspberries and stir gently. Add nuts. Pour into 8 x 11-inch glass dish. Refrigerate until firm.

Serves 8 to 10

creamy pineapple-cheese mold

An excellent luncheon salad.

1 can (1 lb. 4 oz.) crushed pineapple; drain and reserve juice
1 pkg. (3 oz.) lemon gelatin
½ cup finely chopped celery
⅛ tsp. salt
2 pkgs. (3 oz. each) cream cheese
1 cup grated Cheddar cheese
1 jar (2 oz.) pimento, chopped fine
⅔ cup walnuts or pecan pieces
1 cup whipping cream, whipped

In a saucepan, bring reserved pineapple juice to a boil. Dissolve gelatin in boiling liquid. No other liquid is used. Cool gelatin. Add crushed pineapple, celery and salt. Blend cream cheese and Cheddar cheese; add to pineapple gelatin. Stir in pimento and nuts. Fold in whipped cream. Mix thoroughly. Pour into a 6-cup mold. Chill in refrigerator until serving time. Serve on individual lettuce leaves. Mold may be made 24 hours in advance or frozen.

Serves 6 to 8

walnut-cranberry jewel salad

Salad:
½ cup crushed pineapple; drain and reserve juice
1 pkg. (3 oz.) pineapple gelatin
1 cup hot water
½ tsp. salt
1 cup chopped cranberries
½ cup diced celery
½ cup chopped walnuts

Dressing:
1 pkg. (3 oz.) cream cheese
¼ tsp. salt
2 T. honey
¼ cup sour cream

For Salad: Add enough water to reserved pineapple juice to make 1 cup liquid. Dissolve gelatin in 1 cup hot water. Add salt and reserved pineapple juice-water mixture. Chill until slightly thickened. Fold in remaining ingredients. Turn into 1-quart mold; chill until firm. Unmold on bed of lettuce. Garnish with walnut halves and serve with dressing. For Dressing: Combine all ingredients in a small bowl. Whip until smooth.

Serves 6 to 8

holiday salad

A colorful salad . . . delicious with turkey, chicken or ham.

1 pkg. (6 oz.) lime gelatin
1 pkg. (3 oz.) lemon gelatin
2 cups miniature marshmallows or 14 large marshmallows
1 pkg. (3 oz.) cream cheese
½ cup reserved pineapple juice
1 cup whipping cream, whipped
1 can (8 oz.) crushed pineapple; drain and reserve ½ cup juice
1 pkg. (6 oz.) cherry gelatin
frozen dessert topping, thawed
red and green sugar crystals

In a 13 x 9 x 2-inch glass dish, make lime gelatin according to directions. Chill until set. In a blender, combine 1½ cups hot water with lemon gelatin. Add marshmallows, cream cheese and pineapple juice. Cool. Fold whipped cream into crushed pineapple. Combine with *cooled* lemon mixture. Pour over firmly-set lime layer. Chill until firm. Make cherry gelatin according to package directions. When *almost* set, spoon over firm lemon layer. Chill until set. Cut gelatin into squares; top with dessert topping. Sprinkle with red and green sugar crystals.

Serves 12

pear and avocado salad

A refreshingly cool salad.

1 can (16 oz.) pear halves
1 T. vinegar
¼ tsp. salt
1 pkg. (3 oz.) lime gelatin
1 pkg. (3 oz.) softened cream cheese
1 medium avocado, pitted, peeled and diced

Drain and dice pears, reserving juice. Set aside. Add enough water to pear juice to make 1¾ cups liquid. In a saucepan, bring pear liquid, vinegar and salt to boil. Add lime gelatin; stir until dissolved. Gradually add ⅓ cup of hot gelatin to cream cheese. Beat until smooth. Pour into 1-quart mold. Chill until almost firm. Chill remaining gelatin until partially set. Fold in pears and avocado. Spoon fruit mixture over cream cheese layer. Chill until firm. To serve, unmold on salad greens.

Serves 6

creamy waldorf mold

Wonderfully light and crunchy.

1 pkg. (6 oz.) lemon gelatin
¼ tsp. salt
⅔ cup hot water
3 T. lemon juice, divided
1½ cups sliced, unpeeled, Golden or Red Delicious apples
½ cup mayonnaise
1 cup whipping cream, whipped
¾ cup seeded and halved grapes
¾ cup finely chopped celery
¾ cup chopped pecans, roasted and lightly salted

In a mixing bowl, dissolve gelatin and salt in hot water. Stir in 2 tablespoons of the lemon juice. Chill until partially thickened. Sprinkle remaining lemon juice over apples that have been sliced or diced. Blend mayonnaise into thickened gelatin. Fold in whipped cream. Gently spoon apples, grapes, celery and nuts into gelatin mixture. Pour into a lightly oiled 8-cup mold or into 8 individual molds. Chill until firm. Unmold. Garnish with salad greens and grape clusters.

Serves 6 to 8

guacamole-seafood salad

4 cups torn pieces of romaine, butter or leaf lettuce
2 T. wine vinegar
4 T. olive oil
salt and pepper to taste
1 lb. crabmeat or medium-size cooked shrimp
1 cup guacamole or 1 container (6 oz.) frozen avocado dip, thawed
3 hard-cooked eggs, sliced
⅓ cup sour cream
1 lime, cut in wedges

Toss greens with vinegar, olive oil, salt and pepper; arrange on a plate. Arrange seafood in a ring on top of lettuce, mounding guacamole in the center. Garnish with egg slices. Spoon sour cream onto guacamole. Serve with lime wedges.

Serves 4

tomato aspic with seafood and vegetables

A lovely main dish salad for a luncheon or buffet.

1 envelope unflavored gelatin
¼ cup water
2 cups tomato juice
2 tsp. Worcestershire sauce
1 T. lemon juice
1 bay leaf
½ tsp. celery salt
2 T. minced onion
1 clove garlic, minced
2 tsp. sugar
½ tsp. tarragon
1 T. vinegar
1 tsp. horseradish
½ cup chopped celery
½ cup chopped cucumber, peeled and seeded
1 pkg. (6 oz.) frozen shrimp or crab, thawed
Herb Mayonnaise (see index)

Sprinkle gelatin over water. Let stand 5 minutes. In a small saucepan, combine remaining ingredients, except celery, cucumber and shrimp or crab. Bring to boil; reduce heat and simmer 5 minutes. Strain. Add softened gelatin to hot liquid; stir until dissolved. Pour into a 6-cup mold or 6 individual molds. Chill until partially set. Add celery, cucumber and shrimp or crab; mix gently. Chill until firm. Unmold and serve on lettuce leaves. Garnish with avocado slices, halved artichoke hearts or cold asparagus. Top with Herb Mayonnaise.

Serves 4

curried chicken salad

. . . served on chilled peach halves and crisp greens.

1 can (1 lb. 13 oz.) cling peach halves
¼ cup mayonnaise
¼ cup sour cream
½ tsp. curry powder
½ cup finely chopped, drained chutney
2½ cups diced, cooked chicken
1 cup chopped celery
½ cup toasted coconut chips or flakes (optional)
salt to taste
crisp salad greens

Chill peach halves thoroughly. In a bowl, blend mayonnaise, sour cream, curry powder and chutney. Add chicken, celery and coconut. Toss lightly. Add salt to taste. Drain peaches thoroughly. Arrange cup-side up on salad greens. Top each with a mound of chicken salad.

Serves 6

curried chicken salad mold

4 cups finely chopped chicken
¾ cup French dressing
3 envelopes unflavored gelatin
2½ cups chicken broth, divided
½ cup diced celery
½ cup diced green pepper
¾ cup chopped, roasted pecans
1½ cups mayonnaise
2 T. grated onion
¾ tsp. curry powder
¾ tsp. salt
⅛ tsp. white pepper

Combine chicken and French dressing. Cover and refrigerate 6 hours or overnight. Soften gelatin in 1 cup of the cold chicken broth. In a small saucepan, heat remaining 1½ cups broth to boiling. Add gelatin mixture and stir until dissolved. Cool until partially thickened. In a mixing bowl, combine celery, green pepper, pecans and chicken mixture; toss lightly. In a separate bowl, combine mayonnaise, onion, curry powder, salt and pepper; add to chicken mixture. Stir in gelatin mixture. Mix well, stirring gently. Pour into an oiled 2-quart mold. Cover and chill until firm. Unmold and garnish with watercress or leafy green lettuce. Serve with marinated artichokes or asparagus and assorted rolls.

Serves 8 to 10

hot chicken salad

3 cups chopped, cooked chicken breasts
1 can (10¾ oz.) condensed cream of chicken soup
¾ cup mayonnaise
1 cup diced celery
1 cup bite-size canned pineapple
3 hard-cooked eggs, chopped
½ cup blanched, sliced almonds
1 cup crushed potato chips

In a large mixing bowl, combine chicken, soup, mayonnaise, celery, pineapple and eggs. Pour into a 2-quart baking dish. Sprinkle almonds and potato chips on top of casserole. Bake at 450° for 20 minutes. Serve immediately with hot rolls and a green salad.

Serves 6

hawaiian chicken and rice salad

⅔ cup quick-cooking rice, uncooked
½ tsp. salt
¾ cup boiling water
1 cup mayonnaise
1 tsp. each: lemon juice, grated lemon peel, salt
½ tsp. curry powder, or more to taste
⅛ tsp. pepper
2 cups cubed, cooked chicken
1 cup chopped celery
1 cup pineapple tidbits, drained
½ cup shredded coconut

In a small bowl, mix together rice, salt and water. Let stand 15 minutes, covered. In another bowl, mix together mayonnaise, lemon juice and peel, salt, curry powder and pepper. Set aside. In a large bowl, mix together chicken, celery, pineapple and coconut. Add rice and toss. Add dressing mixture and toss again. Serve on a plate with grapes and melon or papaya slices.

Serves 6

flan de pescado

From Spain . . . a creamy gelatin salad with tuna.

2 envelopes unflavored gelatin
½ cup cold water
1 can (10 oz.) condensed cream of asparagus soup
1 cup mayonnaise
1 pkg. (8 oz.) cream cheese, softened
1 T. lemon juice
1 small onion, minced
½ green pepper, finely chopped
1 can (7 oz.) tuna, drained

In a small bowl, soak gelatin in cold water. In a medium saucepan, heat asparagus soup until hot. Remove from heat. Slowly add gelatin, stirring constantly. Add remaining ingredients. Stir well. Pour mixture into an oiled 1-quart mold. Chill several hours or until set. Unmold onto a bed of lettuce.

Serves 8

reuben salad

The immortal Reuben in a bowl!

1 large head leaf lettuce, torn into bite-size pieces
1 lb. sauerkraut, drained
½ cup cooked corned beef, cut into strips
¼ cup sliced dill pickle
2 tomatoes, cut in wedges
1 cup grated Swiss cheese
1 cup Thousand Island salad dressing
ground pepper to taste

In a salad bowl, combine lettuce, sauerkraut, corned beef, pickles and tomatoes. Toss lightly. Sprinkle with cheese. Heat salad dressing with pepper. Pour over salad mixture and toss lightly. Serve immediately with Campari and soda, plenty of dark bread and sweet butter.

Serves 4 to 6

taco salad with melted cheese

A hit with both family and friends.

1½ lbs. ground beef
1 cup chopped green pepper
1 cup chopped red onion
salt and pepper to taste
1 T. chili powder
½ tsp. cumin powder
1 lb. process American cheese, diced
¼ cup canned tomatoes
1 head iceberg lettuce, torn into pieces
2 tomatoes, chopped
1 pkg. (6 oz.) corn chips, crumbled
½ cup chopped olives

In a large skillet, brown meat; drain off excess fat. Add green pepper, onion, salt and pepper. Brown a few minutes more; add chili powder and cumin. Meanwhile, melt cheese in double boiler and stir in canned tomatoes. In a salad bowl, place in order: lettuce pieces, chopped tomatoes, corn chips, olives, hot meat mixture and cheese mixture. Do not toss. Nice for lunch or a light supper.

Serves 4 to 5

ham and pineapple mold amandine

A refreshing salad combination.

2 pkgs. (3 oz. each) pineapple gelatin
2 cups boiling water
1 can (8 oz.) crushed pineapple, undrained
1 cup mayonnaise
1 pkg. (0.7 oz.) blue cheese salad dressing mix
1½ cups coarsely chopped, cooked ham
½ cup coarsely chopped celery
¼ cup finely chopped green pepper
2 T. chopped, toasted, slivered almonds
1 T. chopped pimento
salad greens

In a bowl, dissolve gelatin in boiling water. Add pineapple, mayonnaise and salad dressing mix. Beat with a rotary beater until thoroughly blended. Chill until slightly thickened. Fold in ham, celery, green pepper, almonds and pimento. Pour into a 6-cup mold and chill until firm. Unmold onto a serving plate lined with salad greens. Serve with assorted fresh fruit and cheese.

Serves 6

pasta salad

Perfect for summer entertaining on the patio with a charcoal grilled steak.

1 lb. penne (pen-shaped pasta)
1 T. salt
1 T. olive oil
½ cup bottled Italian salad dressing
1 cup peeled, seeded, finely diced tomato
½ cup finely chopped red onion
¾ cup finely chopped celery
½ cup finely chopped sweet red pepper
¼ cup finely chopped carrots
¾ cup unpeeled, seeded, finely chopped cucumber
¾ cup unpeeled, finely chopped zucchini
2 T. finely chopped fresh basil (or 2 tsp. dried)
salt and pepper

In a large pot, cook penne in 4 quarts boiling water to which salt and olive oil have been added. Cook until tender, about 8 to 10 minutes. Drain. Put pasta into a large bowl and toss with salad dressing. Toss the vegetables together and sprinkle over top of pasta, ending with basil. Toss well. Season to taste with salt and pepper. Serve immediately. Salad may also be refrigerated and served cold the next day.

Serves 16

olive and macaroni salad

You will be pleased to serve this in either of two ways.

1 cup sliced, stuffed green olives, drained
¼ cup chopped onion
¼ cup finely chopped green onions
½ cup chopped celery
2 T. lemon juice
⅔ cup mayonnaise
1 T. Dijon mustard
½ tsp. sugar
2 cups cooked macaroni, drained

Combine all the ingredients in a mixing bowl. Mix gently but thoroughly. Cover and refrigerate for at least 4 hours before serving. Serve from a bowl lined with lettuce greens or use as a stuffing for fresh, chilled tomatoes.

Serves 4 to 6

rice salad

3 cups water
1 bay leaf
1 tsp. salt
1 pinch saffron
½ cup converted rice
½ cup vegetable oil
2-3 T. wine vinegar
freshly ground black pepper
⅓ cup each: finely chopped onion, seeded tomato, celery, green pepper
¼ cup dark raisins
½ cup pinenuts or slivered almonds
⅓ cup chopped fresh parsley

Bring water to boil. Add bay leaf, salt and saffron. Stir in rice. Simmer covered, for 12 minutes; drain. Add oil, vinegar and pepper. Let the rice cook with the sauce for a few minutes; add remaining ingredients. Toss well and chill. Spoon into a lettuce-lined salad bowl; garnish with sliced eggs and tomatoes. Serve very cold with grilled lamb or beef and a chilled Beaujolais. May also be served as a luncheon salad.

Serves 6

aunt martha's salad dressing

Delicious over vegetables and green salads.

¼ cup each: sugar, ketchup, mayonnaise, salad oil, tarragon vinegar
2 T. Worcestershire sauce
2 T. steak sauce
2 tsp. minced onion

Combine all the ingredients in a glass pint jar or blender. Shake or blend until well mixed. Refrigerate in a covered container until ready to serve.

Makes 1½ cups

blender caesar salad dressing

1 can (1¾ oz.) anchovies, drained
1 T. peppercorns
2 cloves garlic
1 T. Dijon mustard
1 T. Worcestershire sauce
1½ tsp. lemon juice
2 cups vegetable oil, divided
2 raw eggs

Place first 6 ingredients in an electric blender. Blend with 1 cup of the oil. Add the eggs and remaining cup of oil; blend well.

Makes 2½ cups

blue cheese salad dressing

4 oz. blue cheese
2 cups real mayonnaise
1 clove garlic, minced
3 T. chives
1 T. freshly ground pepper
½ tsp. A-1 sauce
1 cup sour cream
½ cup buttermilk

In a bowl, combine all ingredients, except sour cream and buttermilk. Stir gently; do not beat. Add sour cream and buttermilk. Stir gently until well blended. Add a little milk, if too thick.

Makes 1 quart

sweet-sour salad dressing

1 cup oil
½ cup each: cider vinegar, honey, brown sugar
⅓ cup ketchup
1 T. Worcestershire sauce
1 medium onion, finely chopped
½ tsp. salt

Place all ingredients in an electric blender; blend until well mixed. Serve over fresh spinach, garnished with finely chopped egg and chopped, crisp bacon.

Makes 2½ cups

creamy french dressing with bacon

1 onion, grated
1 cup sugar
½ cup chili sauce
½ cup ketchup
2 cups vegetable oil
½ cup vinegar
1 tsp. dry mustard
2 tsp. salt
1 clove garlic
bacon, fried crisp and crumbled

In an electric blender, blend onion, sugar, chili sauce and ketchup. The longer you blend the better. Add oil slowly. Add remaining ingredients. Blend until well mixed. Serve on salad greens or on avocado and grapefruit salad.

Makes 1 quart

red wine vinaigrette with chopped eggs

¾ cup vegetable oil
¼ cup red wine vinegar
2 hard-cooked eggs, chopped
1 tsp. salt
1 tsp. dry mustard
½ tsp. pepper

In a jar, mix salad oil and vinegar. Then add the remaining indredients. Cover and chill in refrigerator for at least 20 minutes. Especially good with bibb lettuce or spinach.

Serves 6

peppercorn dressing

Delicious with mixed greens, cherry tomatoes and sliced avocados.

1 celery stalk, chopped
½ onion, chopped
1 T. peppercorns
2 cloves garlic
1 T. Dijon mustard
1 T. Worcestershire sauce
1½ tsp. lemon juice
2 tsp. salt
2 cups vegetable oil, divided
2 raw eggs

Place the first 8 ingredients in an electric blender and blend with 1 cup of the oil. Add the eggs and remaining cup of oil. Blend well. Refrigerate.

Makes 2½ cups

sweet cream and vinegar dressing

Prepare in a minute! So good you'll wish you had made more!

¼ cup whipping cream
3 T. white wine vinegar
1-2 T. sugar
2 tsp. chopped fresh chives

In a glass jar, combine the cream, vinegar, sugar and chives. Shake to blend and dissolve sugar. Refrigerate. Serve over tender butter lettuce.

Makes ½ cup

fruit salad marinade

Especially good for a brunch.

¼ cup each: lemon juice, orange juice, lime juice
⅔ cup water
1⅓ cups sugar

Place all ingredients in a bowl and mix thoroughly. Pour over fruits of any kind, using fresh or frozen or a combination. Chill thoroughly for about 4 hours.

Makes enough dressing for a large 4 to 5 quart fruit bowl.

herb mayonnaise

2 eggs, at room temperature
1 tsp. salt
⅛ tsp. white pepper
¼ tsp. dry mustard
½ tsp. basil
¼ tsp. oregano
2 cups vegetable oil, at room temperature
1 T. lemon juice
2 dashes Tabasco

Place eggs and seasonings in a medium mixing bowl. Beat with an electric mixer at medium speed until thick, pale and fluffy. Add oil in ¼ cup portions in very thin stream. Beat constantly until thickened and oil is absorbed. Beat in lemon juice. Continue beating until well-blended. Sauce will be very thick. Place in glass refrigerator container. Cut wax paper to fit over top; rinse in cold water. Place paper over sauce; cover and refrigerate until ready to use. Serve cold over garden-fresh tomato and cucumber slices or molded vegetable salads.

Makes 1¾ cups

honey-lime fruit salad dressing

Especially good with citrus fruit.

½ tsp. grated lime peel
⅓ cup lime juice
¼ cup honey
1 T. cider vinegar
⅔ cup salad oil
½ tsp. each: dry mustard, paprika, salt
3 drops Tabasco

Combine all ingredients in a blender. Blend for 30 seconds. Store in a covered container and refrigerate. Shake before serving.

Makes 1 cup

honey-poppy seed dressing

Wonderful on fresh fruit or grapefruit and avocado salad.

½ cup sugar
½ cup strained honey
1 T. dry mustard
1 T. poppy seed
¼ tsp. salt
1 tsp. celery seed
6 T. lemon juice
1 cup vegetable oil

Combine all ingredients in a bowl, beating well until sugar dissolves.

Makes 2½ cups

mushroom relish

A make-ahead delight!

½ lb. fresh mushrooms, sliced
1 celery stalk, sliced
1 carrot, sliced
¼ cup sliced dill pickle
1 jar (2 oz.) pimento, undrained
¾ cup olive or vegetable oil
¼ cup vinegar
1¼ tsp. salt
¾ tsp. Italian seasonings
¼ tsp. instant minced garlic

Place vegetables, pickle and pimento in a quart jar or crock. Set aside. Prepare marinade by combining the remaining ingredients in a small saucepan. Bring to a boil then reduce heat and simmer 10 minutes. Pour over vegetable mixture. Cover tightly and refrigerate at least 2 days before using.

Serves 8

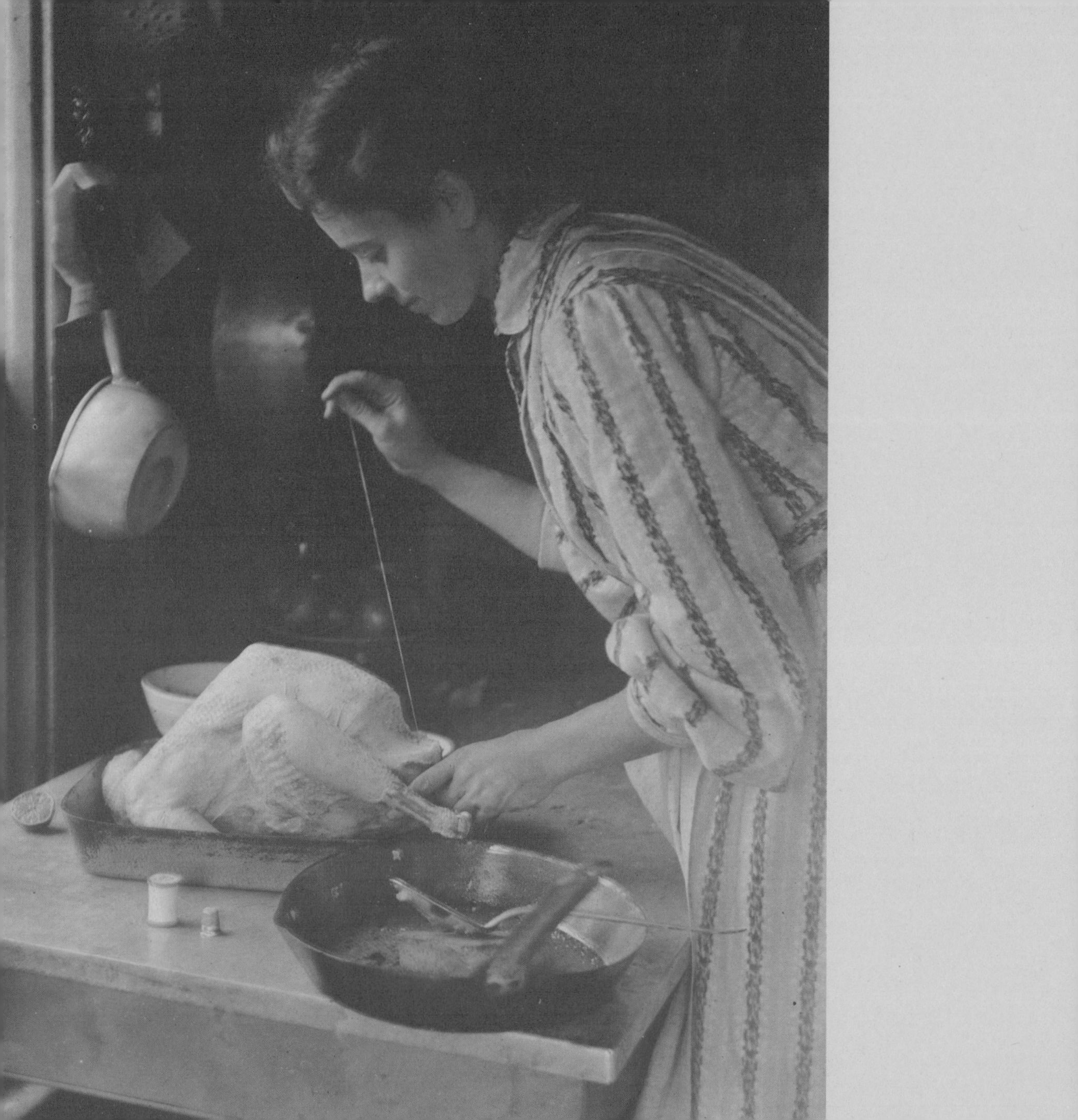

poultry and game

"Work done *quietly* about the house seems easier.
A slamming of oven doors, and the rattle and clatter
of dishes, tire and bewilder everybody.
Those who accomplish much in housekeeping—
and the same is true of every other walk in life—
are the quiet workers."

CULVER PICTURES

artichoke-chicken elegant

A casserole of unique flavors.

6 T. butter, divided
3 whole chicken breasts, boned, halved and skinned
salt and pepper
paprika
¼ cup chopped onion
½ lb. mushrooms, sliced
2 T. flour
⅔ cup chicken broth
¼ cup dry white wine
¼ cup dry sherry
¾ tsp. dried rosemary, crumbled
1 can (16 oz.) artichoke hearts, drained

In a large skillet, melt 4 tablespoons of the butter. Sprinkle chicken with salt, pepper and paprika. Place in skillet and brown on all sides. Transfer to a 3-quart covered casserole. In the same skillet, add remaining 2 tablespoons butter. Saute onion and mushrooms until tender. Sprinkle with flour and stir. Add chicken broth, wine, sherry and rosemary. Cook over low heat, stirring constantly, until liquid is blended and slightly thickened. Add artichoke hearts. Heat through. Pour over chicken. Cover and bake at 375° for 40 minutes. Serve with rice or noodles.

Serves 4

baked chicken with apple-currant stuffing

Apple-Currant Stuffing:
½ cup butter
1 large onion, finely chopped
¼ cup chopped celery
4 cooking apples, cored and diced
1 cup chopped hazelnuts
½ cup currants, plumped in boiling water, then drained
1 cup soft breadcrumbs
1 tsp. salt
½ tsp. pepper
1 tsp. grated lemon rind
½ tsp. coriander
½ tsp. thyme
¼ tsp. nutmeg

Chicken:
3 whole chicken breasts, halved
flour
salt and pepper
½ cup butter

For Apple-Currant Stuffing: Melt butter in a large skillet. Saute onion until tender. Add remaining stuffing ingredients. Stir to blend. Place in bottom of a buttered 13 x 9 x 2-inch baking dish.

For Chicken: Coat chicken pieces with flour, salt and pepper. Melt ½ cup butter in the same skillet and brown chicken slowly. Place on top of Apple-Currant Stuffing. Cover with foil and bake at 350° for 10 minutes. Remove foil and bake 15 minutes longer or until chicken is done and stuffing is lightly browned.

Serves 6

asparagus-chicken casserole

Easy, make-ahead luncheon dish.

2 pkgs. (10 oz. each) frozen asparagus or 2 lbs. fresh
2 cups dry noodles, cooked according to package directions
2 cans (10½ oz. each) condensed cream of chicken soup
2 whole chickens, cooked, boned and diced (5-6 cups)
1 cup real mayonnaise
1 can (8 oz.) mushrooms
1 tsp. lemon juice
1 cup sliced green olives with pimentos
½ cup shredded Colby cheese
½ cup breadcrumbs
1 T. butter

In a medium saucepan, cook asparagus until tender. Drain. Arrange in a 13 x 9 x 2-inch casserole. Combine cooked noodles, soup, chicken, mayonnaise, mushrooms, lemon juice and olives. Pour over asparagus. Sprinkle with cheese and breadcrumbs. Dot with butter. Cover and refrigerate overnight. To bake, uncover and place in oven directly from refrigerator. Bake at 350° for 30 to 45 minutes.

Serves 12

barbecued chicken with honey-mustard glaze

Super summer fare.

Marinade:
1 can (8 oz.) tomato sauce
½ cup olive oil
½ cup orange juice
¼ cup vinegar
1½ tsp. oregano
1 tsp. salt
6 peppercorns
1 clove garlic, minced

Chicken:
2 whole chicken breasts, halved
4 chicken legs, including thighs

Glaze:
¼ cup honey
½ tsp. mustard

For Marinade: In a large screw-top jar, combine all ingredients. Cover and shake vigorously to blend.

For Chicken: Pour marinade over chicken in a shallow baking dish. Cover and marinate 2 hours at room temperature, or overnight in refrigerator, turning occasionally. Drain chicken, reserving marinade. Bake chicken at 350° for 30 minutes. Remove to grill and cook over medium to low coals for 30 minutes. Brush with marinade, turning frequently.

For Honey-Mustard Glaze: Combine honey and mustard. Brush chicken with mixture and serve.

Serves 6

cajun gumbo

1 3-lb. frying chicken, cut up; or 12 pieces, 6 thighs and 3 breasts, halved
salt and pepper
3 T. vegetable oil, divided
3 T. butter, divided
1 large onion, chopped
2 cloves garlic, minced
3 T. flour
1½ cups chicken broth
2 T. chopped parsley
¼ tsp. thyme
2 cups cooked, diced ham
1 lb. cooked shrimp
1 lb. sliced, cooked okra

Season chicken with salt and pepper. In a 3-quart pan, melt 2 tablespoons each of oil and butter; brown chicken pieces. In a separate pan, saute onion and garlic in remaining 2 tablespoons of oil and butter until tender. Add to chicken. Remove excess fat. Sprinkle chicken with flour. Stir in chicken broth, parsley and thyme. Cook over medium-low heat until chicken is tender. Add ham, shrimp and okra. Cook slowly, 15 to 20 minutes, to blend flavors. Spoon into a large serving dish. Serve hot with fluffy white rice, French bread and red wine.

Serves 8 to 10

chutney chicken breasts a la creme

4 whole chicken breasts, halved
2 T. butter
2 cups whipping cream
2 tsp. Worcestershire sauce
½ cup chutney, chopped
1 T. flour
salt and pepper to taste

Remove skin from chicken. Place in a single layer in a shallow, buttered 10-inch baking dish. Rub with butter. Brown under broiler 5 to 10 minutes. Meanwhile, blend together remaining ingredients with a whisk. Pour over chicken. Place in a 350° oven, basting frequently, for 45 minutes or until done. Serve with rice.

Serves 6 to 8

curried chicken breasts with mushroom sauce

Great for the calorie counters.

4 whole chicken breasts, boned and halved
¾ tsp. seasoned salt
½ tsp. paprika
2 chicken bouillon cubes
2 cups boiling water
½ cup sauterne
1 tsp. curry powder
dash pepper
1 T. minced onion

Mushroom Sauce:
2 T. flour
¼ cup water
1 jar (4 oz.) mushroom pieces

In a 9 x 13-inch casserole, place the chicken breasts. Sprinkle each breast with seasoned salt and paprika. In a saucepan, dissolve the chicken bouillon in boiling water. Add the wine, curry powder, pepper and onion to the bouillon. Pour mixture over chicken. Cover casserole with foil. Bake at 350° for 30 minutes. Uncover and bake 45 minutes longer or until tender. Remove chicken to serving platter, reserving pan juices.

For Mushroom Sauce: Into a small saucepan, strain pan juices. Blend flour and water; add slowly to the pan juices, stirring constantly. Boil 3 to 4 minutes or until thickened. Add undrained mushrooms. Spoon half the Mushroom Sauce over the chicken. Serve the remaining sauce as a gravy. The sauce is excellent over rice.

Serves 4

grilled marinated chicken

14-16 chicken pieces

Marinade:
½ cup each: vegetable oil, lemon juice, wine vinegar
¼ cup soy sauce
1 tsp. salt
½ tsp. pepper
1 tsp. each: basil, marjoram, savory, thyme

In a shallow baking dish large enough to hold the chicken pieces in a single layer, mix ingredients for Marinade. Place chicken in dish and marinate for 4 hours, turning occasionally. Drain Marinade and reserve. Bake chicken in same dish for 30 minutes at 325°. Place chicken on grill and baste often with Marinade. Cook for 30 minutes, turning occasionally.

Serves 6 to 8

fancy chicken casserole

Delicious, make-ahead brunch dish.

2 medium stewing chickens
2 cups water
2 cups dry sherry
1½ tsp. salt
½ tsp. curry powder
1 medium onion, chopped
½ cup finely chopped celery
1 can (16 oz.) mushrooms, drained
½ cup butter
2 pkgs. (6 oz. each) long-grain and wild rice
½ cup sour cream
½ cup milk
1 can (10¾ oz.) condensed cream of mushroom soup

Place chickens in a deep kettle or Dutch oven with water, sherry, salt, curry powder, onion and celery. Bring to a boil; reduce heat. Simmer 1 hour. Remove chicken from broth and cool. Reserve broth. Cut chicken into small pieces, removing skin and bones. Saute mushrooms with butter. Use reserved broth to prepare rice, following package directions. Allow chicken to soak in remaining broth. Drain chicken; mix with rice, mushrooms, sour cream, milk and soup. Bake at 350° for 45 minutes. Casserole may be frozen before baking.

Serves 8

herbed oven-fried chicken

An easy and elegant company or family dish.

6 chicken breasts, halved
1 cup crumbled herb-seasoned croutons
⅔ cup grated Parmesan cheese
¼ cup fresh or 2 T. dried parsley
garlic powder to taste
½ cup melted butter

Combine croutons, cheese, parsley and garlic powder in a mixing bowl; mix thoroughly. Dip chicken first in melted butter and then in crumb mixture. Place in a buttered 12-inch, shallow baking dish. Pour remaining butter over chicken. Top with remaining crumbs. Do not turn. Bake, uncovered, at 350° for 1 hour 15 minutes. Serve immediately.

Serves 4 to 6

chicken normandy

This rich and creamy sauce can be prepared with veal, also.

3 large Golden Delicious apples
¼ cup lemon juice
3 whole chicken breasts, skinned, boned and halved
salt and pepper
½ cup flour
2 T. butter
2 T. oil
½ cup apple brandy
1 cup whipping cream
pinch of brown sugar
dash nutmeg

Peel, core and slice the apples. Toss with lemon juice in a medium bowl. Set aside. Sprinkle chicken with salt and pepper. Dredge with flour, shaking off excess. Melt butter in a heavy skillet. Saute chicken about 8 minutes on each side or until golden brown. Remove and keep warm. In the same skillet, combine apple mixture and apple brandy. Cook 5 minutes, scraping brown bits loose from pan. Add cream, brown sugar and nutmeg. Cook, stirring often, until rich and creamy and reduced by half, about 20 minutes. Sauce should coat spoon. Pour hot sauce over chicken and serve immediately.

Variation: Just as delicious substituting 12 veal scallops for chicken. Saute scallops 2 to 3 minutes per side.

Serves 4 to 6

lime-broiled chicken

A most unusual flavored chicken, good served either hot or cold with zucchini and tomatoes and rice pilaf.

4 whole chicken breasts, boned, skinned and halved
2½ tsp. salt
MSG
1¼ cups corn oil
1¼ cups lime juice
5 T. chopped onion
1 T. tarragon
1¼ tsp. Tabasco

Sprinkle chicken with salt and a dash of MSG. Combine remaining ingredients in a deep baking dish. Lay the breasts in the dish in a single layer. Turn to coat well with the marinade. Marinate for at least 4 hours. Broil breasts in same dish with marinade for 2 to 3 minutes on each side.

Serves 6 to 8

kotopoulo me kremidakia kai tirie

In English, chicken with onions and cheese.

1 3-3½-lb. frying chicken, cut up
salt
freshly ground pepper
½ cup butter, divided
2 T. vegetable oil
1 can (16 oz.) whole, peeled tomatoes with liquid
¼ cup water
2 lbs. yellow onions, quartered
1 bay leaf
dash cinnamon
12 1-inch cubes Kasseri cheese

Season chicken with salt and pepper. In a large skillet, melt ¼ cup of the butter with oil. Add chicken and brown slowly. Meanwhile, simmer tomatoes in a covered saucepan. Remove chicken to a Dutch oven. Add water to the skillet. Heat and scrape brown bits loose from bottom. Pour over chicken. Melt remaining ¼ cup butter in the skillet and slowly brown onions. When tender, add to chicken. While onions are cooking, put simmering tomatoes through a sieve. Simmer a little longer with bay leaf and cinnamon. Pour over chicken and onions. Cover Dutch oven and simmer gently, about 1 hour. Add cheese and simmer until soft, about 10 minutes. Serve immediately.

Serves 6

chicken teriyaki

Great on the grill.

1 3-lb. frying chicken, cut up
garlic salt and pepper to taste

Teriyaki Marinade:
⅔ cup soy sauce
⅔ cup bourbon
⅔ cup vegetable oil
1 tsp. ginger

Season chicken with garlic salt and pepper.

For Teriyaki Marinade: Combine soy sauce, bourbon, oil and ginger in a large bowl. Place chicken in marinade for several hours. Grill over medium heat about 45 minutes. Baste with marinade every 15 minutes. To bake in oven, place chicken on a rack in a shallow pan. Bake at 325° for 45 minutes, turning frequently and basting with Teriyaki Marinade.

Serves 4

stuffed chicken breasts a l'orange

Easy and elegant company fare.

4 whole chicken breasts, boned and halved
1 cup herb-seasoned stuffing
¾ cup butter, divided
water
1 cup finely crushed corn-flake cereal

Orange Sauce:
½ cup white granulated sugar
½ cup brown sugar
¼ tsp. salt
1 T. cornstarch
1 tsp. grated orange peel
1 cup orange juice

In a small bowl, toss the dry stuffing mix with ¼ cup of the butter. Add enough water to moisten slightly. Place 2 tablespoons of stuffing in each cavity of the chicken breasts. Pull the skin over to cover stuffing. Dip each breast in remaining ½ cup butter which has been melted in the oven in a 9 x 13 x 2-inch casserole. Roll breasts in corn-flake cereal crumbs and return to the casserole, skin-side up.

For Orange Sauce: In a small saucepan, combine the dry ingredients. Add orange juice slowly, stirring constantly. Continue stirring as mixture comes to a boil. Simmer until sauce is clear and transparent. Pour the Orange Sauce over the chicken and bake at 325° for 1 hour or until chicken is very tender and glazed. Baste often.

Serves 6

chicken breasts supreme

Quail may be substituted for the chicken breasts.

1 pkg. (4 oz.) dried beef
4 whole chicken breasts, boned and halved
8 slices bacon
1 can (10¾ oz.) condensed cream of mushroom soup
1 cup sour cream
½ lb. fresh mushrooms, sauteed

On 2 to 3 slices of dried beef, place one-half chicken breast. Wrap chicken and beef with one bacon slice. Secure bacon with a toothpick, if necessary. Place breast in a greased 13 x 9 x 2-inch casserole, seam side down. Repeat for the remaining seven breasts. Bake, uncovered, at 350° for 30 minutes. In a small bowl, combine soup, sour cream and mushrooms. Mix well. Pour this mixture over chicken and continue baking for 30 minutes. Serve with wild rice and a spinach salad.

Serves 6 to 8

chicken a la veronique

The criss-cross pastry top makes this as attractive as it is delicious.

⅔ cup chopped onion
3 T. margarine
3 whole chicken breasts, cooked, boned and diced
2 jars (4 oz. each) sliced mushrooms, drained
1 can (10½ oz.) condensed cream of chicken soup
1 cup sour cream
1½ cups green grapes, halved
1 T. brown sugar
1½ tsp. salt
¼ tsp. nutmeg
¼ tsp. pepper

Criss-Cross Pastry:
1½ cups self-rising flour
¼ cup self-rising cornmeal
¼ cup vegetable shortening
1 egg
¼-⅓ cup milk

In a large skillet, saute onion in margarine until tender. Stir in remaining 9 ingredients. Spoon mixture into a 11 x 7-inch baking dish.

For Criss-Cross Pastry: Cut shortening into flour and cornmeal until mixture resembles small peas. In a small bowl, combine egg and milk. Add this mixture to the flour mixture gradually until the dough is soft. On a floured surface, knead the dough gently for 30 seconds. Roll out dough and cut into ½-inch strips. Arrange strips on top of casserole in lattice design. Bake at 450° for 15 minutes or until pastry is lightly browned.

Serves 6

chicken tropicale

Easy luncheon or supper dish.

2 (3-lb. each) frying chickens, cut into pieces
½ cup flour
1 tsp. salt
½ tsp. pepper
½ tsp. paprika
1 tsp. MSG
½ cup butter
¼ cup vegetable oil
1 clove garlic, minced
1 can (8 oz.) pineapple slices, drained and cut into bite-size pieces
1 can (4 oz.) mushrooms, drained
4 green onions with tops, chopped
1 can (4 oz.) water chestnuts, drained and sliced
½ cup dry white wine or pineapple juice
1 T. brown sugar
½ cup chopped macadamia nuts or almonds

Shake chicken in paper bag with flour, salt, pepper, paprika and MSG. Melt butter and mix with oil and garlic in a glass baking dish large enough for a single layer of chicken. Coat all sides of chicken in butter and oil. Place in dish skin-side down. Bake at 400° for 30 minutes. Turn chicken. Add pineapple, mushrooms, onions and water chestnuts. Combine wine and sugar. Pour into casserole. Top with nuts. Bake at 375° for 45 minutes. Can be reheated. May substitute 14 to 16 chicken pieces for 2 whole frying chickens.

Serves 6

herbed chicken

3 whole chicken breasts, boned and halved
salt
¼ cup butter
1 can (10½ oz). condensed cream of chicken soup
½ cup sauterne
½ cup water
1 can (5 oz.) water chestnuts, drained
1 can (3 oz.) mushrooms, drained
2 T. chopped green pepper
¼ tsp. thyme

Season chicken with salt. In a large skillet, melt butter and brown chicken slowly. Remove chicken to a 13 x 9 x 2-inch casserole. Reserve pan juices in skillet. Stir soup into the pan juices and slowly add wine, stirring until smooth. Add remaining ingredients and bring to a boil. Pour over chicken. Cover and bake at 350° for 25 minutes. Uncover and continue baking 25 to 35 minutes. Serve immediately, or refrigerate and reheat at serving time.

Serves 4

chicken in sherry-cream sauce

Special and easy. The sliced black olives may fool your guests into thinking they are French truffles!

1 frying chicken, cut up
¼ cup butter
1 tsp. salt
¼ tsp. pepper
pinch of basil
1 cup dry sherry
1 cup sour cream
1 cup sliced ripe olives

In a large skillet, brown chicken in butter. Sprinkle with seasonings. Remove chicken to a 10 x 6 x 2-inch casserole. Add sherry to drippings in skillet. Stir in sour cream. Pour over chicken. Cover with foil and bake at 350° for 45 minutes or until tender. Add olives and bake 5 minutes longer.

Serves 4

chicken and wine

An easy, inexpensive main dish for family or entertaining.

4-6 lbs. chicken pieces
¼ lb. margarine
1 cup sliced mushrooms
1 cup diced onions
1 can (10½ oz.) condensed cream of mushroom soup
¾ cup dry sherry or *dry* vermouth
1 lemon, thinly sliced

Brown chicken pieces in margarine in a large skillet. Remove chicken and place in a 13 x 9 x 2-inch glass casserole. Mix mushrooms, onions, soup and sherry or vermouth in skillet. Pour over chicken. Top with lemon slices. Bake at 350° for 1 hour. Make early in the day and refrigerate until baking time.

Serves 6 to 8

chicken with pea pods

2 whole chicken breasts, boned, skinned and diced
3 tsp. cornstarch, divided
1 tsp. dry sherry
¼ tsp. MSG
2 tsp. salt
5 T. cold water
¼ cup vegetable oil
1 clove garlic, crushed
½ cup water chestnuts, sliced
½ cup bamboo shoots
1 pkg. (10 oz.) frozen pea pods, thawed

In a medium bowl, combine 1 tsp. of the cornstarch, sherry, MSG and salt. Add diced chicken and mix. Set aside. In a small bowl, mix remaining 2 teaspoons cornstarch and cold water. Set aside. Pour oil into a hot skillet or wok over medium-high heat. Add garlic and chicken mixture. Stir constantly until almost done, about 2 minutes. Add water chestnuts and bamboo shoots. Stir 1 minute. Add pea pods and stir thoroughly. Add cornstarch mixture and stir a few seconds until gravy thickens. Pea pods should remain crisp and green. Remove from heat and serve immediately over rice.

Note: A stiff spatula makes a good stirring tool, as the chicken tends to stick to the pan. Ingredients may be cooked a day ahead except for the pea pods. At serving time, reheat chicken and add pea pods.

Serves 2 to 3

orange-baked chicken casserole

2 frying chickens, cut into pieces
1 tsp. salt
¼ tsp. pepper
½ cup flour
⅓ cup butter and oil combined
1 can (6 oz.) frozen orange juice concentrate, thawed
1 juice can water
¼ cup brown sugar
1 tsp. oregano
½ tsp. nutmeg
1 onion, thinly sliced

In a bag, shake chicken pieces with salt, pepper and flour. Remove. Heat butter and oil in a large skillet. Brown chicken, a few pieces at a time. Place in a buttered 13-inch casserole. Combine remaining ingredients in a separate bowl. Pour over chicken. Cover and bake at 350° for 45 minutes or until done. Serve with noodles.

Serves 6

cornish hen delight

Wonderful dish for a special occasion.

4 1-lb. Cornish hens, thawed
6 T. butter, divided
1 tsp. each: salt, pepper, thyme
1 T. flour
1 T. Worcestershire sauce
2 T. lemon juice
1 cup red wine
8 small onions
8 small mushrooms
fresh parsley or dill

In a large Dutch oven, melt 3 tablespoons of the butter. Saute hens until golden on all sides. Sprinkle hens with salt, pepper and thyme. Stir flour into butter around hens. Add Worcestershire sauce, lemon juice and wine. Simmer, covered, 40 to 50 minutes. While hens are simmering, melt remaining 3 tablespoons of butter in a medium-size skillet. Saute onions until golden. Add onions to hens, reserving liquid. In same skillet, saute mushrooms and add to hens. Cook, covered, until hens and vegetables are tender, about 15 to 20 minutes. At serving time, garnish with fresh parsley or dill. Hens, mushrooms and onions can be prepared in the morning and reheated 30 minutes before serving.

Serves 4

oriental chicken

¼ cup peanut or vegetable oil
1 cup carrots, cut into 2-inch strips
1 cup celery, cut into 2-inch strips
2 medium onions, sliced and separated into rings
½ tsp. ginger
½ tsp. garlic salt
2 whole chicken breasts, skinned, boned and cut into 2-inch strips
1 tsp. MSG
1 cup thinly sliced mushrooms
1 tsp. lemon juice
½ cup sliced water chestnuts, drained
½ lb. fresh broccoli or 2 pkgs. (8 oz. each) frozen broccoli spears, flowerets only
Tabasco sauce
⅓ cup soy sauce
¼ cup chopped parsley
⅓ cup sake or sherry

In a large wok or frying pan, heat peanut or vegetable oil. When hot, add carrots, celery and onion rings. Reduce heat and stir until vegetables are glazed, about 5 minutes. Sprinkle with ginger and garlic salt. Remove and set aside. Add chicken and MSG. Cook 8 minutes or until chicken lightens in color. Add mushrooms sprinkled with lemon juice, water chestnuts, fresh or frozen broccoli, Tabasco and soy sauce. Add reserved vegetables. Cover all and steam for 5 minutes. Remove cover; add parsley and sake or sherry. Cook, uncovered, about 5 minutes, until vegetables are tender-crisp. Serve with or without rice and additional soy sauce.

Serves 4 to 6

chicken and vegetables with horseradish sauce

The cooking aroma will definitely whet any and all appetites.

1 4-lb. chicken
4 carrots, cut into 2-inch strips
6 small turnips, quartered
3 leeks, white part only, cut into 3-inch strips; or 2 medium onions, cut into rings and separated
3 stalks celery, cut into 2-inch strips
1 small white cabbage, cut into 6 wedges
2 small potatoes, quartered
3 cups chicken broth
1 cup dry white wine
1 clove garlic, minced
salt and pepper to taste

Horseradish Sauce:
2 T. butter
1 T. plus 2 tsp. flour
1 cup chicken broth
¼ cup horseradish
½ cup cream

Place chicken in a soup kettle. Add vegetables. Pour broth and wine over all. Add garlic. Season with salt and pepper. Bring to boil. Reduce heat, cover and simmer 40 minutes or until chicken and vegetables are tender. Drain the chicken and vegetables. Arrange on hot platter with chicken in center and vegetables surrounding. Keep warm.

For Horseradish Sauce: In a saucepan, make a roux of the butter and flour. Stir in chicken broth, stirring constantly, with wire whisk. Bring to boil and reduce heat. Stir in horseradish and cook over low heat until sauce thickens. Gradually stir in cream. Pour small amount of sauce over chicken. Serve remaining sauce separately.

Serves 6

cornish hens with almond-raisin rice and chutney sauce

4 Cornish hens, thawed
¼ cup melted butter
salt and pepper

Almond-Raisin Rice:
1¼ cups long-grain rice
2½ cups chicken broth
½ tsp. salt
1 T. butter
⅓ cup seedless white raisins
pinch of sugar
⅓ cup toasted chopped almonds
1 T. chopped parsley

Chutney Sauce:
1 cup water
½ cup cider vinegar
⅔ cup sugar
2 T. cornstarch
1 T. soy sauce
⅓ cup chutney
1 T. brandy

Brush the hens with melted butter. Sprinkle with salt and pepper. Place hens on a rack in a shallow roasting pan. Bake at 400° for 1 hour and 15 minutes or until tender. Baste frequently with the pan juices or additional butter, if necessary.

For Almond-Raisin Rice: In a medium saucepan, combine rice, broth, salt and butter. Bring to a boil. Reduce heat, add raisins and sugar. Cover pan and simmer until the broth is absorbed by the rice, approximately 20 minutes. Add the almonds and parsley before serving.

For Chutney Sauce: Combine the first 5 ingredients in a saucepan. Bring to a boil, stirring constantly with a wire whisk. Reduce heat; simmer 2 to 3 minutes. Stir in the chutney and brandy. Sauce may be made in advance and heated before serving. Add additional water, if sauce is too thick. Serve the hens on a platter with the rice in the center. Garnish with fresh parsley. Serve the Chutney Sauce separately.

Serves 4

roast duck with cherry sauce and coconut

Cherry Sauce preparation must begin while duck roasts.

1 5-lb. duck
1 small white onion, sliced
½ tsp. salt
¼ tsp. pepper

Cherry Sauce:
3 T. sugar
¼ cup red wine vinegar
2 cups chicken stock, divided
2 T. cornstarch
3 T. cherry liqueur
1 cup dark sweet cherries
1 T. lemon juice
2 T. wine
½ cup coconut, optional

Clean and dry duck. Stuff with sliced onions, pepper and salt. Place in shallow roasting pan. Cook at 350° for 30 minutes. Pour off fat. Increase heat to 425°. Cook 1 to 1½ hours, draining fat frequently. Turn duck over last 20 minutes of cooking. Cook until tender but not dry. Remove duck to warm, ovenproof serving platter. Keep warm. Spoon Cherry Sauce over duck. If desired, sprinkle duck with coconut. Place under broiler to brown coconut. Serve immediateiy.

For Cherry Sauce: Place sugar and red wine vinegar in a small saucepan. Boil over medium-high heat until it becomes a dark, thick syrup. Add one cup chicken stock. Simmer one minute, stirring constantly. Add remaining cup of chicken stock, cornstarch and cherry liqueur. Allow cherries to sit in lemon juice for 30 minutes. Add cherry mixture to stock mixture. When duck is finished, pour out all but 2 tablespoons of fat. Deglaze with wine. Add to sauce. Heat 3 to 4 minutes and pour over duck.

Serves 2

roast duckling with mandarin orange sauce

1 5-5½-lb. duck
salt and pepper
1 orange, peeled and sliced
1 apple, peeled and sliced
1 small onion, sliced
1 small clove garlic, slivered

Mandarin Orange Sauce:
2 cups mandarin oranges, drained
½ cup orange juice
1 cup pineapple juice
1 T. cornstarch
1 T. soy sauce
⅛ tsp. ground cloves
¼ tsp. ginger
2 T. orange brandy
¼ cup orange marmalade
toasted, slivered almonds

Preheat oven to 450°. Remove chunks of fat from inside of duck, if any. Discard. Rinse duckling inside and out with water. Pat dry with paper toweling. Place duck breast-side up on rack in a shallow roasting pan. Sprinkle inside and outside with salt and pepper. Stuff cavity with the orange, apple, onion and garlic. Prick well with fork. Roast at 450° for 20 minutes. Remove from oven to pour off excess fat. Cover legs and wing tips with foil to prevent burning. Reduce temperature to 350°. Return to oven and continue roasting for 1½ hours. Pour off excess fat as needed. Remove stuffing from cavity; discard. Place duckling on warm serving platter. Keep warm.

For Mandarin Orange Sauce: Drain oranges and set aside. In a saucepan, combine remaining ingredients, except brandy. Heat, stirring constantly with wire whisk, until mixture comes to boil. Reduce heat; simmer 3 minutes until mixture thickens. Stir in oranges and brandy. Cook for 2 minutes. Pour small amount of sauce over duck. Top with toasted slivered almonds. Serve remaining sauce separately.

Note: To prepare in advance, follow above procedures. Remove from oven and cool to room temperature. Wrap and store in refrigerator. When ready to serve, place, uncovered, in shallow roasting pan; bake at 450° for 20 minutes. Serve with sauce.

Serves 2 to 3

currant sauce for duck and game

¾ cup dry currants
½ cup water
1 cup beef broth
1 T. sugar
1 small whole onion
1 small whole clove garlic
1 bay leaf
2 T. red wine vinegar
⅓ cup red currant jelly
2 T. cornstarch
⅓ cup orange juice
1 T. chili sauce
¼ tsp. ground cloves
salt and pepper to taste
3 T. creme de cassis (black currant liqueur)

Place the first 7 ingredients in a saucepan. Bring to boil. Reduce heat; simmer, covered, for 10 minutes. Strain. Stir in vinegar and currant jelly. Combine cornstarch with orange juice. Stir into currant liquid with a wire whisk. Add remaining ingredients except the liqueur. Bring to boil, stirring constantly. Reduce heat; simmer, uncovered for 10 minutes. Stir in creme de cassis. Pour sauce over duck or game or serve separately.

Makes 2¼ cups sauce

lapin au vin

Rabbit baked in wine.

1 whole rabbit, cut into pieces
6 T. butter, divided
1 cup sliced onions
1 cup diced carrots
2-3 slices thick bacon
1 lb. salt pork, cut into ¾ x ¼-inch strips
1 cup white wine
2 cups chicken stock
6 cups breadcrumbs
2-3 T. chopped parsley
1 tsp. thyme
1 clove garlic, minced
salt

In a large skillet, melt 4 tablespoons of the butter. Saute rabbit until browned. In a large, deep oven-to-table casserole, combine the vegetables, bacon and salt pork. Place the rabbit and pan juices over the vegetables. Add the wine and stock to the casserole. In a separate bowl, mix the crumbs, parsley, thyme, garlic and salt. Cover the rabbit with bread mixture and dot with remaining butter. Bake at 350° for 1 hour. Serve with red cabbage and fried apples.

Serves 6

roast pheasant

2 3-lb. young pheasants
salt
freshly ground black pepper
¼ cup butter or margarine
1 small onion, finely chopped
¼ cup chopped celery with leaves
1 T. chopped parsley
½ tsp. thyme
3 cups soft breadcrumbs
¼ cup chicken broth
3 T. vegetable oil
12 slices bacon
½ cup dry white wine

Sprinkle birds inside and out with salt and pepper. In a medium skillet, melt butter and cook onion until tender. Add celery and cook 3 minutes. Add parsley, thyme, breadcrumbs and broth. Season with additional salt and pepper. Stuff birds with the bread mixture. Sew cavity closed and tie legs together with string. Rub birds with oil. Place bacon slices over the birds and tie in place with string. Place birds, breast-side up, on a rack in a shallow roasting pan. Roast at 350° about 1½ hours, basting frequently with pan juices. Add wine during last half hour of roasting and baste frequently. Remove birds to a serving platter. Skim off fat and serve pan juices separately.

Serves 4

pecan-herb stuffing

So good with turkey!

½ cup butter
1¾ cups chopped onion
½ cup chopped celery
2 tsp. thyme
½ tsp. rosemary
1 T. salt
1 tsp. pepper
¼ tsp. nutmeg
½ cup chopped parsley
1 cup chopped pecans
10 cups breadcrumbs or cubes
water or chicken broth (optional)

Melt butter in a large skillet. Saute onion and celery 5 minutes. Stir in remaining ingredients except breadcrumbs and water. Place breadcrumbs or cubes into a large bowl. Add sauteed mixture and toss well. Moisten, if desired, with a little water or chicken broth.

Note: Remember never to stuff a turkey until roasting time.

Makes stuffing for a 16 pound turkey

fish and seafood

"In the country, Knickerbockers are fashionable day suits.
Felt hats, rough coats, leggings and substantial boots may be worn.
A gentleman, if he ride or walk may pay a visit to familiar acquaintances
in such attire, but if he drive, he must wear a morning dress."

LIBRARY OF CONGRESS

scampi a la creme

Bechamel Sauce:
1 T. butter
1 T. flour
½ cup milk
½ small bay leaf
pinch of ground cloves

Scampi:
4 fresh tomatoes, peeled
2½ T. butter
1 medium onion, finely chopped
2 dozen shrimp, shelled and deveined, seasoned with salt and pepper
1½ T. brandy
1 T. sherry
½ cup Bechamel Sauce
½ cup whipping cream
1 egg, beaten

For Bechamel Sauce: In a small saucepan, melt butter over low heat. Blend in flour. Cook 3 to 5 minutes. Slowly stir in milk over low heat. Add the bay leaf and cloves. Stir with wire whisk or wooden spoon until sauce is thickened and smooth. Remove bay leaf before serving. Makes ½ cup.

For Scampi: Cut each tomato into 4 pieces and remove seeds. Cut into small squares. Place in a bowl and set aside. In a 10-inch skillet, melt butter being careful not to let it brown. Add onion. Cook for 1 minute. Add seasoned shrimp. Cook 4 minutes, shaking pan so shrimp will not stick. Add brandy and flame. Cook 2 minutes. Add sherry and warm Bechamel Sauce. Bring to boil. Remove pan from heat. In a small bowl, combine whipping cream and egg. Add mixture to shrimp. Mix and heat. Garnish with tomatoes. Serve with rice and a crisp green salad.

Serves 3

herbed shrimp with garlic butter

2 lbs. fresh shrimp, shelled and deveined
1 T. salt
1 tsp. oregano
1 tsp. thyme
1 cup softened butter, divided
4 cloves garlic, crushed
1 T. minced parsley
¼ lb. mushrooms

In a bowl, toss shrimp with salt, oregano and thyme. Chill at least 20 minutes. In a separate small bowl, cream together ½ cup of the softened butter, garlic and parsley. In a skillet, saute mushrooms in remaining ½ cup butter 3 to 4 minutes. Place shrimp in 6 individual baking dishes. Top with mushrooms. Dot with garlic butter. Bake at 375° for 20 minutes or until shrimp are pink and shiny.

Serves 6

tuna casserole

The mayonnaise, soy sauce, sherry combination gives this a very special flavor.

2 cups cooked wild rice
1 can (16 oz.) French style green beans, drained
½ cup diced green pepper
1 cup diced celery
½ cup chopped onion
1 can (8 oz.) mushrooms, drained
1 can (8 oz.) water chestnuts, drained and sliced
2 cans (7 oz. each) tuna
1 jar (2 oz.) pimento strips
1 cup real mayonnaise
2 T. soy sauce
1 can (10¾ oz.) condensed cream of mushroom soup
⅓ cup dry sherry
1 T. lemon juice
2 cups grated Cheddar cheese

Place the cooked rice in a greased 13 x 9 x 2-inch casserole. Cover with the vegetables and tuna. In a medium-size mixing bowl, combine the pimento, mayonnaise, soy sauce, mushroom soup, sherry and lemon juice. Pour over ingredients in the casserole. Cover with the cheese. Bake at 350° for 30 minutes or until casserole is thoroughly heated.

Variation: 2 cups of cooked chicken can be substituted for the tuna.

Serves 4 to 6

crab and shrimp casserole

1 pkg. (6 oz.) frozen crab, thawed
1 pkg. (6 oz.) frozen shrimp, thawed
1 can (10¾ oz.) condensed cream of mushroom soup or cream of shrimp soup
½ cup real mayonnaise
⅔ cup milk
¼ cup sherry or orange juice
1 can (4 oz.) mushrooms
2 cups uncooked very thin noodles
½ cup grated Cheddar cheese

In a 2-quart saucepan, combine the first 7 ingredients and heat until well blended. Place uncooked noodles in a greased 1½-quart casserole. Pour heated ingredients over noodles. Top with grated cheese. Bake at 350° for 35 minutes.

Serves 4

marianne's cannelloni shells

A crepe that tastes like pasta!

6 eggs
2 cups water
2 cups flour
dash salt
½ cup oil for frying shells

Put eggs, water, flour and salt in blender jar. Blend at high speed for 30 seconds. Scrape down sides. Blend at high speed 10 to 15 seconds more. Cover and refrigerate 2 hours. Brush a 6-inch crepe pan with oil and place over medium-high heat. Add about 2 tablespoons of batter to pan, tipping in a circular fashion to coat the bottom. Cook until edges begin to brown. Turn and cook other side. Slide onto a platter and repeat. Fill and serve as desired. The shells can be made up to 48 hours ahead of time, wrapped and stored in the refrigerator. They may also be frozen, properly wrapped.

Makes about 2 dozen shells

seafood cannelloni

12 cannelloni shells (see index) or 12 prepared cannelloni shells, cooked and drained.

Filling:
2 cups ricotta cheese
1 pkg. (3 oz.) cream cheese
⅔ cup Parmesan cheese
½ cup chopped parsley
2 eggs, well beaten

Sauce:
½ cup butter
1 medium onion, chopped
1 clove garlic, minced
½ cup flour
1 cup milk
2 cups half-and-half cream
1 cup chicken broth
¼ cup dry white wine
1 bay leaf
¼ tsp. oregano
salt to taste
dash cayenne pepper
2 pkgs. (6 oz. each) frozen crab or shrimp, thawed
1 cup grated mozzarella cheese
½ cup Parmesan cheese

Prepare shells according to directions.

For Filling: Combine all ingredients in a mixing bowl. Blend thoroughly. Stuff shells with filling. Place in a buttered 13 x 9-inch casserole.

For Sauce: Melt butter in a saucepan. Saute onion and garlic until tender. Stir in flour. Gradually add milk, cream and broth, stirring constantly. Cook until thick. Stir in wine, bay leaf and seasonings. Cover and cook over low heat 10 minutes. Remove bay leaf. Stir in crab or shrimp. Pour sauce over cannelloni. Sprinkle with mozzarella. Top with Parmesan. Bake at 400° until golden. Serve immediately. Shells can be stuffed and frozen. Thaw in refrigerator. Add the Sauce and bake as stated.

Serves 6 to 8

scalloped oysters

Recipe doubles or triples easily.

1 pint fresh oysters
¼ cup oyster liquid (reserved from above oysters)
2 T. cream
½ cup day-old breadcrumbs
1 cup cracker crumbs
½ cup butter, melted
salt and pepper
paprika

Drain oysters, reserving oyster liquid. Mix oyster liquid and cream; set aside. Mix bread and cracker crumbs with melted butter; sprinkle a thin layer of crumbs into a small greased 8 x 8 x 2-inch baking dish. Add half the drained oysters and half the cream mixture; salt lightly. Add another layer of crumbs. Repeat layers. Top with crumb mixture. Do not make more than two layers of oysters. Sprinkle with paprika. Bake at 425° for 30 minutes. If doubling recipe, bake in a 9 x 13-inch baking dish.

Serves 6

scalloped oysters with cream sauce

A great addition to a holiday meal.

2 cups coarse cracker crumbs
½ cup butter, melted
1 pint oysters; drain and reserve liquid
pepper
¾ cup half-and-half cream
¼ cup oyster liquid
¼ tsp. Worcestershire sauce
½ tsp. salt

In a small bowl, combine cracker crumbs and melted butter. Spread one-third of the crumb mixture in a greased 8 x 1¼-inch round casserole. Cover with half of the oysters. Sprinkle with pepper. Spread another one-third of the crumb mixture over oysters. Cover with remaining oysters. Sprinkle with pepper. In a separate bowl, combine cream, oyster liquid, Worcestershire sauce and salt. Pour into casserole. Top with remaining crumb mixture. Bake at 350° for 40 minutes.

Serves 4

salmon roulade with lemon sauce

A savory souffle roll, so special it is worth every minute of preparation time.

Cheese Souffle:
5 T. butter
5 T. flour
1 tsp. salt
1¼ cups milk
½ cup grated Cheddar cheese
½ cup grated Parmesan cheese
6 eggs, separated
¼ tsp. cream of tartar
grated Parmesan cheese

Salmon Filling:
1 can (15½ oz.) salmon; drain and reserve liquid
¾ cup diced, fresh mushrooms
½ cup diced celery
¼ cup minced onion
1½ T. butter
¼ tsp. salt
⅛ tsp. pepper
⅓ cup sour cream

Lemon Sauce:
2 T. butter
2 T. flour
1¼ cups chicken broth
reserved salmon liquid
¼ tsp. salt
2 egg yolks, beaten
1 T. finely minced parsley
2 T. lemon juice

For Cheese Souffle: In a heavy saucepan, melt butter. Blend in flour and salt. Gradually add milk. Cook, stirring constantly, until thick and smooth. Add cheeses. Heat, stirring constantly, until cheese melts. In a large bowl, beat egg yolks. Gradually beat in cheese sauce. In a separate bowl, beat egg whites with cream of tartar until stiff peaks form. Fold one-half of the beaten egg whites into cheese mixture. Carefully fold in remaining egg whites. Turn into oiled 15 x 10 x 1-inch jelly roll pan lined with greased wax paper. Bake at 350° for 12 minutes or until firm. Turn out onto a linen towel sprinkled with Parmesan cheese. Carefully remove wax paper. Roll up souffle and towel together lengthwise. Cool at room temperature. Unroll. Spread with Salmon Filling.

For Salmon Filling: Flake drained salmon. In a 10-inch skillet, saute mushrooms, celery and onion in butter. Cool slightly. Combine with salmon, salt, pepper and sour cream. Spread on unrolled souffle. Roll up. Place seam-side down on baking sheet. Bake at 350° for 15 to 20 minutes or until heated through. Slice. Serve with Lemon Sauce.

For Lemon Sauce: In a heavy saucepan, melt butter. Blend in flour. Gradually stir in chicken broth and salmon liquid. Add salt. Cook, stirring constantly, until thick and smooth. Add small amount of sauce to beaten egg yolks. Then add egg yolk mixture to sauce. Cook over low heat until thickened. Blend in parsley and lemon juice. Serve over Salmon Roulade.

Note: Roulade may be prepared beforehand to the point of final baking. Lemon Sauce is also excellent over a salmon loaf. The Roulade is nicely complemented by the color of fresh spinach salad.

Serves 6 to 8

fish and broccoli roll-ups

Delightfully simple and elegant.

2-2½ lbs. fresh or frozen thin sole or flounder fillets
2 pkgs. (10 oz. each) frozen broccoli spears, cooked and drained
juice of 1 lemon (3 T.)
salt and pepper
slivered almonds
lemon wedges

Cream Sauce:
3 T. butter
3 T. flour
½ tsp. salt
2 cups half-and-half cream
1 lemon peel, grated
⅛ tsp. dry mustard
2 T. sherry

Thaw fillets, if frozen. Wrap one fillet around each cooked broccoli spear. In a greased 12 x 8 x 2-inch glass baking dish, arrange roll-ups seam-side down. Sprinkle with lemon juice, salt and pepper. Pour Cream Sauce over fillets. Top with slivered almonds. Bake at 350° for 20 to 25 minutes. Garnish with lemon wedges. Serve with rice.

For Cream Sauce: In a medium saucepan, melt butter. Gradually stir in flour and salt until smooth. Remove from heat. Gradually add cream. Cook and stir over medium heat until sauce boils. Stir in lemon peel, dry mustard and sherry. Pour over fillets.

Serves 4 to 6

fillet of sole mornay

A subtle combination of simple ingredients makes this very special and very French!

1½ lbs. sole fillets
1 T. lemon juice
2 bay leaves
½ cup water
⅛ tsp. thyme
1 cup milk
1 slice onion
1 clove garlic
6 whole peppercorns
2 T. butter
1½ T. flour
salt and pepper
2 T. whipping cream
3 T. grated Parmesan cheese

Wash fillets and dry well with paper towels. Fold both ends under and place in a well-buttered, shallow baking dish. Add lemon juice, 1 bay leaf, ½ cup water and the thyme. Cover with foil and poach in a 350° oven for 12 to 15 minutes or until fish flakes when nudged with a fork. Meanwhile, put milk, onion, garlic, 1 bay leaf and whole peppercorns into a saucepan. Bring to a boil and remove from heat. In another saucepan, melt butter. Remove from heat and add flour, salt and pepper, stirring with a whisk. Strain and add hot milk. Stir over medium heat until sauce comes to a boil. Add cream for enrichment and simmer 2 minutes. Arrange drained fillets on an ovenproof serving dish. Pour over sauce. Sprinkle with Parmesan cheese and brown lightly under the broiler.

Serves 4

rolled flounder fillets with mushroom-caper sauce

Easy way to make "just fish" elegant!

1 pkg. (8 oz.) herb stuffing mix or 2 cups of your favorite stuffing
6 strips bacon, fried crisp and crumbled
2 T. bacon drippings
2 T. melted butter
2 T. minced parsley
¼ cup minced onion
6 thin flounder fillets or any white fish
melted butter

Mushroom-Caper Sauce:
1 can (4 oz.) sliced mushrooms; drain and reserve liquid
⅓ cup mushroom liquid
1 can (10¾ oz.) condensed cream of mushroom soup
2 T. capers
¼ cup dry sherry
salt and pepper to taste

For Fillets: Prepare stuffing mix according to package directions. In a medium bowl, mix stuffing, bacon, bacon drippings, butter, parsley and onion. Spread equal amount of mixture on each fillet. Roll up. Secure with wooden toothpick. In well-greased muffin cups, place each roll upright. Brush with additional melted butter. Bake at 375° for 30 minutes. If necessary, brush again with melted butter. Put under broiler to brown. Serve with Mushroom-Caper Sauce.

For Mushroom-Caper Sauce: In a medium saucepan, mix all ingredients together. Heat and pour over fillets.

Note: For quick preparation, place 3 fillets in a well-greased 12-inch casserole. Cover with equal amount of stuffing mixture. Top with remaining 3 fillets. Brush with melted butter. Bake at 350° for 20 to 30 minutes. Serve with Mushroom-Caper Sauce.

Serves 4 to 6

fillet of sole with tomatoes and mushrooms

1 lb. frozen fillet of sole, thawed
salt and pepper
2 T. butter
½ cup chopped onion
1 clove garlic, minced
1 T. plus 2 tsp. flour
½ cup each: dry white wine, milk, cream
2 medium tomatoes, peeled, seeded, diced
1 can (4 oz.) mushrooms, drained
½ tsp. each: tarragon, thyme, basil
1 cup grated Swiss cheese

Place fillets of sole in well-buttered baking dish; season with salt and pepper. Melt butter in saucepan; add onions and garlic. Saute until tender. Stir in flour; add wine. Slowly add milk and cream. Simmer over low heat for 3 minutes. Stir in tomatoes, mushrooms and seasonings. Pour sauce over fish. Sprinkle with Swiss cheese. Bake at 350° for 30 minutes. To serve, lift fish carefully with slotted serving utensil.

Serves 4

jim's favorite baked walleye or northern pike

2-3 lbs. fresh or frozen walleye or northern pike fillets
salt and pepper
1 cup White Sauce (recipe below)
1 can (4½ oz.) tiny shrimp
¼ cup (1 oz.) shredded Swiss cheese

White Sauce:
2 T. butter
2 T. flour
¼ tsp. salt
¾ cup milk
¼ cup sherry or white wine

Place fillets in generously buttered, shallow casserole. Season with salt and pepper. Cover tightly with buttered aluminum foil. Bake at 350° for 45 minutes. Add tiny shrimp and Swiss cheese to White Sauce. When fish has finished baking, remove foil. Add White Sauce mixture. Broil until lightly browned and bubbly. Serve with asparagus, crusty French bread and chilled white wine.

For White Sauce: In a small, heavy saucepan, melt butter. Blend in flour and salt. Cook over low heat until mixture is smooth and bubbly. Remove from heat. Stir in milk and sherry or white wine. Bring to boil, stirring constantly. Boil 1 minute.

Serves 4 to 6

southern snapper

1 5-6 lb. red snapper, cleaned and scaled with head and tail on (or pieces, if preferred)
butter
salt
freshly ground black pepper
⅛ tsp. thyme
1 bay leaf, crushed
¾ cup chopped celery
1 cup chopped green pepper
½ cup chopped parsley
½ cup butter
1 onion, thinly sliced
1 clove garlic, minced
½ cup flour
4 cups canned tomatoes, cut into quarters

Rub fish with butter. Sprinkle with salt and pepper. Place in a foil lined pan. Sprinkle with thyme, bay leaf, celery, green pepper and parsley. In a 10-inch skillet, melt butter. Add onion and garlic. Saute until golden. Blend in flour. Add tomatoes. Bring to boil. Cook slowly until slightly thickened. Add salt and pepper to taste. Pour over fish. Bake at 325° for 1 hour or until fish flakes easily with fork. Serve with rice or boiled potatoes.

Serves 6

buttery baked fish

Tender and moist!

1 lb. fish fillets (allow ⅓-lb. per serving)
¼ cup melted butter
½ tsp. salt
¼ tsp. lemon-and-pepper marinade seasoning
¼ tsp. paprika
1 small onion, thinly sliced

Wash and dry fillets. Place fish in a shallow, foil-lined pan. Mix butter, salt, lemon-and-pepper seasoning and paprika. Pour over fish. Bake at 350° for 20 to 25 minutes or until fish flakes easily with fork. Add onion 5 minutes before fish is done. Do not overcook. Pour pan juices over fish when serving.

Variation: Toasted almonds or mushrooms may be substituted for onion. Add when fish is almost done.

Serves 3

baked halibut with chutney sauce

. . . intriguingly served in a delicious sauce.

1 lb. frozen halibut, thawed
salt and pepper
3 T. butter, divided
2 T. dry white wine
½ cup chutney
2 T. sherry
2 tsp. lemon juice
pinch of mace
⅛ tsp. cinnamon
⅛ tsp. ground cloves

Blot fish dry with paper toweling. Season with salt and pepper. Melt 2 tablespoons of the butter in a large skillet. Saute the fish lightly on both sides. Remove fish and butter to a buttered 10-inch casserole. Pour wine over fish. Cover and bake at 350° for 15 minutes. In the same skillet, combine remaining 1 tablespoon of butter with remaining ingredients. Warm over low heat until well blended. Transfer baked fish with slotted spatula to a warm platter. Pour sauce over fish. Serve immediately.

Serves 2 to 3

broiled fish with deviled cheese

2 lbs. fresh or frozen fish fillets, thawed
2 T. melted butter
salt and pepper
1 cup shredded Cheddar cheese
2 T. chili sauce
1 T. prepared mustard
½ tsp. Worcestershire sauce
1 tsp. prepared horseradish

Place fish fillets on a foil covered broiling pan. Brush foil and fillets with melted butter. Season lightly with salt and pepper. Broil 3 to 4 inches from heat 3 to 4 minutes on each side or until lightly browned and easily flaked with fork. Combine and mix the remaining ingredients in a small bowl. Spread mixture over fish. Return fish to broiler for approximately 3 minutes or until cheese melts and begins to brown. Place on warm serving platter. Serve immediately.

Serves 4 to 6

Kleckner.
age 20 months.
Kansas Farmers' Alliance Presidential Candidate for 1892

a dinner fit for a president

"The napkin should be unfolded and laid across the knee, and only one corner should be lifted to wipe the mouth. It should never be tucked under the chin."

camembert mousse

fresh mushroom soup

elegant beef tenderloin

fluffy-herbed potatoes

spinach-stuffed tomatoes

bibb lettuce and red wine vinaigrette with chopped eggs

home-baked crescent rolls

chocolate angel strata pie

LIBRARY OF CONGRESS

soup to warm a snowman's heart

"The simplest soup may have only pepper and salt,
while the richest may have a little of every savor.
No measure can be given,
because the good soup-maker must be a skillful taster."

picnic in the snow

winter warmer

sausage-tomato soup

swedish rye bread

cubes of cheese

grandmother gilmore's skillet cookies

hearty soup supper

dutch punch

liptauer cheese

czechoslovakian cabbage soup

dilly french bread

fresh apple cake with caramel frosting

ladies luncheons with a flair

"If a lawn-party is given, the hostess and her daughters should receive on the lawn in their bonnets. . . . But whatever costume a lady assumes, she must wear gloves. This rule is absolute."

spring

salmon roulade

asparagus vinaigrette

daiquiri chiffon with spirited custard sauce

summer

curried chicken salad

sliced fresh zucchini with blue cheese dressing

banana-pecan bread

sunny silver pie

fall

crabmeat quiche

oriental spinach salad

tippecanoe tea bread

applesauce cake with warm rum sauce

winter

ham crepes with hot mustard sauce

tomatoes stuffed with pea salad

"blizzard-blues" ice cream pie

1902

haute cuisine for the "horsey set"

"A bow should be according to circumstances. Among formal acquaintances the lady bows first. Between intimate friends either may bow first. It should be prompt, as soon as the eyes meet. . . . Nearsighted people ought to be made an exception to this rule."

derby day cocktail buffet

mint juleps

hot crab dip

guacamole dip with vegetables

asparagus-blue cheese roll-ups

sliced baked ham with grandma's mustard sauce and melt-in-your-mouth biscuits

laura's marinated vegetables

spinach-filled mushrooms

tray of assorted cheese and crackers

candy coated pecan halves

tiny cheesecakes

bev's creamy chocolate wafers

bluegrass brunch

strawberry spritzers

salmon asparagus pie

ham and cheese souffle with golden mushroom sauce

fresh fruit with fruit salad marinade

melt-in-your-mouth biscuits

currant-pecan crown

danish puff

rhubarb coffee cake

S.S. Picknic.

the family reunion

"To make lemonade, roll six lemons well, slice thin in an earthen vessel. Put over them two tea-cups white sugar and let stand fifteen minutes. Add one gallon water and lumps of ice. Pour into a pitcher and set aside in the ice-chest until ready to serve."

everyone's favorite barbecue

grilled marinated chicken

corn-on-the-cob

alice's hot potato salad

layered vegetables and cheese casserole

summer slaw

olive and macaroni salad

fresh fruit with honey-poppy seed dressing

old-fashioned biscuits with homemade apple butter

zucchini-pineapple bread

ann's herb bread

peach cobbler

grandmother's graham cracker cake

lemonade

summer fun

"For archery, croquet and lawn-tennis, the players dress in flannel made for the purpose.
The dress for the lady is a short skirt and a jersey,
the latter being indispensible to the free use of the arms. . . .
For yachting, ladies wear flannel suits of navy blue or white,
or serge or tweed, with jaunty sailor hats.

a sporting luncheon

tomato aspic with seafood and vegetables and herb mayonnaise

cucumber salad finlandia

pecan sticky buns

lemon-sour cream pie

picnic for land or sea

zucchini soup

italian casserole for a crowd

epicurian vegetable salad

dilly french bread

glazed fresh fruit pie

an evening on the patio or at poolside

san fernando salad soup

tenderloin on the grill

rice salad

parmesan-baked zucchini with tomatoes and onions

rhubarb cheesecake

prize winning dinners

"Gentlemen and ladies go to a dinner-party in full dress, the gentlemen in regulation 'swallow-tail and white choker'."

spring

caviar mousse

veal oscar for company

buttered rice

carrots amandine

mixed salad greens and creamy french dressing with bacon

herb crescent rolls

strawberries with grand marnier sauce

summer

carrot soup

lemon broiled lamb

fettucine with zucchini and mushrooms

lettuce and tomato salad with sweet cream and vinegar dressing

blueberries with lemon mousse

fall

cold cucumber-watercress soup

chicken normandy

cashew rice ring

buttered peas

mandarin orange and avocado salad

mocha charlotte

winter

cream of leek and carrot soup

roast duck with cherry sauce and coconut

wild rice

broccoli fantastic

cucumber ring mold

fresh pear pie

PHOTOGRAPHIC ARCHIVES, UNIVERSITY OF LOUISVILLE

gentlemen's choice

"Loud conversation or uproarious laughter should not be indulged in:
they are characteristics of vulgarity.
At the same time there should be a 'cheerful chatting',
good nature, a general freedom from care and anxiety and a social time."

the gourmand's delight

new england clam chowder

rare roast ribs of beef

wild rice au vin

green beans a la nicoise

mixed green salad

herb french bread

mocha cake

before or after the game

trilby

onion-tomato soup

sandwich beef brisket

broccoli and cauliflower salad

cheese ripple fudge cake

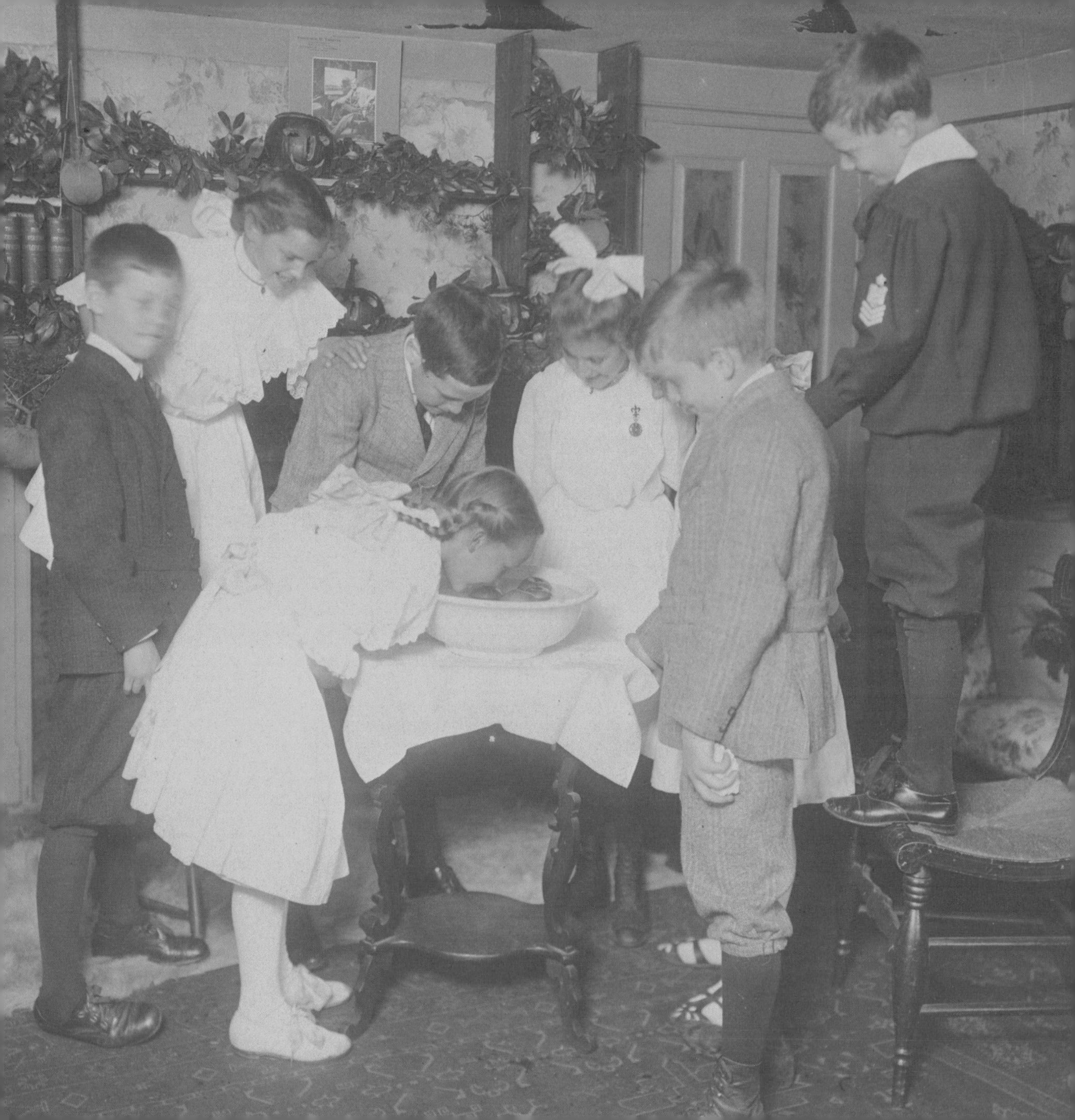

"trick or treat" fare

"Don't sit with elbows akimbo, but
keep them down close to your side."

hot mulled cider

marinated country-style ribs

hasselback potatoes

tray of fresh vegetable relishes

frozen island salad

pumpkin bread

make-your-own ice cream sundaes

monster cookies

THE BETTMANN ARCHIVE

home for the holidays

"New Year's calling is a beautiful custom and,
while hearts are warm and friends are true,
will never wholly disappear."

christmas dinner

scalloped oysters

roast turkey with pecan and herb stuffing

crunch topped sweet potatoes

cranberry-raspberry mold

elegant peas

snowballs served in champagne glasses

holiday buffet

cheddar cheese and olive canape

marinated artichokes with curry dip

roast pork tenderloin au vin

mushroom noodle casserole

seasoned brussels sprouts

walnut-cranberry jewel salad

pumpkin spice roll or creamy pumpkin praline pie

BROWN BROTHERS

VICTOR JOE
5¢ CIGAR
JOHN KOONS
CLUB-HOUSE
LUNCH-ROOM
CLUB
HOUSE
RESTAURANT.
Ribs of Beef
Veal Pot Pie
Dinner
15¢
Soup
5¢

beef and veal

"If conversation is a fine art, so is listening,
for without a good listener there can be no good conversation.
If silence in company is a vice, inattention is a crime.
Absent-mindedness is unpardonable.
What right has a man or woman to accept an invitation,
and then selfishly employ the time in 'wool-gathering'."

tournedos with madeira sauce

Elegant!

Madeira Sauce:
¼ cup butter
2 cloves garlic, minced
¼ cup chopped onion
2 stalks celery with leaves, chopped
1 small carrot, diced
¼ cup flour
3 cups beef consomme, divided
2 T. red wine vinegar
⅓ cup Madeira sherry
2 T. ketchup
¼ tsp. thyme
1 bay leaf
ground black pepper

Meat:
6 (8 oz.) 2-inch thick beef tenderloin slices
salt and pepper
¼ cup butter
2 T. olive oil
chopped parsley

For Madeira Sauce: In heavy saucepan, melt butter; saute garlic, onion, celery and carrot over low heat for 10 minutes. Stir in flour; cook 3 minutes. Add 1 cup of the consomme; bring to boil. Pour mixture into blender jar. Cover and blend until vegetables are pureed. Pour mixture into saucepan. Add remaining consomme and ingredients. Cook, uncovered, over low heat for 30 minutes. Remove and discard bay leaf.

Makes 2 cups.

For Meat: Pat beef dry with paper toweling. Season with salt and pepper. Heat butter and olive oil in large skillet. When hot, cook meat over high heat for about 5 minutes on each side until well browned, but rare. Transfer to a warm serving platter. Spoon small amount of Madeira Sauce over meat. Sprinkle with parsley. Serve remaining Madeira Sauce separately in a sauceboat.

Serves 6

tenderloin on the grill

1 4-5 lb. whole beef tenderloin
1 clove garlic
4 T. Worcestershire sauce
juice of 1 lime (3 T.)
salt and pepper to taste
¼ tsp. MSG

Rub tenderloin with garlic. Place in pan. In a small bowl, mix Worcestershire sauce with lime juice, salt, pepper and MSG. Pour over meat. Let stand 1 hour. Broil to taste on grill. Baste frequently. Slice to serve. Heat remaining marinade. Pour over sliced tenderloin. Tenderloin may be wrapped in foil after it is grilled until ready to serve.

Serves 8

elegant beef tenderloin

For that very special dinner.

1 2-lb. whole beef tenderloin
½ cup softened butter, divided
¼ cup chopped scallions
2 T. soy sauce
1 tsp. Dijon mustard
dash of pepper
¾ cup dry sherry or dry white wine

Rub tenderloin with 2 tablespoons softened butter. On a rack in a shallow pan, place tenderloin. Bake at 400° for 20 minutes. In a small saucepan, cook scallions in remaining butter until tender. Add soy sauce, mustard and pepper. Stir in sherry. Heat just to boiling. Pour sauce over tenderloin. Return tenderloin to oven. Bake 25 to 30 minutes for medium rare. Baste frequently while cooking.

Serves 4

marinated flank steak

A variation of a Korean dish.

1 1½-lb. flank steak

Marinade:
1 cup Kikkoman soy sauce
½ cup brown sugar
¾ cup vegetable oil
1 tsp. sesame seeds
4 cloves garlic, pressed
1 tsp. ginger

Mix all ingredients for marinade in shallow baking dish. Place steak in marinade. Marinate steak all day or at least 4 hours. Broil flank steak on grill 7 to 8 minutes on each side. Cut diagonally into thin slices and serve.

Serves 4

flank steak supreme

They will ask for more . . .

1 1½-lb. flank steak, scored on both sides
½ tsp. MSG
2 T. prepared mustard
5 T. butter, divided
⅓ cup chopped onion
⅓ cup chopped celery
1½ cups dry bread cubes or croutons
½ tsp. poultry seasoning
¼ tsp. salt
pepper
clear French salad dressing, enough for basting

Pound steak to flatten. Sprinkle meat with MSG to tenderize. Spread mustard on one side of steak. In a small skillet, melt 2 tablespoons of the butter. Saute onion and celery until golden. Add croutons, remaining butter and seasonings to onion mixture. Spread mixture over mustard side of steak. Roll up jelly roll fashion. Secure with metal skewers. Tie with string. Brush with clear French dressing. Roast over medium coals on a spit about 35 minutes or until done to taste, basting frequently. Also can cook steak on covered grill by indirect method.

Serves 4

herbed flank steak in wine sauce

An old-favorite highlighted with a special blend of herbs.

1 1½-lb. flank steak
2 T. butter or margarine
1 small onion, finely chopped
½ cup sliced, fresh mushrooms
½ cup dry red wine
2 beef bouillon cubes
½ cup water
¾ tsp. seasoned salt
1 tsp. Herb Meat Seasoning

Herb Meat Seasoning:
1 tsp. parsley flakes
1 tsp. rosemary
1 tsp. sweet basil
1 tsp. marjoram
1 tsp. thyme

Cut flank steak across grain at a 45° angle into paper thin slices. Set aside. In a large skillet, melt butter. Saute onion and mushrooms until slightly browned. Add meat. Brown quickly. Reduce heat to simmer. Add wine, bouillon, water, salt and Herb Seasoning. Simmer 15 minutes. Serve over rice or noodles.

For Herb Meat Seasonings: Mix seasoning ingredients. Store leftover seasoning in a glass jar for later use. Great seasoning for pork and roast beef also!

Serves 4

stir-fried beef with chinese pea pods

The delicate sherry-oyster sauce makes this unusual and delicious.

1 1½-lb. flank steak, partially frozen
8 scallions with tops
6 T. bottled oyster sauce
2 T. dry sherry
1 tsp. sugar
4 tsp. cornstarch
3 T. peanut oil
1 pkg. (6 oz.) frozen Chinese pea pods, thawed, or fresh Chinese pea pods

Slice partially frozen flank steak at a 45° angle across the grain into ¼-inch slices. Cut scallions at an angle into 1-inch pieces. In a small bowl, mix the oyster sauce, sherry, sugar and cornstarch until blended. Set aside. Heat a wok or skillet over high heat until very hot. Pour in oil. Heat until hot. Add steak slices; stir quickly, coating all surfaces with oil. Stir-fry over high heat to desired doneness. Stir in sauce mixture quickly and thoroughly. Add pea pods and scallions. Stir-fry 1 minute. Serve immediately with hot rice.

Note: If bottled oyster sauce is not available, substitute by adding 6 T. of canned oysters which have been blended in a blender.

Serves 4

rare roast ribs of beef

This is absolutely foolproof.

2, 3 or 4 standing ribs of beef
salt
pepper
red wine, optional
water

Preheat oven to 375°. Place roast, fat-side up, on rack in a shallow roasting pan. Sprinkle with salt and pepper. Put into preheated oven for exactly 1 hour. Turn off oven. This may be done hours before serving. Do not open the oven door until ready to serve. Before serving, set oven to 300°. Preheat a 2-rib roast for 22 minutes, a 3-rib roast for 25 to 30 minutes, and a 4-rib roast for 35 minutes. Remove to a heated platter. Let stand a few minutes before slicing and serving. Meat will be rare with juices all the way through. Drain excess fat from pan. Add ¼ to ¾ cup red wine or water or combination of both (depending on size of roast) to the pan; stir to loosen the meat sediment. Cook on top of stove until liquid boils. Simmer for 2 minutes. Add salt and pepper to taste. Strain, if necessary. Pour into heated gravy boat. Serve with beef.

2 ribs serve 4 to 6
3 ribs serve 8
4 ribs serve 10 to 12

brandy beef with burgundy

A "spirited" version for budget beef.

1 4-lb. chuck or pot roast
2 cloves garlic, quartered
salt
freshly ground pepper
flour
2 T. bacon drippings
2 T. olive oil
1 cup brandy
1 bay leaf, crushed
pinch of thyme
pinch of marjoram
8 carrots, sliced
8 onions, sliced
2 tomatoes, sliced
1 cup burgundy
¼ cup butter
½ lb. fresh mushrooms, sliced
2 cups sour cream

Make small cuts in top of roast. Insert quartered garlic cloves in cuts. Season flour with salt and pepper. Coat roast on all sides with seasoned flour. In a Dutch oven, heat bacon drippings and olive oil. Add meat and brown on all sides. Add next 8 ingredients. Cover and simmer 3½ to 4 hours. In a small skillet, melt butter. Saute mushrooms 4 to 6 minutes. Before serving, add mushrooms and sour cream to beef. Mix well. If gravy becomes too thick, add more burgundy or water. Beef mixture may be made a day ahead.

Serves 6 to 8

colombian beef with prunes

A typical dish from South America. Must be prepared in advance to allow beef to marinate overnight.

2 medium onions, sliced
2 cloves garlic, minced
2 T. olive oil
2½ lbs. beef stew meat, cut into cubes
2 cups beef stock
1 cup red wine
1 tsp. salt
½ tsp. pepper
2 bay leaves
20 dry prunes, pitted

In an electric frying pan or large 12-inch skillet, brown onion and garlic in oil. Remove onion and garlic. Set aside. In same skillet, brown beef. Add stock, wine, salt, pepper, bay leaves and reserved onions and garlic. Cook over low heat for 1 hour. Stir occasionally to avoid sticking. Add prunes. Cook for another hour. Pour into a 3-quart casserole. Cover and refrigerate overnight. Bake at 325° for 30 minutes. Add some water if too dry. Serve over rice.

Serves 6 to 8

snowy day pot roast

Perfect when you're snowed under.

1 4-lb. arm or blade pot roast
3 T. bacon drippings
2 tsp. salt
1 tsp. pepper
2 medium onions, sliced
½ can (11 oz.) condensed Cheddar cheese soup
1 can (8 oz.) tomato sauce
1 can (4 oz.) pieces and stems mushrooms, drained
¼ tsp. basil
¼ tsp. oregano

In a Dutch oven or an electric skillet, heat bacon drippings. Brown pot roast. Pour off drippings. Season roast with salt and pepper. In a medium bowl, combine remaining ingredients. Pour over meat. Cover tightly. Cook slowly for 3 to 3½ hours or until meat is tender. Serve with the gravy.

Serves 6

hunter's stew

A hearty winter dish.

8 slices bacon, chopped
1½ cups finely chopped onions
1 tsp. finely chopped garlic
2 large carrots, sliced
2 cups water
¼ cup red wine vinegar
3 lbs. boneless beef chuck, cut into 2-inch cubes
1 tsp. salt
freshly ground black pepper
1 cup converted rice
2 medium green peppers, sliced
1¼ cups beef stock, divided

In a 12-inch skillet, fry bacon for 6 to 8 minutes. Remove from skillet. Discard bacon fat, leaving just a thin film in skillet. Add onions to skillet. Cook 4 minutes. Add garlic and carrots. Cook 5 to 6 minutes more. In a large pan or Dutch oven, place the onion-carrot mixture. Add the cooked bacon. Stir in water, vinegar, beef, salt and pepper. Cover and simmer for 1½ hours. Gradually stir in rice. Add peppers. Add 1 cup of beef stock. Bring liquid to boil. Reduce heat to low. Cover and simmer for 20 minutes or until rice is tender. If rice becomes too dry, add remaining stock.

Note: May be frozen after cooking. Reheat.

Serves 8

beer braised beef

This is good made a day ahead and reheated.

¼ cup flour
¼ tsp. salt
3 lbs. beef chuck, cut into 1-inch cubes
3 T. vegetable oil
2 large onions, thinly sliced
1 can (8 oz.) sliced mushrooms, drained
1 can (10½ oz.) condensed beef broth
1 can (12 oz.) beer
1 T. vinegar
2 tsp. sugar
1 clove garlic, minced
1 tsp. crushed dried thyme
1 bay leaf
1 T. parsley

Mix flour and salt. Coat beef cubes with flour mixture. Reserve any remaining flour. Heat oil in a large skillet and set aside. Brown beef, one-half at a time. Remove beef from skillet and set aside. Add the next 9 ingredients to the skillet. Return beef to skillet. Cover and simmer for 2 hours or until meat is tender. Remove bay leaf. Thicken slightly with remaining flour. Stir in parsley.

Serves 8

madras beef curry

Easy, spicy and special!

1 lb. sirloin, cubed
¼ cup vegetable oil
1 large onion, chopped
1 tsp. garlic powder
1 T. curry powder
3 green chilies, chopped
2 T. tomato paste
1 cup hot water
1 T. lemon juice
salt

Condiments:
bananas, sliced
bacon, cooked and crumbled
coconut
chutney
peanuts

In a large skillet, brown meat in oil. Remove meat from skillet. Set aside. Add onion, garlic, curry and chilies to skillet. Cook for 10 minutes over low heat. Add meat, tomato paste and water. Simmer until meat is tender, about 20 minutes. Add lemon juice and salt. Serve over rice with condiments on the side.

Serves 3 to 4

marinated beef brisket

An economical meal that will receive raves from the entire family.

1 6-8 lb. brisket of beef
salt and pepper
garlic powder
1 bottle (8 oz.) French dressing
1 bottle (12 oz.) chili sauce
1 cup dry sherry or red wine
3 medium onions, sliced
½ lb. fresh mushrooms, sliced, or 1 can (4 oz.) sliced mushrooms, drained

Place brisket in a shallow pan. Season with salt, pepper and garlic powder. Pour French dressing over beef. Cover and marinate several hours or overnight in refrigerator. Turn meat at least twice. In a large roasting pan, place brisket. Roast at 325° for 3 to 4 hours. Allow at least 30 minutes per pound. When brisket is half cooked, add chili sauce, sherry and onions. Return to oven and finish roasting. Remove meat from pan, cool and slice. Add mushrooms to gravy remaining in pan. Return sliced meat to pan. Bake at 325° for 30 minutes. Can be made ahead and reheated or frozen for later use.

Serves 10 to 12

suzie's kabobs

Great on the grill or under the broiler.

Kabobs:
½ lb. fresh mushroom caps
cut into bite-size pieces the following:
2 lbs. round steak
2 medium green peppers
2 medium onions
3 medium fresh tomatoes

Marinade:
1½ cups vegetable oil
¾ cup soy sauce
4 T. Worcestershire sauce
2 T. dry mustard
1 tsp. salt
½ cup wine vinegar
2 tsp. dried parsley flakes
2 cloves garlic, crushed
½ cup lemon juice
1 can (10½ oz.) condensed tomato soup

In a large bowl, combine all marinade ingredients. Stir to blend. Add meat. Cover and marinate overnight. To prepare, place meat and vegetables on metal skewers in any combination. Brush with marinade. Broil 4 inches from heat, 7 minutes on each side. While broiling, brush frequently with marinade. In a small saucepan, warm extra marinade. Serve with Kabobs and rice. Marinade is delicious with other cuts of beef.

Serves 6

steak parmigiana

A hit with the children.

1 1½-lb. round steak, flattened and cut into 4 to 6 pieces
1 egg, slightly beaten
½ cup flour
½ cup shredded Cheddar cheese
½ cup vegetable oil
1 large onion, chopped
1 can (6 oz.) tomato paste
1 clove garlic, pressed or finely chopped
salt and pepper to taste
2 cups hot water
1 cup shredded mozzarella cheese

Dip steak in beaten egg until evenly coated. In a small shallow dish, combine flour and Cheddar cheese. Dredge steak in cheese mixture. In an electric skillet, heat oil. Brown steak in oil 2 to 3 minutes per side. Place steak in a 13x9x2-inch greased casserole; saute onion in remaining oil in skillet. Stir in tomato paste, garlic, salt, pepper and water. Simmer 10 minutes. Pour over steak. Top with mozzarella cheese. Cover and bake at 350° for 1 hour. Serve with noodles.

Serves 4 to 6

braccioli (beef roll-ups)

An excellent combination of flavors.

Roll-ups:
1 2-lb. ¼-inch thick round steak, cut into 4 to 6 pieces
1½ T. oregano
2½ T. grated Parmesan cheese
3 T. chopped parsley
1 clove garlic, minced
1 tsp. basil
¾ tsp. salt
½ tsp. pepper
¼ cup chopped salami, ham or cooked sausage
¼ cup olive oil
3 cups Tomato Sauce

Tomato Sauce:
1 can (15 oz.) tomato sauce
15 oz. water
1 can (6 oz.) tomato paste
1 small onion, cut in half
½ tsp. basil
¼ tsp. oregano
1 tsp. parsley
½ clove garlic, minced
salt and pepper to taste

For Roll-ups: Mix oregano, cheese, parsley, garlic, basil, salt, pepper and salami. Spread mixture on top of steak. Fold in edges and roll. Tie securely with string. Heat oil in a medium-size skillet. Saute steak on all sides until brown. Place steak in a 2-quart casserole. Add Tomato Sauce. Cover. Bake at 325° for 2 hours. Serve over pasta.

For Tomato Sauce: In a large pan or electric skillet, mix tomato sauce, water, tomato paste, onion and seasonings. Watch the salt. Simmer for 2 hours over low heat. Remove onion. Sauce can be made a day ahead. Leftover sauce can be frozen for later use.

Serves 4 to 6

steak diane

For the connoisseur!

4 ½-inch thick New York strip or Delmonico steaks
salt
freshly ground black pepper to taste
1 tsp. dry mustard
¼ cup butter
3 T. lemon juice (juice of 1 lemon)
2 tsp. chopped chives
1 tsp. Worcestershire sauce

Score edges of steaks so sides will not curl when cooking. Sprinkle one side of steak with salt, pepper and half of mustard. Pound seasonings into steaks. Turn steaks over and repeat procedure. In an electric skillet, melt butter. Add steaks. Cook 2 minutes on each side over high heat. Remove to platter. Lower heat. Add lemon juice, chives and Worcestershire sauce to skillet. Bring to boil. Pour over meat. Serve immediately.

Serves 4

italian casserole for a crowd

Casserole:
½ cup plus 1 T. butter, divided
2 oz. salt pork, diced
2 T. chopped onions
2 lbs. lean ground beef
1 lb. fresh mushrooms
1 large can (1 lb. 12 oz.) tomatoes
1 T. corn syrup
salt and pepper
1½ cups dry red wine
1½ lbs. green spinach noodles, cooked and drained
1 cup grated Parmesan cheese

White Sauce:
½ cup butter
1 cup flour
1 tsp. nutmeg
dash of bitters
salt and pepper
1 tsp. thyme
1 T. corn syrup
6 cups milk

For Casserole: In a large skillet, combine ½ cup of the butter, salt pork and onions; simmer for 25 minutes. Remove from skillet. In same skillet, brown ground beef and mushrooms. Combine first mixture with meat and mushrooms. Add tomatoes, remaining 1 tablespoon of butter, corn syrup, salt, pepper and red wine. Simmer for 2½ hours. In a large roasting pan, layer one-half of the noodles and one-half of the meat sauce; repeat layers. Cover with White Sauce. Sprinkle top with Parmesan cheese. Bake at 350° for 1 hour.

For White Sauce: In a saucepan, melt butter. Add flour, nutmeg, bitters, salt, pepper, thyme and corn syrup. Add milk and stir over low heat until sauce begins to thicken.

Serves 18 to 20

hamburger stroganoff

Gourmet flavor at budget prices.

1 lb. ground beef
1 can (2¼ oz.) sliced mushrooms, drained, or 1 cup fresh mushrooms, sauteed
1 tsp. salt
dash Tabasco
½ cup hot beef bouillon
1 can (3 oz.) French fried onions
2 T. parsley flakes
2 cups sour cream

In a large skillet, brown ground beef. Drain excess fat. Add remaining ingredients. Heat, but do not boil. Serve over cooked noodles or rice. Can be made in advance, omitting sour cream. May also be frozen. Thaw, if frozen; add sour cream and heat.

Serves 4

meat, spinach and noodle bake

Prepare a day ahead to save time on the day you entertain.

¼ cup butter or margarine
¼ cup vegetable oil or olive oil
1 cup finely chopped celery
½ cup finely chopped onion
½ cup finely chopped carrots
2½ lbs. lean ground chuck
1 tsp. dry garlic chips or 1 clove garlic, diced
1 can (6 oz.) tomato paste
3 cups canned stewed tomatoes or tomato puree
2 tsp. salt
1½ tsp. oregano
1 tsp. basil
½ tsp. thyme
few drops hot pepper sauce (optional)
1 pkg. (6 oz.) green noodles, cooked and drained
2 pkgs. (10 oz. each) frozen spinach, cooked and squeezed dry by hand when cool
½ cup grated Parmesan cheese

In a large skillet or saucepan, combine the butter, oil, celery, onion and carrots. Cook over low heat for 1 hour, stirring frequently. Add beef and garlic. Cook until beef is brown. Stir in the tomato paste, tomatoes, seasonings and hot sauce. Simmer 1½ hours. Combine the noodles and spinach with the meat mixture. Turn into a greased 9 x 13 x 2-inch casserole. Sprinkle top with cheese. Bake at 350° for 25 to 30 minutes. Allow additional baking time if casserole has been refrigerated.

Serves 10 to 12

spaghetti pie

6 oz. spaghetti, cooked according to package directions
2 T. butter or margarine
⅓ cup grated Parmesan cheese
2 eggs, well beaten
¾ lb. ground beef
¼ lb. bulk pork sausage
¼ cup chopped onion
¼ cup chopped green pepper
1 cup stewed tomatoes
1 can (6 oz.) tomato paste
1 tsp. dried oregano, crushed
⅛ tsp. celery salt
⅛ tsp. dry mustard
½ tsp. salt
½ tsp. seasoned salt
⅛ tsp. pepper
1 tsp. parsley flakes
2 T. Worcestershire sauce
1 can (4 oz.) mushrooms, drained
1 cup cottage cheese
1 cup shredded mozzarella cheese

In a large bowl, stir the butter into the hot spaghetti. Add Parmesan cheese and eggs to this mixture. In a buttered 10-inch pie plate, form the spaghetti mixture into a "crust". In a large skillet, cook beef, sausage, onion and green pepper until vegetables are tender and the meat is browned. Drain excess fat. Stir in tomatoes, tomato paste, seasonings and mushrooms. Heat through. Spread cottage cheese over bottom of spaghetti crust. Fill pie with the meat sauce. Bake, uncovered, at 350° for 20 minutes. Sprinkle mozzarella cheese on top and bake 5 minutes longer. This may be frozen before adding the cheese and baking.

Serves 6

burger bundles

A hearty dish for a winter supper.

1 lb. ground chuck
⅔ cup milk, divided
1 cup herb-seasoned stuffing mix, prepared according to package directions
1 can (10¾ oz.) condensed cream of mushroom soup
1 T. ketchup
2 tsp. Worcestershire sauce
1 can (16 oz.) cut green beans, drained

Thoroughly mix the ground chuck with ⅓ cup of the milk. On wax paper, make 6 to 8 six-inch patties. In the center of each patty spoon approximately 1 tablespoon of stuffing mix. Fold edges up and seal. In an 11 x 7-inch casserole, place the bundles sealed-edge down. Combine soup, remaining milk, ketchup, Worcestershire sauce and beans in a saucepan. Bring to boil. Pour over bundles. Bake at 350° for 45 to 50 minutes.

Serves 4 to 6

calico casserole

A testing favorite of the children!

½ lb. bacon, fried and crumbled
1 T. bacon drippings
1 lb. ground beef
½ cup chopped onion
½ cup firmly packed brown sugar
½ cup ketchup or chili sauce
2 T. vinegar
2 T. prepared mustard
1 tsp. salt
1 can (16 oz.) lima beans, drained
1 can (15½ oz.) red kidney beans
1 can (16 oz.) pork and beans

In a large skillet, brown the beef and onion in bacon drippings. Add the bacon to meat mixture. Add remaining ingredients; mix well. Spoon mixture into a 3-quart casserole. Bake at 300° for 1½ hours. Tastes better each time it is reheated.

Serves 6

joe's special

A favorite dish in San Francisco.

1½ lbs. ground chuck
2 medium onions, finely chopped
2 cloves garlic, minced
½ lb. fresh mushrooms, sliced
1¼ tsp. salt
½ tsp. each: nutmeg, pepper, oregano
1 pkg. (10 oz.) frozen chopped spinach, thawed and well drained; or ½ lb. fresh spinach, washed and drained
4-6 eggs, beaten

In a large skillet, brown the ground chuck well. Drain excess fat. Add onions, garlic and mushrooms. Cook until onions and mushrooms are tender. Stir in seasonings and spinach. Cook an additional 5 minutes. Add eggs and stir over low heat until eggs begin to set. Remove to serving dish and serve with French bread.

Serves 4 to 6

enchilada verde

This is spicy-hot and delicious.

12 frozen corn tortillas, thawed
¾ cup vegetable oil
3 cups shredded Monterey Jack cheese
1 cup chopped onions
1 lb. ground beef, cooked and drained
¼ cup butter or margarine
¼ cup flour
2 cups chicken broth
1 cup sour cream
1 can (4 oz.) chopped green chilies
sliced black olives

In a skillet, cook tortillas one at a time in hot oil for 10 to 15 seconds on each side. (Be careful not to overcook or tortillas will not roll.) Place 2 to 3 tablespoons of cheese, 1 tablespoon onion and 2 to 3 tablespoons ground beef on each tortilla. Roll up. Place seam-side down in a 9 x 13-inch baking dish. In a saucepan, melt butter and blend in flour. Add chicken broth; stir until mixture thickens. Stir in sour cream and chilies; heat thoroughly. *Do not boil.* Pour sauce over tortillas in casserole dish. Bake at 400° for 20 minutes. Sprinkle remaining cheese on top. (Add more cheese, if desired.) Top with black olives for color. Return to oven for 5 minutes, or until cheese melts. Serve with sour cream or green taco sauce as a condiment. To make ahead, prepare tortillas, fill and place in casserole dish. Make sauce *except* for adding sour cream; refrigerate. When ready to serve, heat sauce. Stir in sour cream. Pour over tortillas and continue as directed.

Serves 6

charlotte's sour cream enchiladas

Can be prepared in advance and frozen.

2 T. vegetable oil
1½ lbs. ground beef
1 medium onion, chopped
1 can (16 oz.) frijoles
1 tsp. salt
⅛ tsp. garlic salt
⅓ cup mild taco sauce
1 cup pitted black olives, quartered
2 cans (10 oz. each) mild or hot enchilada sauce
12 flour tortillas
3 cups shredded Cheddar or Monterey Jack cheese
sliced black olives for garnish
1 cup sour cream

In a large skillet, brown the ground beef and onions in the oil. Stir in frijoles, salts, taco sauce and olives. Heat until bubbly. In a separate pan, heat the enchilada sauce. Pour half the enchilada sauce into a large shallow casserole. Spoon ⅓ cup filling onto each tortilla and roll like a crepe. Place the tortillas, seam-side down, in the casserole. Pour on remaining sauce, being sure to cover all the tortillas. Top with cheese and garnish with sliced rings of black olives. Bake at 350° for 15 minutes or until hot. Serve with sour cream, if desired.

Serves 6

indiana meat loaf

For the best Hoosier home-style cooking . . .

2 slices rye bread, cubed
2 slices white bread, cubed
1 cup water
1 lb. ground beef
1 medium onion, chopped
1 tsp. snipped parsley
3 T. grated Parmesan cheese
1 egg, slightly beaten
1 tsp. salt
¼ tsp. pepper
2 T. butter
1 can (8 oz.) tomato sauce
1 tsp. oregano

In a large bowl, combine bread and water. When water has been absorbed, mash with fork. Stir in meat, onion, parsley and cheese. Add the egg, salt and pepper. Mix well. Place the mixture in a 9 x 5 x 3-inch pan. Dot with butter. Bake at 375° for 40 minutes. Combine tomato sauce and oregano. Pour on top of meat loaf. Continue baking for 20 minutes. Can be prepared in advance.

Serves 4 to 6

ravioli rolls

A quick and easy make-ahead dinner.

1 pkg. refrigerated crescent rolls
1 egg, beaten
1 T. water
1 pkg. (10 oz.) frozen spinach, cooked and drained
½ lb. ground chuck or sausage or 1 can (4½ oz.) deviled ham
⅓ cup grated Parmesan cheese
1 cup spaghetti sauce
1 tsp. dried oregano, crushed

Unroll crescent roll dough and separate into 8 triangles. In a small bowl, combine the egg and water. Brush half of it lightly over dough. In another bowl, combine the spinach, meat and cheese; mix well. Place two tablespoons of spinach mixture in center of each triangle. Roll up, starting at wide end. Arrange rolls, point-side down, on greased baking sheet or dish. Brush again with the egg-water mixture. Bake at 375° for 25 minutes. In a small saucepan, heat the spaghetti sauce with the oregano. Spoon over rolls after baking. Can be made ahead and refrigerated.

Serves 4

italian tomato sauce

A favorite sauce for any Italian dish. Will keep in the freezer indefinitely.

¼ cup olive oil
½ cup finely chopped onion
½ cup finely chopped celery
2 cloves garlic, minced
2 cans (1 lb. 12 oz. each) tomatoes
4 cans (6 oz. each) tomato paste
3 tsp. salt
1 tsp. sugar
½ tsp. nutmeg
1 tsp. oregano
¼ tsp. pepper
½ cup parsley
½ cup grated Parmesan or Romano cheese

In a Dutch oven or large soup kettle, heat oil. Saute onion, celery and garlic slowly in olive oil for about 5 minutes. Put tomatoes through a food mill and discard seeds. Add tomatoes and tomato paste to kettle; mix well. Add all other ingredients; simmer in partially covered pan for at least 4 hours. Stir often to prevent burning. The sauce can be cooked partially, cooled overnight and refrigerated. Continue the cooking 1 to 6 days later. Water can be added to thin the sauce, if desired.

Makes 2 quarts

barbecue sauce for leftover meat

½ cup finely chopped onion
1 T. butter
2 T. vinegar
2½-3 T. brown sugar
1-2 T. prepared mustard
1 T. Worcestershire sauce
2 T. bottled steak sauce
1 tsp. A-1 sauce (optional)
¾ cup ketchup
¼ cup water
1½ tsp. salt
dash pepper
dash garlic salt
¼ tsp. chili powder (more if desired)
2-3 cups leftover meat, cut into strips

Saute onion in butter until soft. Add all other ingredients, mixing well. Bring to a boil. Simmer 35 to 45 minutes until the sauce has thickened. Serve warm.

Makes 2 to 3 cups

soy marinade for beef shish-kabobs

1½ cups vegetable oil
¼ cup Worcestershire sauce
¼ cup soy sauce
⅓ cup lemon juice
½ cup wine vinegar
2½ tsp. salt
1 tsp. pepper
1½ tsp. parsley flakes
2 cloves garlic, minced
2 tsp. dry mustard
1 tsp. MSG

Put all ingredients in blender. Mix well for 1 minute. Makes enough for 3 lbs. of beef shish-kabobs. Marinate for 8 to 24 hours depending on cut of meat. More time is needed for less tender cuts of meat.

tomato-mushroom sauce for meat

Serve over chops, steaks or sausages.

2 T. butter
1 T. olive oil
1 clove garlic, minced
½ cup chopped onion
2 medium tomatoes, peeled, seeded and diced
1 can (4 oz.) mushrooms, drained
1 tsp. Worcestershire sauce
1 T. chopped parsley
1 T. chili sauce
salt and pepper to taste

Heat butter and oil in a skillet. Saute garlic and onion until tender. Add remaining ingredients. Simmer until tomatoes are tender. Stir gently with fork. Serve hot over cooked meats or serve separately with cooked meats.

Makes 1⅓ cups

teriyaki marinade

Simple and superb for beef, pork, fish or poultry.

⅔ cup Kikkoman soy sauce
6 T. sugar
½ cup sake or white wine
½ tsp. MSG
2 cloves garlic, crushed, or ¼ tsp. garlic powder
1 small piece ginger root, crushed, or ½ tsp. powdered ginger
1 T. vegetable oil

Combine all of the above ingredients; blend well. Cover and set aside at least 6 hours before using. Marinate any cut of meat, fish or poultry for at least 1 hour. Cook as desired.

Makes ¾ cup

baked liver and onions

Delicious and moist.

1 large onion, sliced
salt
pepper
flour
2 lbs. calves liver
2 T. minced parsley
¼ tsp. thyme
1 bay leaf
1 can (4 oz.) sliced mushrooms, drained
salt and pepper to taste
4 T. melted butter or margarine
¼ cup beef bouillon
2 T. dry red wine (optional)

In the bottom of a 2-quart casserole, place half of onion slices. Season liver. Dredge in flour. Place liver on onion slices. Sprinkle parsley and thyme on liver. Place bay leaf on top. Place mushrooms over liver. Cover with remaining onions. Season slightly with salt and pepper. Pour butter over last layer. Pour bouillon and wine over all. Cover. Bake at 350° for 30 minutes. Remove cover. Bake 30 minutes longer or until liver is completely done.

Serves 6

veal a la madeira

The pate makes this very special.

6 veal cutlets, pounded thin
1 can (2¾ oz.) pate de foie gras
3 T. butter
1 T. chopped parsley
¼ tsp. rosemary
½ tsp. garlic salt
2 T. flour
½ cup grated Parmesan cheese
2 T. olive oil
½ cup Madeira or dry sherry
1 cup chicken bouillon
1 T. cornstarch, dissolved in ⅓ cup cold water
½ lb. fresh mushrooms, sliced and sauteed in 2 T. butter

Mash pate, butter and parsley together. Spread evenly over cutlets. Roll up and secure with toothpicks. Mix rosemary, garlic salt, flour and cheese. Coat veal rolls with this mixture. In a large skillet, heat olive oil. Brown veal rolls on all sides until done, about 2 minutes. Add wine; ignite. Let flame burn out. Transfer veal rolls to a heated platter. Add chicken bouillon, cornstarch and water mixture to the pan juices. Cook, stirring constantly, until thickened. Add mushrooms. Pour sauce over rolls. Serve with a hot fruit compote and small white potatoes with parsley.

Serves 4 to 6

veal marsala

As served at "Michael's Backyard" in Naples, Florida.

12 (2 oz. each) veal scallops
3 eggs, beaten
½ cup vegetable oil
¼ cup butter
juice of 2 lemons (6 T.)
¼ cup Marsala wine
6 fresh mushrooms, halved
Parmesan cheese, grated
lemon wedges

Dip veal in eggs until well coated. In a large oven-proof skillet, heat oil and butter together until hot. Brown veal quickly on both sides. Add lemon juice and wine. Top each scallop with sliced mushrooms. Place skillet in 350° oven for 3 minutes. Remove from oven and sprinkle with Parmesan cheese, if desired. Place under broiler quickly to melt cheese. Remove to platter. Garnish with lemon wedges.

Serves 4

veal parmigiana

Its tantalizing aroma embraces your kitchen.

4 veal patties
1 egg, beaten
salt and pepper
½ cup breadcrumbs
1 cup grated Parmesan cheese, divided
2 T. olive oil
½ tsp. oregano
1 can (8 oz.) tomato sauce
4 slices mozzarella cheese

In a small bowl, combine the egg with the salt and pepper. In another bowl, combine breadcrumbs with ½ cup of the Parmesan cheese. Dip each veal patty into egg, then into breadcrumb mixture. Heat olive oil in a small skillet. Brown each breaded patty on both sides. Drain on paper towels. Place patties in a 11 x 7 x 1½-inch casserole. Sprinkle patties with oregano and the remaining ½ cup Parmesan cheese. Cover with tomato sauce. Top each patty with a slice of mozzarella cheese. Add more Parmesan cheese, if desired. Bake at 350° for 30 minutes.

Serves 4

veal chops with lemon sauce

Enhanced by slow braising and flavorful sauce.

1 T. butter
1 T. vegetable oil
4 veal chops, ¾-inch thick
salt and pepper
1 clove garlic, minced
2 T. finely chopped onion
1 T. chopped parsley
½ tsp. tarragon
½ cup dry white wine
½ cup water
3 egg yolks, well beaten
1½ tsp. lemon juice
chopped parsley for garnish

In a large skillet, heat butter and oil. Season chops with salt and pepper. Brown on both sides. Add garlic, onion, parsley, tarragon, wine and water. Cover and cook over low heat for 20 minutes or until veal is tender. Remove meat to a warm platter. Keep warm. Cook liquid until reduced by one-half. Stir lemon juice into beaten egg yolks. Stir a small amount of hot liquid into egg mixture. Pour egg mixture into skillet. Cook over low heat, stirring constantly, until slightly thickened. Pour over veal chops. Sprinkle with chopped parsley. Serve immediately. If sauce is too thick, add additional water or wine.

Variation: Lamb chops may be substituted for the veal.

Serves 4

french veal with mushrooms

A delicious and easy gourmet dish.

2 lbs. boneless veal shoulder, cut into 1½-inch cubes
2 T. vegetable oil
4 medium-size onions, chopped into small pieces
2 T. flour
1 cup chicken bouillon, heated
2 T. tomato puree
1 cup dry white wine
salt, pepper and parsley to taste
1 lb. mushrooms, sauteed slightly

Heat oil in a large skillet. Brown veal and onions together. Sprinkle flour gradually over the meat mixture. Add bouillon and tomato puree. Mix well. Add wine and seasonings. Simmer on low heat for 30 minutes. Add mushrooms and continue cooking for another 30 minutes. Remove to casserole dish. Serve with rice or noodles.

Serves 4 to 6

veal paprika

1½ lbs. veal scallops, pounded to ¼-inch thick
salt
garlic salt
MSG
4 T. butter, divided
½ cup chopped onion
1½ tsp. paprika
3 T. flour
1 cup chicken broth
½ cup sour cream
1 T. sauterne
salt and pepper to taste
½ cup (4 oz.) mushrooms, drained
1 cup whole baby onions, drained
1 can (14 oz.) artichoke hearts (6 to 8), drained
¼ lb. bacon, fried crisp and crumbled
toasted slivered almonds

Sprinkle both sides of veal with salt, garlic salt and MSG. In a heavy skillet, melt 3 tablespoons of the butter. Saute veal, cooking 2 to 3 minutes on each side. Arrange the veal in a 11 x 7-inch casserole. Add the remaining tablespoon of butter, onion and paprika to the skillet. Cook until onion is soft. Remove pan from heat. Stir in flour. Return to heat and cook 1 minute. Gradually add broth, stirring constantly, until mixture boils and thickens. Reduce heat. Add sour cream, wine and seasoning. Do not boil. Place mushrooms, onions and artichokes in casserole with veal. Top with sauce. Cover and bake at 350° for 30 minutes. Garnish with bacon and almonds. May be made ahead and refrigerated. Add 10 minutes to baking time.

Serves 4

veal aix-en-provence

An adaption of a recipe from a French family in Aix.

2 T. butter
1 T. vegetable oil
½ tsp. each: garlic salt, marjoram, thyme, MSG
4 veal chops, ¾-inch thick
¼ cup dry white wine
1 cup mushrooms, drained
1 T. flour
¾ cup half-and-half cream
½ cup grated Gruyere cheese

In a large skillet, heat butter and oil. Combine seasonings. Sprinkle over chops. Brown chops on both sides. Add wine to skillet. Cover. Cook for 10 minutes over low heat. Place chops in a 12-inch casserole. Cover with mushrooms. Loosen meat sediment from bottom of skillet. Stir in flour. Add cream and cheese. Stir until sauce is well blended and begins to thicken. Pour over veal and mushrooms. Bake at 350° for 20 to 25 minutes. Serve immediately.

Serves 4

veal oscar for company

A dish for all seasons . . . prepare in advance.

4 lbs. veal steaks, pounded
½ cup flour
½ cup clarified butter
2 pkgs. (6 oz. each) frozen crabmeat, defrosted and drained
2 pkgs. (8 oz. each) asparagus spears, cooked and drained

Bearnaise Sauce:
6 egg yolks
2 T. tarragon vinegar
2 tsp. lemon juice
½ tsp. salt
dash cayenne
1½ tsp. tarragon
1 cup melted butter
2 T. chopped parsley

Cut veal into 2-inch strips. Dredge in flour. Heat butter in a large skillet. Saute meat until brown, about 2 minutes on each side. Do not overcook. Remove meat from skillet. Place in two 13 x 9 x 2-inch greased casseroles. Layer veal with asparagus spears. Top with crabmeat. Bake at 350° for 20 minutes. Serve with Bearnaise Sauce.

For Bearnaise Sauce: Combine egg yolks, vinegar, lemon juice, salt, cayenne and tarragon in a blender. Blend for 30 seconds. Heat butter to foaming. Turn blender to high speed and slowly pour in butter. Blend until well mixed. Stir in parsley. Pour over veal and serve immediately. Makes 1½ to 2 cups sauce.

Note: To make ahead, prepare recipe according to directions to point of baking. Cover and refrigerate. Then bring to room temperature before baking. Uncover and bake for 30 minutes.

Serves 10

veal stew

A real treat on a cold winter evening.

2-2½ lbs. veal, cut into 1-inch cubes
6 T. butter
1 lb. small white onions, peeled
12 oz. fresh mushrooms, sliced
1 clove garlic, minced
1 tsp. salt
⅛ tsp. freshly ground pepper
⅓ cup flour
1 can (10 oz.) chicken broth
¾ cup dry white wine
1 carrot, halved
1 leek, sliced
1 stalk celery, halved
2 sprigs parsley
¼ tsp. thyme
1 bay leaf
3 T. lemon juice
2 egg yolks
¾ cup whipping cream
grated nutmeg
lemon wedges

In a Dutch oven, simmer veal, uncovered, in the butter for 10 minutes. Do not brown the meat. Add onions, mushrooms, garlic, salt and pepper. Simmer, uncovered, another 10 minutes. Sprinkle flour over meat. Stir until blended. Add chicken broth, wine, carrot, leek and celery. Tie parsley, thyme and bay leaf in cheesecloth. Add to the meat mixture. Cover and simmer, stirring occasionally, for 30 minutes or until meat is tender. Remove and discard bag, carrot, leek and celery. Stir in lemon juice. Beat together egg yolks and cream. Stir ½ cup of the hot mixture into the cream and egg yolk mixture. Return all to the hot mixture and stir constantly until bubbly and slightly thickened. Transfer to serving dish. Sprinkle with nutmeg. Serve with lemon wedges.

Serves 6 to 8

osso buco

½ cup flour
salt and pepper
3-4 veal shanks, sawn into 2-inch pieces
3 T. vegetable oil, divided
3 T. butter, divided
½ cup each: chopped carrots, celery, onion
1 cup dry white wine
¾ cup chicken broth, approximately
2 cloves garlic, minced
1 tsp. basil
½ tsp. thyme
2 bay leaves
peel of 1 orange
peel of 1 lemon
1 quart boiling water
chopped parsley

Combine flour, salt and pepper in plastic bag or small paper sack. Add veal shanks to seasoned flour; shake well until lightly coated. Heat 2 tablespoons each of oil and butter in large skillet. Brown meat on all sides over medium heat. Don't crowd meat. Brown in several batches, if necessary. Place meat in baking dish large enough to arrange veal in a single layer. In a separate skillet, heat remaining 2 tablespoons of oil and butter; saute carrots, celery and onions over medium heat until tender. Spoon vegetables over meat. Pour oil and butter out of skillets. Deglaze skillets with wine; cook and stir to boiling. Pour over meat. Add chicken broth until liquids are half way up meat. Add garlic, basil, thyme and bay leaves. Peel orange and lemon into very fine julienne strips 1/16-inch wide. Simmer strips in 1 quart boiling water for 5 minutes. Drain and sprinkle over meat. Bake, covered, at 350° for 1¼ to 1½ hours. Do not overcook. Meat should not fall from bones. Uncover pan for last 20 minutes to allow meat to brown and juices to cook down. When tender, remove meat to serving platter. Skim off fat and reduce juices to sauce consistency. Pour over meat. Sprinkle with chopped parsley. Serve with risotto.

Serves 4 to 6

veal and butter-crumb dumplings

Veal:
2 lbs. veal round, cubed
⅓ cup flour
1 tsp. paprika
¼ cup vegetable shortening
⅛ tsp. pepper
½ tsp. salt
2¾ cups water, divided
1 can (10¾ oz.) condensed cream of chicken soup
1¾ cups (1 lb. can) small, cooked onions

Butter-Crumb Dumplings:
2 cups flour
4 tsp. baking powder
1 T. poppy seed
1 tsp. each: celery seed, instant minced onion, poultry seasoning
½ tsp. salt
1 cup milk
¼ cup vegetable oil
¼ cup melted butter
1 cup dry breadcrumbs

Sauce:
1 can (10¾ oz.) condensed cream of chicken soup
1 cup sour cream

For Veal: Coat veal with flour and paprika. Brown in oil in skillet. Add pepper, salt and 1 cup of the water. Cover and simmer 30 minutes or until tender. Transfer to a 13 x 9-inch baking dish. Heat 1 can of the soup in brown drippings in skillet. Gradually blend in remaining 1¾ cup of water and bring to boil. Pour over meat in baking dish. Add onions. Top with Butter-Crumb Dumplings. Bake, uncovered, at 350° for 1 hour. Serve with Sauce.

For Butter-Crumb Dumplings: In a large mixing bowl, combine all dry ingredients except the breadcrumbs. Add milk and oil. Stir just until moistened. Drop rounded tablespoons of dough into mixture of butter and breadcrumbs. Roll and coat well with crumbs. Place 14 to 16 dumplings on top of veal and onions in baking dish.

For Sauce: Heat the soup and sour cream in a saucepan. Add milk if too thick.

Serves 6 to 8

pork and lamb

"To take what others say in easy comment,
to give in return something which will please,
to stimulate the silent and the morose out of their vapours,
and surprize them into good humor,
to lead while one seems to follow—
this is the real aim of conversation."

HISTORICAL ROOM OF THE NAPPANEE PUBLIC LIBRARY

new york lamb

The aroma while simmering is wonderful.

2 T. vegetable oil
3 lbs. lamb shoulder or leg, cubed
1 medium onion, sliced
1 stalk celery, diced
1 tsp. salt
1 tsp. pepper
2 cloves garlic, minced
2 cups dry red wine, divided
1 can (6 oz.) tomato paste
1 cup beef broth
1 T. chopped parsley
¼ tsp. oregano

In a large skillet, heat oil. Brown lamb cubes. Add onions, celery, salt, pepper and garlic. Cook until onions and celery are soft. Add 1 cup of the wine and simmer, uncovered, until wine evaporates. Add tomato paste and beef broth. Simmer, covered, for one hour. Add remaining wine, parsley and oregano. Simmer an additional 30 minutes. Serve.

Serves 4 to 6

lemon-broiled lamb

Even lamb haters will like this recipe.

1 4-5-lb. leg of lamb, boned and rolled
chopped garlic
powdered ginger
cracked black pepper
juice of 2 lemons (6 T.)

Using a sharp knife, make 7 or 8 slits in the leg of lamb about 2-inches apart. Fill each slit with finely chopped garlic, a pinch of ginger and pinch of black pepper. Generously rub the surface of the lamb with the lemon juice. Save the juice that is not absorbed into the lamb. Place lamb on a rack in a shallow roasting pan. Brown under a preheated broiler until sides and top are browned, 3 to 5 minutes. Bake at 300° for 2 hours or to desired degree of doneness. Brush the lamb occasionally with the leftover lemon juice.

Serves 10

stuffed shoulder of lamb

A classic and delicately flavored roast.

1 4-lb. shoulder or leg of lamb, boned and butterflied
6 T. butter, divided
2 T. chopped parsley
1 T. chopped mint
1 T. chopped chives
1 tsp. thyme
2 T. breadcrumbs
salt and pepper
½ cup white wine
1 egg, well beaten
1 cup chicken broth

Preheat oven to 400°. In a small mixing bowl, combine 4 tablespoons of the butter with the herbs, breadcrumbs, salt and pepper. Mash until smooth. Stir in egg gradually. When well mixed, spread the open and flattened meat with the stuffing. Roll meat and tie. Place in roasting pan. Spread remaining butter over meat. Sprinkle with salt and pepper. Pour wine and broth into roasting pan. Bake at 400° for 15 minutes. Reduce heat to 350°; bake for 1 to 1½ hours or to desired degree of doneness. Serve with gravy made with stock.

Serves 6

grilled marinated lamb steaks

An interesting way to serve lamb for those who love shish-kabob.

1 6-lb. leg of lamb, boned, rolled and tied
salt and freshly ground black pepper
1 large onion, thinly sliced
1 T. thyme
1 T. rosemary
6 sprigs fresh parsley
rind of 1 lemon, grated
1-2 cloves garlic, minced
2 bay leaves, broken
1 cup olive oil
⅓ cup red wine vinegar

Have butcher bone the lamb, roll and tie it securely with string at four or five intervals. Using a sharp knife, cut between the strings to make four or five steaks, each one about 1½ to 2-inches thick. Place the steaks in one layer in a flat container. In a medium mixing bowl, combine the remaining ingredients and pour mixture over meat. Cover and let stand at least an hour. Grill the steaks over hot charcoal, turning carefully once or twice. Cook to desired degree of doneness. Remove the string and cut into desired number of portions.

Variation: Oregano may be substituted for the rosemary and thyme if you prefer a change in flavor.

Serves 8 to 10

roast leg of lamb with vegetables and herb butter

A beautiful and delicious lamb and vegetable platter.

1 4-lb. leg of lamb, boned
2 cloves garlic, slivered
1 tsp. each: rosemary, basil, thyme
salt to taste
ground black pepper

Herb Butter:
1 cup butter
3 cloves garlic, pressed
¼ cup lemon juice
1 tsp. Worcestershire sauce
1 tsp. each: thyme, marjoram, savory, oregano
½ cup finely chopped parsley
dash Tabasco

Vegetables:
1 lb. fresh broccoli or 2 pkgs. (8 oz. each) frozen broccoli spears
1 lb. carrots, cut into 2-inch strips
1 lb. small, whole onions

Cut 7 to 8 tiny slits in lamb with point of sharp knife. Insert garlic slivers. Combine seasonings and sprinkle over lamb. Place meat on rack in shallow roasting pan. Bake at 325°, allowing 20 to 35 minutes per pound depending on desired degree of doneness. Serve with Herb Butter and Vegetables.

For Herb Butter: Combine all ingredients in a mixing bowl; beat with electric mixer on low speed until well blended. Gradually increase speed until mixture is light and fluffy. To serve whipped, scrape into serving bowl. To serve warm, place in a small saucepan over low heat. Pour a small amount over meat and vegetables. Serve remaining butter separately in sauceboat. To serve cold, scrape whipped mixture onto wax paper. Form into 2 rolls, 1½-inches in diameter. Chill. Cut into ½ to ¾-inch slices. Place on hot meats, fish or vegetables. Makes 1½ cups whipped or approximately 18 slices and 1 cup warm. Can prepare in advance and use as needed.

For Vegetables: Prepare vegetables according to favorite method of cooking or according to package directions. Drain and keep warm. To serve, slice lamb and place overlapping pieces on a large platter. Arrange vegetables around meat. Serve with warm or whipped Herb Butter.

Serves 6 to 8

mint-glazed lamb chops

8 loin lamb chops

Marinade:
½ cup mint jelly
½ cup firmly packed brown sugar
½ cup cider vinegar
1 T. vegetable oil
1 T. lemon juice
1 tsp. prepared mustard
2 cloves garlic, minced
½ tsp. salt
mint sprigs or fresh watercress

Trim chops well. Curl tail-end around and secure each with toothpick or skewer. Sprinkle with salt and pepper, if desired; place in large shallow baking dish. Set aside.

For Marinade: In a small saucepan, combine ingredients. Cook over medium heat. Stir constantly until sugar is dissolved and mixture just begins to boil. Remove from heat; cool completely. Pour marinade over chops. Marinate at room temperature 2 to 3 hours, turning several times. Remove chops from marinade; place on grill over hot coals. Grill 3 to 5 minutes on each side, depending on thickness of chops and desired doneness. Best if well browned on the outside and light pink on the inside. Place on warm platter. Garnish with mint sprigs or watercress. Heat marinade and serve in bowl to spoon over chops. Nicely complemented by scalloped potatoes or a rice pilaf and whole green beans topped with buttered, toasted almonds. Chops also may be grilled under broiler, quickly, so they will not be overdone.

Serves 4 to 8

lamb shanks with white wine

Flavorful and easy.

6 lamb shanks
1 cup dry white wine
1 cup vegetable oil
1 T. lemon juice
¼ cup chopped onion
2 cloves garlic, minced
1 tsp. each: tarragon, basil, oregano, salt
10 crushed peppercorns

Place lamb shanks in a 13 x 9 x 2-inch casserole dish; set aside. In a medium-size mixing bowl, combine the remaining ingredients; pour mixture over lamb. Let stand at room temperature for at least 4 hours. Turn lamb shanks once or twice and spoon marinade over them. Broil lamb for about 30 minutes, turning frequently, basting with the marinade.

Serves 6

lamb ragout

An interesting twist to lamb prepared the French way.

2 T. drippings or margarine
1 2-lb. lamb shoulder, neck or other inexpensive cut, cubed
2 medium onions, quartered
2 medium carrots, cut into ½-inch slices
2 small turnips, cut into ½-inch slices
1 tsp. sugar
1 T. flour
2 cups water or lamb stock, divided
bouquet garni (chopped bay leaf, thyme and parsley tied in bag)
salt and pepper to taste
chopped parsley

Heat drippings or margarine in a large, shallow skillet. Brown meat on all sides. Remove. Add vegetables to the skillet. Sprinkle with sugar. Saute until the vegetables are a bright color. Shake pan frequently to prevent over browning and bitter flavor. Stir in flour gradually. Continue to saute for 2 to 3 minutes. Add 1½ cups of the water or stock and bring to a boil. Return meat to skillet. Add remaining ½ cup water or stock so that the meat is barely covered. Add the bouquet garni and seasonings. Simmer, covered, for 30 minutes. Turn pieces over; continue to simmer, uncovered, for 30 minutes. When meat is tender and gravy is reduced to half, put into a serving dish and sprinkle with parsley. Serve with rice or small roasted potatoes.

Serves 4

lamb curry

A nice way to prepare leftover lamb.

2 cups cooked, cubed lamb
3 T. butter
1 medium onion, diced
1 clove garlic, minced
1 medium apple, cored and diced
2 stalks celery, diced
2 T. flour
1 tsp. salt
2-2½ tsp. curry powder
2 cups lamb stock or canned beef gravy
Variety of chopped condiments: chopped hard-cooked eggs, peanuts, bacon, bananas, chutney

In a medium-size saucepan, melt butter. Add onion, garlic, apple and celery. Cook until transparent. Add flour, salt and curry powder. Stir until well mixed. Add lamb stock or gravy and lamb cubes. Simmer ten minutes. Serve over rice. Garnish with condiments or pass condiments in bowls when ready to serve. This recipe can be easily doubled, but do not double curry powder. It tastes even better if made ahead and reheated.

Serves 4

moussaka

Gourmet flare for a traditional Greek dish.

3 medium eggplants
boiling water
¾ cup butter, divided
3 large onions, finely chopped
2 lbs. ground lamb
3 T. tomato paste
½ cup dry red wine
½ cup chopped parsley
½ tsp. cinnamon
salt and pepper
6 T. flour
1 quart milk
½ tsp. nutmeg
¼ tsp. ground cloves
4 eggs, beaten until foamy
2 cups ricotta cheese
1 cup fine breadcrumbs
1 cup grated Parmesan cheese

Cut unpeeled eggplants in halves lengthwise. Slice crosswise ¼-inch thick. Place in shallow baking pan. Cover with boiling water. Let stand 5 minutes. Pour off water. Drain slices well on paper towel. Set aside. In large, heavy skillet, melt ¼ cup of the butter. Saute onions until brown. Add ground lamb. Cook 10 minutes. Stir in tomato paste, wine, parsley, cinnamon, salt and pepper. Simmer, stirring often, until liquid is absorbed. Remove from heat. In medium saucepan, melt the remaining ½ cup butter. Blend in flour. In a separate pan, bring milk to boil. Add boiling milk to flour mixture, stirring constantly. Add nutmeg and cloves. When mixture is thickened and smooth, remove from heat. Cool slightly. Stir in beaten eggs and ricotta cheese. Grease an 11 x 16 x 2½-inch pan. Layer half the breadcrumbs, eggplant, meat mixture and Parmesan cheese in the pan. Repeat layers. Pour ricotta cheese sauce over top. Bake at 375° for 1 hour or until golden. Remove from oven. Cool slightly. Cut into squares.

Serves 8 to 10

lamb-rice casserole

Tasty leftover lamb dish.

2 cups tomato sauce
1 T. brown sugar
2 bay leaves
2 stalks celery with leaves
1 tsp. each: oregano, marjoram, basil, paprika
½ tsp. garlic salt
salt and pepper to taste
4 cups cooked rice
2 cups cooked, diced lamb
½ cup grated Parmesan cheese

In a heavy saucepan, combine tomato sauce, brown sugar, bay leaves, celery and seasonings. Cover and simmer over low heat for 45 minutes. Remove bay leaves and celery stalks. Combine the sauce, rice and lamb. Place in a greased 2-quart casserole. Sprinkle cheese over top. Bake at 350° for 25 minutes.

Serves 6

lamb meatballs with orange-curry sauce

Meatballs:
1½ lbs. finely ground lamb
½ cup fine breadcrumbs
1 egg, lightly beaten
½ cup water
2 tsp. salt
½ tsp. pepper
⅔ cup grated onion
3 T. butter

Orange-Curry Sauce:
2 T. butter
2 T. flour
½ tsp. curry powder
2 cups chicken broth
1 cup lamb stock or bouillon
grated peel of small orange

For Meatballs: In a mixing bowl, combine all ingredients except butter. Mix until well blended. Shape into 2-inch balls. Heat butter in a large skillet; brown meatballs on all sides. Cook over low heat to desired degree of doneness. Drain. Place into warm chafing dish. Keep warm.

For Orange-Curry Sauce: Melt butter in a saucepan; stir in flour and blend. Add curry, broth, stock and orange peel, stirring constantly. Cook until thickened. Pour sauce over meatballs. Serve with rice. Recipe can be doubled or tripled easily and can be made ahead. Reheat meatballs, covered, at 350° for 15 to 20 minutes. Warm sauce over low heat or, covered, in oven. Combine in chafing dish and serve.

Serves 4 to 6

roast pork tenderloin au vin

Certain to please the most discriminating palates.

1 T. salt
1 tsp. pepper
1 tsp. sage or thyme
½ tsp. nutmeg
1 6-lb. pork tenderloin
1 T. butter
1 clove garlic, minced
¼ cup chopped parsley
1 large onion, sliced
1 bay leaf
2 cups red wine
1 can (10½ oz.) beef consomme
1 cup water

In small bowl, combine salt, pepper, sage or thyme and nutmeg. Rub this mixture into tenderloin. In skillet, melt butter. Add garlic. Add tenderloin and brown. Remove tenderloin from skillet. Set skillet aside for later use. Place tenderloin in small roasting pan. Add parsley, onion, bay leaf and wine. Bake at 350° for 2 hours or until done. Turn the meat twice. Baste frequently. If wine evaporates completely, add some of the consomme to pan to prevent burning. Add remaining consomme during last 20 minutes of roasting. Remove tenderloin to serving platter. Scrape pan drippings into skillet used to brown tenderloin. Add water to dilute concentrated juices. Bring to boil, stirring constantly. Strain. Serve with tenderloin.

Serves 6 to 8

pork braised with bourbon

An unusual and delicious meat and sauce.

18 prunes
1½ cups warm beef bouillon, divided
1 4-lb. pork loin, boned and tied
½ cup Dijon mustard
⅔ cup brown sugar
2 T. vegetable oil
⅔ cup bourbon whiskey, divided
salt and freshly ground pepper
bouquet garni of thyme, sage and parsley
½ tsp. cornstarch (optional)

In a small bowl, place prunes and 1 cup of the bouillon. Cover and set aside. Dry meat with paper towel. Brush meat with mustard and roll in brown sugar. In a Dutch oven, heat oil and brown meat. Turn when one side is colored so that it browns evenly, approximately 10 minutes. The sugar will caramelize. Be careful not to burn. Pour ⅓ cup of the bourbon over the meat and set aflame. When flame goes out, pour in the remaining ½ cup bouillon. Cover the Dutch oven and put into the oven. Bake at 375° for 45 minutes. Turn meat and season with salt and pepper. Add the bouquet garni. Lower the oven temperature to 350° and bake, covered, another 30 minutes. Add prunes and their liquid. Return to the oven for 10 minutes or until meat is tender. Remove meat and prunes to a warm platter. Strain the cooking liquid and skim off excess fat. Return liquid to the Dutch oven and place on stove burner. Bring sauce to a boil. Add remaining ⅓ cup bourbon, stirring to dislodge pan sediments. The sauce can be thickened by adding cornstarch mixed with a little cold water. Add seasonings to taste. Serve sauce separately with prunes and pork.

Serves 6

pork tenderloin a l'asparagus

1 2-lb. pork tenderloin, cut into 8 slices
2 T. butter or margarine
1 can (10½ oz.) condensed cream of asparagus soup
¼ cup milk
½ cup chopped onion
1 can (3 oz.) sliced mushrooms, drained
½ tsp. curry powder
dash pepper

Pound pork slices to flatten. In a large skillet, melt butter and brown meat well. Remove meat. In the same skillet, heat together the soup and milk. Stir in the remaining ingredients. Return meat to the skillet. Cover and simmer 45 minutes or until meat is tender. Place in serving dish and serve with sauce on top.

Serves 4

chinese pork steaks with mustard sauce

Delicious with or without the sauce.

1 beef bouillon cube
⅓ cup hot water
1 tsp. ginger
2 tsp. salt
1 T. sugar
¼ cup honey
¼ cup soy sauce
4-6 pork arm or blade steaks

Mustard Sauce:
1 T. butter
1 T. flour
¼ tsp. salt
½ cup milk
1 tsp. prepared mustard
1 egg yolk
1 T. cream
1 T. lemon juice

Dissolve bouillon in hot water. Combine with remaining ingredients in a glass dish. Place pork in marinade. Cover and marinate in refrigerator 2 hours or overnight, turning occasionally. Remove steaks from marinade and place on rack in shallow roasting pan. Bake at 350° for 1 hour or until done. Serve with Mustard Sauce.

For Mustard Sauce: Melt butter in heavy saucepan. Stir in flour, salt and milk. Add mustard. Cook until smooth and thickened. Combine egg yolk with cream. Stir slowly into hot mixture. Cook until thick, stirring constantly. Stir in lemon juice. Pour into serving dish. Makes ¾ cup.

Note: The marinade keeps the steaks moist while baking. The Mustard Sauce may be served with fish and vegetable dishes.

Serves 4 to 6

broiled marinated pork chops

The seasoned rice vinegar makes this special.

Marinade:
⅔ cup seasoned rice vinegar
1 T. plus 1 tsp. soy sauce
¼ tsp. garlic salt
¼ tsp. dry mustard
1 tsp. MSG

4 1-inch thick pork chops

Combine all the ingredients for the marinade in a glass dish. Add the pork chops. Cover and marinate at room temperature for 1 to 2 hours, turning chops several times to cover with marinade, or refrigerate 4 to 6 hours. Remove from marinade. Broil about 4 inches from heat 12 to 15 minutes each side or until juices run clear. Brush each side with marinade at least once while broiling.

Serves 4

sweet and pungent pork

2 lbs. pork shoulder, cubed
2 eggs, beaten
1 cup flour
⅛ tsp. dry mustard
½ tsp. salt
1 cup water, divided
peanut or vegetable oil
2 cups chunk pineapple; drain and reserve juice
1 cup reserved pineapple juice
⅔ cup vinegar
¾ cup sugar
dash Tabasco
1 T. soy sauce
2 T. minced green onions
½ tsp. ginger
2 T. cornstarch
1 tsp. salt
2 T. orange marmalade
2 green peppers, sliced and seeded
2 oranges, peeled and cut into chunks
2 tomatoes, peeled, seeded and diced

In a mixing bowl, combine eggs, flour, mustard, salt and ⅓ cup water. Add pork cubes; stir until well coated. Fry pork in 3 inches of hot oil (400°) for 2 to 3 minutes or until golden brown. Drain pork; keep hot. In a large saucepan, combine pineapple juice, vinegar, remaining ⅔ cup water, sugar, Tabasco, soy sauce, onions, ginger, cornstarch and salt. Bring to boil; reduce heat and simmer for 5 minutes. Stir in marmalade, green peppers and oranges. Cook 3 minutes. Stir in tomatoes, pineapple chunks and pork. Simmer 8 to 10 minutes until well heated and flavors are blended. Spoon into a large serving or chafing dish. Serve with rice. Can be made in advance to point of adding fruits, vegetables and pork. Pork can be fried and refrigerated a day ahead. Place on baking sheet, reheat and crispen in oven at 400° for 10 minutes. Proceed and complete at point of adding fruit, vegetables and pork.

Serves 8 to 10

chutney orange pork chops

4 ½- to ¾-inch thick smoked pork chops
1 T. vegetable oil
½ cup dry white wine, divided
2 oranges, peeled and sliced
½ cup mango chutney, chopped, with syrup
¼ cup sugar
2 T. lemon juice
1 tsp. grated orange peel

In a large skillet, heat oil and brown chops. Pour off any excess oil. Add ¼ cup of the wine. Cover. Simmer over low heat for 10 minutes or until chops are tender. Arrange orange slices over chops. In a small bowl, combine chutney, remaining wine, sugar, lemon juice and orange peel. Pour over chops. Simmer, uncovered, spooning liquid over chops for about 10 minutes or until liquid becomes syrupy.

Serves 2 to 4

apricot glazed pork chops with apricot-apple stuffing

1 cup diced, dried apricots
½ cup boiling water
1 T. brown sugar
6 pork chops, 1-inch thick
¼ cup flour
¼ tsp. dry mustard
salt and pepper
3 T. vegetable oil
¼ cup butter
½ cup diced celery
½ cup finely chopped onion
4 cups ¼-inch stale bread cubes
1 large, tart apple, peeled and diced
2 T. chopped parsley
½ tsp. thyme
½ tsp. marjoram

Apricot Glaze:
1 cup apricot preserves
2 T. orange juice
1 T. brandy (optional)

Place apricots in a small bowl. Add boiling water and sugar. Set aside. Coat pork chops with the flour seasoned with dry mustard, salt and pepper. Heat oil in a large skillet. Brown chops on both sides; remove and set aside. Add butter to skillet; saute celery and onion until soft but not brown.

In a mixing bowl, combine bread cubes, apple, parsley and seasonings. Stir in apricot mixture and sauteed vegetables; toss lightly. Place stuffing in bottom of a shallow baking dish, large enough to place pork chops in a single layer. Place chops on top; cover and bake at 325° for 30 minutes. Remove from oven; spoon thin layer of Apricot Glaze over chops. Cover; return to oven. Bake for 1 hour or until chops are thoroughly cooked.

For Apricot Glaze: Combine ingredients in a small saucepan; heat until blended. Spoon over chops as stated above. Use additional glaze, if desired.

Serves 4 to 6

fruit stuffed pork chops with raisin-ginger sauce

Fruit Stuffing:
1 cup diced apples
¼ cup seedless raisins
¾ cup breadcrumbs
½ tsp. salt
1½ T. sugar
1 T. minced onion
2 T. butter
3 T. hot water

Meat:
4 rib pork chops, 1½-inches thick, with pocket
salt and pepper
½ cup water

Raisin-Ginger Sauce:
½ cup orange juice
½ cup water
¼ cup cider vinegar
1 T. cornstarch
2 T. soy sauce
½ tsp. dry mustard
¼ tsp. ginger
½ cup brown sugar
½ cup seedless raisins

For Fruit Stuffing: In small bowl, mix together apples, raisins, breadcrumbs, salt and sugar. In large skillet, saute onions in butter until soft. Add onions to bread mixture. Add water and mix well.

For Meat: Salt and pepper inside of pocket of chops. Fill pockets with stuffing. Close opening with skewers or toothpicks. In same skillet, brown chops on both sides. Place in an 8 x 8 x 2-inch casserole. Add water to drippings in skillet and stir to loosen brown bits. Pour over chops. Cover and bake at 375° for 45 minutes. Uncover and bake 15 minutes longer.

For Raisin-Ginger Sauce: In small saucepan, combine all ingredients *except raisins*. Cook, stirring constantly, until mixture boils. Add raisins; simmer 2 to 3 minutes or until mixture thickens. If too thick, thin with additional orange juice or water. Pour small amount of sauce over chops and serve. Serve remaining sauce separately.

Serves 4

mother's pork chops

Just as easy to make for two or twelve.

4 pork chops (½-inch or thicker)
1 T. seasoned salt
½ tsp. pepper
¼ cup chopped, frozen onions
1 can (10¾ oz.) condensed cream of mushroom soup

In a large skillet, brown chops evenly on both sides. Sprinkle chops generously with salt and pepper. Top with onions. Spread undiluted soup over chops. Cover and simmer over low heat for 1½ hours.

Variation: Cream of chicken or cream of celery soup may be used instead of the mushroom. The soup makes a good gravy to serve over mashed potatoes or rice.

Serves 2 or 3

pork chop and green bean skillet

An easy and delicious family meal.

8 thinly sliced pork chops
½ cup flour
salt and pepper
2 T. vegetable oil
2 cans (16 oz. each) green beans

Place flour, salt and pepper in bag. Shake pork chops in bag until coated. Heat oil in skillet; brown pork chops. Pour undrained green beans over chops. Bring to boil. Cover and reduce heat. Simmer until tender, about 1 hour. Remove pork chops to platter and beans to serving dish. Boil juices to reduce to sauce. Pour over pork chops and serve.

Serves 4

grandma's mustard sauce

1 cup sugar
2 tsp. prepared mustard
1 egg, beaten
¼ cup white vinegar
¼ cup milk

Combine all ingredients in order in a small saucepan. Simmer over low heat until bubbly, stirring constantly. Remove from heat. Serve immediately or refrigerate and serve cold. The sauce keeps for one week in the refrigerator.

Makes about 1½ cups

pizza pork chops

A family favorite.

6 1½-inch thick pork chops
2 eggs
¼ cup milk
1 cup breadcrumbs
1 tsp. chopped parsley
2 T. grated Parmesan cheese
2 T. vegetable oil
2 cups pizza sauce
6 slices Swiss or mozzarella cheese

Trim fat from the pork chops. In a medium-size bowl, combine the eggs and milk. In another bowl, combine the breadcrumbs, parsley and Parmesan cheese. Dip each chop into the egg mixture, then coat thoroughly with the breadcrumb mixture. Brown in vegetable oil in a skillet. Pour pizza sauce over the chops. Cook, covered, at 200° to 225° for 1½ hours. Add a small amount of water to the skillet occasionally to prevent chops from sticking. Just before serving, place one slice of cheese on each chop.

Serves 4 to 6

plum-sauced spareribs

8-10 lbs. spareribs, cut into 3-inch pieces.
1 tsp. salt
hot water

Plum Sauce:
2 T. margarine
1 medium-size onion, chopped
1 can (17 oz.) pitted purple plums, undrained
¼ cup chili sauce or ketchup
¼ cup soy sauce
1 can (6 oz.) frozen lemonade concentrate, thawed
1 tsp. ginger
2 tsp. prepared mustard
1 tsp. Worcestershire sauce
2 drops hot pepper sauce

Place ribs in a large kettle. Add salt and cover with hot water. Cover kettle and simmer ribs for 1½ hours. Drain ribs. Place in a large shallow roasting pan. Set aside.

For Plum Sauce: In a medium-size saucepan, saute onions in the margarine until tender. In a blender, puree the plums and their syrup. Add plums and the remaining ingredients to the onions in the pan. Simmer for 15 minutes. Pour Plum Sauce over the ribs. Bake at 325° for 1 to 1½ hours, basting often with the Plum Sauce. Turn ribs occasionally. Serve remaining sauce separately.

Serves 10 to 12

country ribs a la mario

A perfect meat dish when you're hungry for something different.

4 lbs. country-style pork ribs
4 Idaho baking potatoes, thinly sliced
¼ tsp. rosemary
salt and pepper to taste
garlic powder (optional)

Place ribs in large roasting pan. Bake at 300° for 30 minutes. Remove ribs from pan and pour off excess fat. Tip pan so that a small amount of fat coats the roasting pan. Add potatoes to pan. Sprinkle rosemary evenly over the potatoes. Place ribs on top of potatoes. Add salt and pepper to the meat to taste. Add more rosemary and garlic powder, if desired. Bake, covered, at 325° for 2 hours. Uncover and bake an additional 15 minutes. Drain excess fat before serving. This recipe can be doubled or tripled, depending on the number of people being served.

Serves 4

marinated country-style ribs

A real crowd-pleaser.

3 lbs. country-style ribs
1 large onion, sliced and separated into rings

Marinade:
1 can (12 oz.) tomato soup
1 tsp. dry mustard
½ cup brown sugar
2 T. vinegar
1 T. Worcestershire sauce
1 tsp. salt
1 tsp. paprika
¼ tsp. pepper

Cut ribs into easy-to-handle serving pieces. Place in one or two 13 x 9 x 2-inch pans. Ribs should lay as flat as possible. Place onions over top of meat. In a medium-size mixing bowl, combine and mix thoroughly the ingredients for the Marinade. Pour over the meat. Marinate overnight. Bake at 350° for 2 hours.

Serves 6

pork picadillo (pee-kah-thee-yoh)

Currants are a sweet accent in this Mexican stew.

2 tsp. butter
2 tsp. vegetable oil
1 large onion, chopped
3½ lbs. pork, cut into ¾-inch squares
1 clove garlic, minced
2 cans (8 oz. each) tomato sauce
½ cup chili sauce
1 tsp. cinnamon
2 tsp. salt
¼ tsp. ground cumin
½ cup currants
3 T. vinegar
3 T. brown sugar
2 green onions, thinly sliced
2 avocados, diced
2 limes, cut in wedges

In a Dutch oven, heat butter and oil together. Saute onion until soft. Remove to a bowl. Add meat and brown well. Return onions to meat. Add garlic, tomato sauce, chili sauce, cinnamon, salt, cumin, currants, vinegar and brown sugar. Cover and simmer for 45 minutes or until meat is tender. Stir occasionally. Add water if too thick. Remove to a serving dish. Garnish meat with the green onion. Spoon meat over the avocado (or rice, if preferred) and squeeze lime juice over the top of meat. Can be made ahead, covered and refrigerated. Reheat, covered, at 350° for 45 to 50 minutes.

Serves 6

sausage-rice casserole

Delicious for a casual supper!

1 lb. bulk sausage
½ cup chopped onion
½ cup chopped celery
4 cups water
1 cup raw rice
2 pkgs. (2 oz. each) chicken noodle soup mix
1 can (4 oz.) diced mushrooms
½ cup sliced blanched almonds

In a large skillet, brown the sausage, onion and celery. Drain excess fat. Stir in the water, rice and soup mix. Cover and simmer 15 minutes. Add mushrooms and almonds. Pour into a 3-quart round casserole. Cover and bake at 350° for 45 minutes. Serve immediately.

Serves 10

ham florentine

Easy and versatile.

2 pkgs. (10 oz. each) frozen chopped spinach
½ cup chopped onion
¼ cup butter, divided
½ cup grated Parmesan cheese
1 cup cottage cheese
1 pkg. (3 oz.) cream cheese
4 eggs, beaten
salt and pepper
½ tsp. basil
½ tsp. crushed rosemary
3 cups cooked, diced ham
½ cup buttered breadcrumbs

Cook spinach and drain. Saute onions in 2 tablespoons of the butter until soft. Squeeze spinach dry. Combine spinach with onions, cheeses and eggs which have been beaten with seasonings. Grease a 10-inch casserole. Put half the spinach mixture into the casserole; add ham. Sprinkle with additional salt and pepper, if desired. Top with remaining spinach mixture. Sprinkle with breadcrumbs. Bake at 400° for 20 to 30 minutes or until eggs have set and top is browned.

Serves 6

baked ham with cherry sauce

1 5-lb. precooked boneless ham
cloves
candied cherries, halved

Cherry Sauce:
2 jars (12 oz. each) cherry preserves
¼ cup butter
½ cup honey
½ cup vinegar
1 tsp. each: ginger, nutmeg, cloves
2 T. sherry

Trim ham. Score top and stud with cloves. Decorate with cherries. Place ham in a shallow roasting pan. Bake at 350° for 1 hour, approximately. Baste ham with Cherry Sauce during last 20 minutes of baking. Serve remaining sauce separately.

For Cherry Sauce: Combine all ingredients except sherry in a saucepan. Bring to boil. Reduce heat and simmer for 5 minutes. Stir in sherry.

Serves 10

creamy ham and noodle casserole

Ideal for a family or a crowd.

6 cups cooked ham, cut into 1-inch cubes
2 pkgs. (10 oz. each) frozen peas
1 cup chopped celery
1 cup canned mushrooms, drained
¾ lb. extra fine egg noodles, cooked and drained (6 cups)
½ cup butter
½ cup flour
2 cups half-and-half cream
2 cups milk
1 cup chicken broth
¾ cup grated Cheddar cheese
½ cup grated Parmesan cheese
2 T. lemon juice
3 T. grated onion
1 tsp. dry mustard
2 T. finely chopped parsley
1-2 tsp. salt
¼ tsp. crushed rosemary
½ tsp. savory
⅛ tsp. cayenne pepper
1 cup mayonnaise

Cook peas according to package directions until tender but crisp. Drain. Add celery and mushrooms to peas; set aside. Prepare noodles and set aside. In a saucepan, melt butter and blend in flour. Slowly add the cream, milk and chicken broth. Cook until thickened, stirring constantly. Add the cheeses and lemon juice. Season with the onion, mustard, parsley, salt, rosemary, savory and pepper. Remove sauce from heat and stir in mayonnaise. Mix sauce with ham and noodles. Arrange layers of the ham mixture and vegetables in a 4-quart casserole or in two 2-quart casseroles; top with the ham mixture. Bake, uncovered, at 350° for 30 minutes or until bubbly. Can be made ahead.

Serves 10 to 12

vegetables and side dishes

"Never lay potato skins on the tablecloth.
Put them in a side dish for that purpose, or leave them on your plate."

creamy artichoke and spinach casserole

4 pkgs. (10 oz. each) frozen chopped spinach
2 pkgs. (8 oz. each) cream cheese
¾ cup butter or margarine
2 cans (15 oz. each) artichoke hearts, drained
grated Parmesan cheese
crushed Ritz crackers

Cook spinach according to package directions. Drain. Place in buttered 3-quart casserole. In top of double boiler, melt butter or margarine and cream cheese. Spread over spinach. Arrange artichoke hearts over cheese mixture. Top generously with cracker crumbs and Parmesan cheese. Bake at 350° until bubbly, approximately 25 minutes. May be combined in advance. Add crumbs and Parmesan when ready to bake.

Serves 12

asparagus with herb sauce

3 pkgs. (8 oz. each) frozen asparagus spears
¼ cup butter
1 clove garlic, minced
1 T. minced onion
1 tsp. chopped chives
1 tsp. lemon juice
½ tsp. salt
⅛ tsp. black pepper

Cook asparagus according to package directions. Drain; place in serving dish and keep warm. Melt butter in a small skillet over medium heat. Saute garlic and onion until tender. Remove from heat. Stir in remaining ingredients. Pour sauce over asparagus. Serve immediately.

Serves 6

asparagus mornay

2 lbs. fresh asparagus spears
2 T. butter
1 T. flour
⅛ tsp. salt
dash white pepper
1 cup milk
½ cup shredded sharp process American cheese
¼ cup slivered blanched almonds, toasted

Cook asparagus and drain. Place in warm serving dish; keep warm. Melt butter in small saucepan over low heat. Combine flour, salt and pepper; blend into melted butter. Add milk, stirring constantly until mixture thickens and boils. Reduce heat; cook and stir 2 minutes. Add cheese; stir until melted. Pour cheese sauce over hot asparagus. Top with toasted almonds. Serve immediately.

Serves 6

asparagus casserole

½ cup butter, melted
1½ cups crushed Waverly crackers
4 pkgs. (10 oz. each) asparagus spears, drained
½ cup toasted slivered almonds
4 T. butter
3 T. flour
1½ cups milk
1 jar (5 oz.) Old English cheese

Mix butter and cracker crumbs together in a medium size bowl. Reserve 2 tablespoons of the crumb mixture for the top of the casserole. Pat the remaining crumbs into the bottom of a 2-quart casserole. Arrange asparagus on the crumbs. Sprinkle with the almonds. In a saucepan, combine the 4 tablespoons of butter with the flour. Add milk. Heat thoroughly. Add cheese and simmer until slightly thickened. Pour over the asparagus. Top with the reserved crumbs. Bake at 400° for 30 minutes.

Serves 6

green beans with hot bacon dressing

1 pkg. (10 oz.) frozen green beans
¼ cup mayonnaise
1 T. sugar
¼ cup chopped onion
1 T. melted butter
2 T. vinegar
6 slices bacon, fried crisp and crumbled

Cook beans according to package directions. Drain and set aside. Combine mayonnaise, sugar, onion, butter and vinegar in a small bowl. Microcook for 30 seconds, or combine these ingredients in a small saucepan and heat. Pour over hot cooked beans. Top with crumbled bacon and serve immediately.

Serves 4

green beans a la nicoise

½ cup chopped onion
1 clove garlic, minced
3 T. olive or vegetable oil
2 pkgs. (10 oz. each) frozen French-cut green beans, thawed
1 can (4 oz.) mushrooms, drained
1 tsp. oregano
1 tsp. salt
¼ tsp. pepper

In a large skillet, saute onion and garlic in oil until tender. Stir in green beans and mushrooms. Gently toss to coat well. Add oregano, salt and pepper. Cover and simmer 10 minutes.

Serves 6

fresh green beans and tomatoes en papillote

Super summer dish.

1 lb. fresh green beans, cut into 1-inch pieces
salted water
2 tomatoes, sliced
¼ cup softened butter
2 tsp. prepared mustard
½ cup chopped onion
1 tsp. horseradish
1 T. brown sugar
1 tsp. salt
dash of pepper

Cook beans in boiling, salted water until done, about 10 minutes. Drain. Place alternating layers of beans and tomatoes on a large double-thick square of foil. In a small bowl combine remaining ingredients and beat until fluffy. Spoon over vegetables. Wrap and tightly seal foil into a neat package or papillote. Bake at 350° for 45 minutes. Roll back foil and serve the beans *en papillote.*

Serves 6

horseradish-baked beets

1 can (1 lb.) julienne beets, drained; reserve juice
1 T. cornstarch
¼ cup sugar
½ tsp. salt
2 T. vinegar
1 T. lemon juice
1 T. butter
3 T. prepared horseradish

Place drained beets in a greased 1-quart casserole. In a saucepan mix the beet juice, cornstarch, sugar, salt, vinegar and lemon juice. Cook over medium heat, stirring constantly. Boil for 1 minute. Stir in butter and horseradish; pour over beets. Bake, uncovered, at 350° for 45 minutes. Serve hot or cold. Especially good with fish and grilled meats.

Serves 4

broccoli fantastic

This simple way to prepare broccoli makes a beautiful vegetable become even more special.

1 large bunch fresh broccoli
2 T. melted butter
2 T. white wine or sauterne

Prepare broccoli by cutting into spears or flowerets. Steam until just tender. Add butter and wine; toss together gently. Serve immediately.

Variation: Saute 1 tablespoon finely chopped onion in the butter until tender. Stir mixture into broccoli along with the wine.

Serves 4

honey and orange glazed beets

1 T. finely chopped onion
2 T. butter or margarine
2 T. cornstarch
1 tsp. grated orange rind
1 cup orange juice
¼ cup honey
2 T. lemon juice
salt and pepper
4 cups cooked, sliced beets, drained

In a heavy skillet, saute onion in butter until tender. Stir in cornstarch. Add remaining ingredients, except beets. Heat to boiling, stirring constantly. Boil and stir 1 minute. Reduce heat; add beets and cook until heated through.

Serves 8

broccoli casserole

A very easy main course vegetable.

1 pkg. (20 oz.) frozen chopped broccoli, thawed and thoroughly drained
4 cups cottage cheese
6 T. flour
½ cup melted butter
1 pkg. (8 oz.) process American cheese, diced
salt and pepper
6 eggs, slightly beaten

Put broccoli in a large bowl. In another bowl, combine cottage cheese, flour, butter, cheese, salt and pepper. Stir in eggs. Gently fold mixture into broccoli. Bake in lightly buttered 13 x 9 x 2-inch pan at 350° for 1 hour. Can be refrigerated and reheated.

Serves 10 to 12

creamy cabbage

A great vegetable dish with or without the curry.

½ medium cabbage
½ cup water
2 T. flour
1 cup half-and-half cream
1 tsp. salt
⅛ tsp. pepper
pinch curry powder, optional

Cut cabbage into coarse chunks. In a large saucepan, add water and cabbage. Cook over medium heat for 5 minutes. Sprinkle with flour. Add cream, salt, pepper and curry powder, stirring constantly until sauce thickens. Cabbage should be tender-crisp.

Serves 6

seasoned brussels sprouts

1 small onion, sliced
¼ cup butter or margarine
½ cup sauterne or sherry
¼ tsp. tarragon
dash cayenne
2 tsp. Worcestershire sauce
2 tsp. lemon juice
¼ cup water
salt to taste
2 pkgs. (10 oz. each) frozen Brussels sprouts

Fried Breadcrumbs:
½ cup butter or margarine
2 cups soft breadcrumbs or cubes

In a medium saucepan, saute onion in butter or margarine until crisp and tender. Add wine, tarragon, cayenne, Worcestershire sauce and lemon juice; simmer, uncovered, 5 minutes. Add water and salt; bring to boil. Add Brussels sprouts. Cook, covered, until tender. Do not overcook. Drain seasoned sauce into a serving container. Serve Brussels sprouts on a bed of Fried Breadcrumbs. Top with the seasoned sauce. For Fried Breadcrumbs: In a small skillet, melt butter over high heat. Saute crumbs or cubes until golden brown.

Serves 6 to 8

carrot ring supreme with creamed peas

¾ cup butter or margarine
½ cup brown sugar
2 eggs, beaten
1¼ cups flour
1 tsp. baking powder
1 T. lemon juice
1 T. orange juice
¼ tsp. baking soda
2 T. warm water
1 cup grated carrots
salt
2 pkgs. (10 oz. each) creamed peas

In a mixing bowl, cream butter or margarine and sugar. Add eggs; mix well. Sift together flour and baking powder; add to creamed mixture. Stir in juices, baking soda mixed with water, and carrots which have been lightly salted; mix thoroughly. Turn into a greased and floured 1-quart ring mold. Bake at 350° for 45 minutes. Unmold onto a serving plate. To serve, fill center with creamed peas or serve peas separately and spoon over individual servings, if desired.

Serves 8

pennsylvania dutch red cabbage

¼ lb. uncooked bacon, diced
2 medium tart, red apples, chopped
½ cup chopped onion
2 lbs. red cabbage, shredded (4-5 cups)
¼ cup plus 2 T. red wine vinegar
¼ cup plus 2 T. brown sugar
½ tsp. salt
dash pepper
2 tsp. caraway seeds

In a heavy 2-quart saucepan, cook bacon, apples and onion over low heat until onions become transparent. Add cabbage. Cook, uncovered, over medium heat until cabbage wilts, stirring occasionally. Add remaining ingredients; mix well. Reduce heat; cover and cook 20 minutes, or until tender. Cooking time depends on size of cabbage shreds. Remove lid if liquid accumulates. Cabbage should be moist, but not juicy. Serve warm. Can be made ahead.

Serves 4 to 6

carrots amandine

1 lb. carrots
1 tsp. sugar
1 tsp. salt
¼ cup butter
½ cup slivered, blanched almonds
minced parsley

Peel carrots and cut diagonally in ½-inch slices. In saucepan, place 1 inch of water. Add sugar and salt. Bring to boil. Add carrots and cook, covered, for 10 to 12 minutes, or until tender but still crisp. Drain. Transfer to heated serving dish and keep warm. In a small skillet, saute almonds in the butter over moderate heat. Stir occasionally and cook 3 to 4 minutes or until almonds are golden. Pour almonds and butter over carrots. Toss lightly and sprinkle with minced parsley.

Serves 6

karen's carrots

Compliments of a Danish cook.

1 medium onion, thinly sliced
6 T. butter, divided
4-6 large carrots, peeled and very thinly sliced
salt to taste
¼ tsp. curry powder
⅛ tsp. pepper

In a skillet with a cover, saute onion in 2 tablespoons of the butter until limp. Add carrots, salt, curry, pepper and remaining butter. Cover and cook over moderate heat, stirring occasionally, 15 minutes or until carrots are just tender.

Variation: Substitute ¼ teaspoon dill weed for the curry powder, particularly if served with fish.

Serves 4

creamy corn casserole

Livens up a "plain meat" meal.

1 can (16 oz.) cream-style corn
¼ cup melted butter
½ cup plus 2 T. cornbread mix
¼ cup water
1 medium onion, finely chopped
1 egg, beaten
salt

Combine all of the ingredients and turn into a 1½-quart casserole. Bake at 350° for 40 minutes or until set.

Serves 6

eggplant casserole

¼ cup olive or vegetable oil
1 clove garlic, minced
1 green pepper, chopped
2 peeled eggplants, chopped
1 large onion, chopped
2 cans (15½ oz. each) stewed tomatoes
8-10 slices bread, buttered, toasted and cubed
1 lb. sharp Cheddar cheese, cubed

In a large skillet, heat oil. Saute garlic, pepper, eggplant and onion until soft, not brown. Add tomatoes and stir. In a 3-quart casserole, put layers of the eggplant mixture alternating with layers of bread cubes. Top with cheese. Bake at 350° for 1 hour. Can be made ahead.

Serves 6 to 8

eggplant-zucchini casserole

2 cans (8 oz. each) tomato sauce
¼ cup water
2 tsp. Worcestershire sauce
1 tsp. salt
½ tsp. oregano
2 cloves garlic, minced
2 medium-size zucchini, cut into ¼-inch slices
1 medium eggplant, peeled and cut into ¼-inch strips
1 green pepper, chopped
3 stalks celery, chopped
1 cup grated mozzarella cheese
1 cup 1-inch uncooked spaghetti pieces

Prepare sauce by combining canned tomato sauce, water, Worcestershire sauce, salt, oregano and garlic. Set aside. Prepare vegetables. In a buttered 2-quart casserole, layer the vegetables, cheese, spaghetti pieces and sauce. Repeat, making sure the spaghetti pieces are well covered so they will not dry out. Bake at 350° for 1 hour and 15 minutes. Serve with a charcoal grilled steak and crisp salad.

Serves 8

cheese-baked cauliflower with mushrooms

1 medium cauliflower or 2 pkgs. (10 oz. each) frozen cauliflower
¼ cup each: diced green pepper, butter, flour
2 cups milk
1 tsp. salt
1 can (4 oz.) sliced mushrooms, drained
6 pimento cheese slices
paprika

Separate cauliflower into bite-size pieces and cook in salted water; drain. Saute green pepper in butter until tender. Add flour and stir until smooth. Gradually add the milk and cook over medium-high heat, stirring constantly, until thick and smooth. Add salt and mushrooms. In a 1-quart casserole alternate layers of the cauliflower pieces, sauce and cheese. Sprinkle with paprika. Bake at 350° for approximately 20 minutes or until bubbly.

Serves 6

caramelized onions

1 lb. tiny onions, peeled
2 T. butter
salt
2 T. sugar

Place onions in a pan with enough water to cover. Add the butter, salt and sugar. Bring to a boil. Simmer until water evaporates and onions are tender and caramelized, about 30 minutes.

Serves 4 to 6

baked peas with water chestnuts

⅓ cup chopped onion
⅓ cup chopped green pepper
⅓ cup chopped celery
1½ T. butter or margarine
2 cups frozen peas
1 can (10½ oz.) condensed cream of mushroom soup
¼ cup milk
1 can (5 oz.) water chestnuts, drained and sliced
1 jar (2 oz.) pimento, drained and chopped
1 cup crumbled cheese crackers

Saute onion, green pepper and celery in butter. Cook and drain peas. Dilute soup with milk. Gently combine all ingredients except the cracker crumbs. Cover and refrigerate overnight. Before baking, cover with cracker crumbs. Bake at 350° for 45 minutes or microcook 3 to 5 minutes. If cooked immediately without refrigeration, reduce cooking time to 25 minutes.

Serves 6

elegant peas

1½ cups sliced, fresh mushrooms
¼ cup minced onion
2 T. butter
¼ tsp. salt
dash pepper
¼ tsp. nutmeg
¼ tsp. marjoram
¼ cup dry sherry
2 cups hot cooked peas

Saute mushrooms and onions in butter in skillet until barely tender, about 5 minutes. Add seasonings and sherry. Simmer 5 minutes. Add peas. Cook about 1 minute and serve.

Serves 4 to 6

green peas and olives

So easy and adds a little something different to peas.

1 pkg. (10 oz.) frozen peas
1 T. butter
¼ cup sliced, stuffed green olives
½ cup grated Cheddar cheese
parsley
garlic powder
salt and pepper

Cook peas according to directions; drain. Remove from heat. Add butter, olives, cheese and seasonings. Heat until cheese is melted. Serve immediately.

Serves 4

souffled spinach

2 pkgs. (10 oz. each) frozen, chopped spinach
1 pkg. (8 oz.) Old English cheese slices, cubed
2 T. finely chopped onion
1 T. lemon juice
1 tsp. salt
10 slices white bread, crusts removed
½ cup melted butter
3 eggs, well beaten
1½ cups milk

Cook spinach according to package directions; drain well. Press out additional liquid. Combine spinach with cheese, onion, lemon juice and salt. Dip bread slices in melted butter and line the bottom and sides of a 2-quart casserole with half the slices. Alternately layer spinach and remaining bread, ending with bread slices. Combine beaten eggs with milk. Beat well and pour over casserole. Bake at 325° for 1 hour or until bread is crusty-brown and middle is set.

Note: For decoration, cut pieces of bread for the top into triangles before dipping in butter. Arrange in an attractive fashion.

Serves 6

french fried onion rings

2 eggs, separated
1¼ cups buttermilk
1½ T. vegetable oil
1¼ cups flour
1 tsp. salt
1¼ tsp. baking powder
2 extra large onions, sliced and separated into rings
additional salt

In a large bowl, beat egg yolks. Beat in buttermilk, oil and dry ingredients. In a separate bowl, beat egg whites until stiff. Fold into buttermilk mixture. Dip onion rings into batter. Fry, a few at a time, in deep fat heated to 375°. Drain thoroughly on paper towels. Sprinkle with salt. Keep warm in a slow oven. Prepared onion rings may be frozen. When ready to serve, place on baking sheet. Heat in a 350° oven for 5 minutes.

Serves 4 to 6

peas with "pizazz"

Summer vegetable cooler.

2 pkgs. (10 oz. each) frozen tiny peas
1 cup sour cream
2 green onions (scallions), chopped
6 slices bacon, fried and crumbled
½ tsp. salt
freshly ground pepper

Thaw and drain peas, but do not cook. Toss peas with remaining ingredients. Keep refrigerated until serving time.

Serves 8

spinach-stuffed tomatoes

Great with charcoal broiled steak.

4 slices bacon, fried and crumbled
2-3 T. bacon drippings
¼ cup chopped onion
10 oz. fresh spinach, finely chopped
½ cup sour cream
dash Tabasco sauce
4 large tomatoes
salt
½ cup (2 oz.) shredded mozzarella cheese

Cook onion in bacon drippings until tender. Stir in spinach. Cover and cook until tender, approximately 3 to 5 minutes. Remove from heat. Stir in sour cream, crumbled bacon and Tabasco sauce. Set aside. Cut tops from tomatoes and remove centers, leaving hollow shells. Drain well; salt. Fill tomatoes with spinach mixture. Place in 8 x 8 x 2-inch lightly greased baking dish. Bake at 375° for 20 to 25 minutes. Top with shredded cheese. Bake 2 to 3 more minutes until melted.

Note: If tomato shell starts to split, wrap with narrow strip of aluminum foil.

Serves 4

spinach-pecan bake

Pretty as a picture. Delightful to taste.

3 pkgs. (10 oz. each) frozen chopped spinach
½ cup chopped onions
¼ cup plus 2 tsp. butter
1 cup half-and-half cream
¾ cup breadcrumbs, divided
½ cup coarsely chopped pecans
1 tsp. salt
½ tsp. ground nutmeg
⅛ tsp. pepper

Cook spinach according to directions. Drain well. In a saucepan, saute onions in ¼ cup melted butter. Set aside. In large bowl, combine spinach, sauteed onions, cream, ½ cup of the breadcrumbs, pecans, salt, nutmeg and pepper. Mix thoroughly. Turn into buttered 1½-quart shallow baking dish. Melt remaining 2 teaspoons of the butter and mix with ¼ cup reserved breadcrumbs. Sprinkle over casserole. Bake at 350° for 30 minutes.

Variation: Cauliflower may be substituted for spinach.

Serves 8 to 10

acorn squash with orange-cranberry filling

3 acorn squash, halved
1 pkg. (10 oz.) frozen orange-cranberry relish, thawed
¼ cup plus 2 T. butter, melted
1 T. brown sugar
⅛ tsp. ground cloves
½ tsp. salt
¼ cup roasted, chopped pecans

Cut squash into halves; remove seeds. Bake on a rack over water, cut-side down, at 350° for 50 to 60 minutes, or until tender. Meanwhile, combine the relish, ¼ cup of the butter, sugar, cloves and salt in a small saucepan. Heat until mixture boils. When squash are tender, remove water from pan and brush pan lightly with melted butter. Return squash, cut-side up, to the pan and brush with the remaining melted butter. If necessary, trim bottoms of squash to level. Add pecans to filling and spoon into squash. Bake 15 to 20 minutes. Serve hot. Can be prepared ahead.

Serves 6

summer squash casserole

Simple to prepare . . . "gourmet" to taste.

2 lbs. yellow summer squash, cut into ¼-inch slices
1 medium onion, finely chopped
1 can (10½ oz.) condensed cream of chicken soup
1 cup sour cream
1 cup shredded carrots
1 pkg. (8 oz.) herb stuffing mix
½ cup melted butter
salt and pepper

Cook squash and onion in salted water for 5 minutes. Drain. In large bowl, combine soup and sour cream. Stir in shredded carrots. Gently fold in squash and onion. In a separate bowl, combine stuffing mix and butter. In a 12 x 8-inch shallow baking dish, spread half of the stuffing mixture. Spoon vegetable mixture on top. Sprinkle remaining stuffing mixture on top. Bake at 350° for 30 minutes.

Variation: Substitute sliced zucchini for the summer squash or a combination of both.

Serves 8

spinach lasagne

1 lb. ricotta or small curd cottage cheese
1½ cups shredded mozzarella cheese, divided
1 egg, beaten
1 pkg. (10 oz.) frozen, chopped spinach, thawed and patted dry
½ tsp. salt
⅛ tsp. pepper
¾ tsp. oregano
2 jars (15½ oz. each) spaghetti sauce
½ pkg. (8 oz.) lasagne noodles, uncooked
1 cup water

In a large bowl, mix ricotta, 1 cup of the mozzarella, egg, spinach, salt, pepper and oregano. In a greased 13 x 9 x 2-inch baking dish, layer ½ cup of the spaghetti sauce, one-third of the uncooked noodles and one-half of the cheese mixture. Repeat. Top with remaining noodles and sauce. Sprinkle reserved ½ cup of mozzarella over the top. Pour water around edges. Cover tightly with foil. Bake at 350° for 1 hour and 15 minutes. Let stand 15 minutes to firm before serving. Nice with a large Italian salad. Can be made ahead.

Serves 8

sour cream and cheese baked zucchini

Yummmm!

4 medium zucchini, coarsely grated
salt
4 T. butter
1 medium onion, chopped
2 T. flour
2 T. milk
2 cups sour cream
2 cups grated Cheddar cheese
grated Parmesan cheese

Place grated zucchini in a colander. Sprinkle with salt to taste; stir. Let stand to drain for about three hours. Press out excess moisture. In a large skillet, melt butter. Stir in onion; saute until softened. Stir in zucchini; saute mixture for a few minutes or until it begins to stick to bottom of skillet. Stir in flour and milk. Cook 1 or 2 minutes. Remove from heat. Stir in sour cream and grated Cheddar cheese. Taste for seasoning. Turn into a 2-quart baking dish. Sprinkle lightly with Parmesan cheese. Bake, uncovered, at 350° for 30 minutes. Serve with a steak or roast beef, crusty French bread and a crisp salad.

Serves 6

zucchini and mushrooms with sour cream

1 can (4 oz.) mushrooms, drained
4 medium-size zucchini, cut in ½-inch slices
¼ cup butter
garlic salt
2 T. flour
1 cup sour cream
1 tsp. dill weed

In a 10-inch skillet, saute mushrooms and zucchini in butter for 5 to 10 minutes. Zucchini should be fork-tender but not mushy. Sprinkle with garlic salt and add flour. Stir well and cook for 2 to 3 minutes longer. Add sour cream and dill. Stir gently over medium heat until hot but not boiling or it will curdle. Serve immediately.

Serves 6 to 8

squash supreme

2 lbs. (8 cups) sliced yellow crook-neck squash
¼ cup butter
6 T. flour
2 cups milk
salt and pepper
¾ lb. sharp cheese, grated
2 eggs, lightly beaten
⅓-½ cup buttered breadcrumbs

In a 2½-quart saucepan, steam squash until tender. Drain and set aside. Melt butter in a 1-quart saucepan. Stir in flour; mix well. Add milk, stirring constantly. Add salt and pepper to taste. Add cheese and eggs, cooking slowly until thickened. Add cheese sauce to squash, mixing gently. Pour the vegetable mixture into a 10 x 6 x 1¾-inch casserole. Top with breadcrumbs. Bake at 350° for 30 minutes.

Serves 6 to 8

zippy zucchini

A delicious version of this plentiful summer vegetable.

4 medium-size zucchini
⅔ cup real mayonnaise
1-2 T. crumbled blue cheese
¼ tsp. garlic salt
¼ cup grated Parmesan cheese

Boil zucchini until tender but not mushy; drain. Cut in half lengthwise. Combine remaining ingredients. Spread mixture on zucchini halves. Just before serving, broil 5 to 10 minutes or until lightly browned and bubbly. Excellent with grilled meat.

Serves 4

layered vegetables and cheese casserole

A tremendously popular buffet party dish.

1 pkg. (10 oz.) frozen broccoli spears
1 pkg. (10 oz.) frozen lima beans
1 cup firmly packed shredded Cheddar cheese
1 large onion, finely chopped
4 T. butter or margarine, divided
2 T. flour
1 can (16 oz.) whole tomatoes, drained with liquid reserved
salt and pepper
dried marjoram leaves, crushed
1 cup soft breadcrumbs
3 T. grated Romano or Parmesan cheese

Cook broccoli according to directions. Remove from liquid with slotted spoon and put in greased, shallow 2-quart baking dish. Cook lima beans in same liquid until tender. Drain, reserving liquid, and layer lima beans on top of broccoli. Sprinkle Cheddar cheese over vegetables. Saute onion in 2 tablespoons of the margarine until soft and transparent. Stir in flour and cook for 2 minutes. Gradually add reserved vegetable water and tomato liquid, stirring until smooth and thick. Chop tomatoes coarsely and add to sauce. Add salt, pepper and marjoram to taste. Pour over cheese-topped vegetables. Saute breadcrumbs in remaining margarine until golden brown. Mix with grated cheese and additional marjoram, if desired. Sprinkle on casserole. Bake at 425° for 15 minutes or until topping is browned. Serve with roast beef or ham. Recipe can be doubled or tripled easily.

Variation: Substitute frozen Brussels sprouts or add sauteed celery.

Serves 6 to 8

parmesan-baked zucchini with tomatoes and onions

3 medium-size zucchini, cut in ¼-inch slices
1 large onion, thinly sliced
3 large tomatoes, sliced
1 tsp. salt
2 tsp. basil
1 cup grated Parmesan cheese
5 T. butter or margarine

In a buttered 2-quart casserole, alternate layers of zucchini, onion and tomato slices with combined salt, basil and Parmesan cheese. Dot with butter. Bake, uncovered, at 375° for 45 minutes.

Serves 6

mediterranean vegetable stew

Hearty enough to serve for supper.

1 cup coarsely chopped onion
½ cup coarsely chopped red pepper
4 T. olive oil
1 cup uncooked macaroni
6 cups vegetable stock or water
2 cups coarsely chopped eggplant (1 medium eggplant)
2 cups coarsely chopped zucchini (2 medium zucchini)
1 can (12 oz.) V-8 juice
½ tsp. basil
2 cloves garlic, minced
¼ tsp. oregano
salt and pepper
2 cups shredded mozzarella cheese

Saute onions and red pepper in olive oil until slightly soft. Meanwhile cook macaroni in vegetable stock or water until tender. Drain and rinse macaroni in colander, reserving vegetable water. Place all ingredients *except cheese* in large kettle. Simmer, uncovered, until tender, but not overcooked, about 30 minutes. Ladle into one large or individual casseroles. Top with grated cheese; place under broiler until cheese is melted and bubbly. Serve immediately with a salad and crusty French bread.

Note: Any soft white cheese may be substituted for the mozzarella.

Serves 5 to 6

potato broccoli bake

3 T. butter or margarine, divided
2 T. flour
1 tsp. salt
⅛ tsp. pepper
⅛ tsp. nutmeg
2 cups milk
1 pkg. (3 oz.) cream cheese, cubed
½ cup (2 oz.) shredded Swiss cheese
4 cups (16 oz.) frozen, loose-pack, hash brown potatoes, thawed
1 pkg. (10 oz.) frozen chopped broccoli, cooked and drained
¼ cup fine, dry breadcrumbs

In a large saucepan, melt 2 tablespoons of the butter; blend in flour, salt, pepper and nutmeg. Add milk. Cook and stir until bubbly. Add cheeses, stirring until melted. Stir in potatoes. Turn half the mixture into a 10 x 6 x 2-inch baking dish; cover with broccoli. Spoon remaining cheese mixture over broccoli. Cover with foil and bake at 350° for 35 minutes. Melt remaining tablespoon of butter; mix with crumbs. Sprinkle around edges of dish. Bake, uncovered, for an additional 10 to 15 minutes. Serve with a standing rib roast.

Serves 8

fluffy herbed potatoes

1⅓ cups instant mashed potato flakes, or 2 cups mashed potatoes
1 cup small-curd cottage cheese
1 cup sour cream
3 egg yolks, beaten
1 clove garlic, minced
2 T. minced chives
2 tsp. celery salt
3 egg whites
½ cup chopped fresh parsley
3 T. butter

Prepare instant potatoes according to package directions, or cook and mash regular potatoes. Whip into the prepared potatoes the cottage cheese, sour cream, egg yolks, garlic, chives and celery salt. Mix thoroughly. In separate bowl, beat egg whites until stiff. Fold egg whites and parsley into the potato mixture. Place in a shallow 2-quart casserole. Dot top with butter; bake at 350° for 30 to 40 minutes or until top is slightly browned. Can be made ahead to the point of baking.

Serves 6 to 8

aunt bella's cheese, tomatoes and mushroom toast

2 pkgs. (7 oz. each) Gouda cheese
½ cup melted butter or margarine
4 slices bread, crumbled
2 large tomatoes, sliced
1 lb. fresh mushrooms, sauteed, or 1 can (8 oz.) mushrooms, drained

Shred 2 cups of the Gouda cheese. Cut remaining cheese into thin slices. Mix shredded cheese, melted butter and breadcrumbs. Press firmly on bottom and sides of greased 8 x 12-inch baking dish. Cover with cheese slices, add layer of tomato slices and top with mushrooms. Sprinkle with remaining shredded cheese. Bake at 350° for 20 minutes. Serve with beef and a crisp, tossed salad. Can be made ahead before baking.

Serves 6

hasselback potatoes

Buttery-cheese delight and easier than hash brown potatoes.

8 small baking potatoes, unpeeled
½ cup butter
½ tsp. salt
½ tsp. paprika
¼ cup grated Cheddar cheese
2 T. fine breadcrumbs

Slice potatoes at ⅛-inch intervals, three quarters of the way through so they spread like a fan. Melt butter in an iron skillet. Roll potatoes in the butter in the skillet, arranging them cut side up. Sprinkle with salt and paprika. Bake in skillet in oven at 350° for 45 minutes, basting occasionally. Continue to bake 20 minutes longer without basting. Combine cheese and breadcrumbs; toss to blend together. Sprinkle mixture over potatoes and bake 10 minutes longer. Serve immediately. Tasty with fish, ham or steak.

Serves 8

party-time baked potatoes

4 large baking potatoes
vegetable oil
½ cup cream
¼ cup plus 2 T. butter
½ tsp. salt
dash of pepper
2 eggs
1 T. chopped chives or 1 tsp. grated onion
½ cup grated sharp cheese

Scrub potatoes, rub with oil and bake at 425° until done, approximately 45 minutes to 1 hour. Cut potatoes in half lengthwise. Scoop out potato pulp leaving shells intact. Mash potatoes with electric mixer until lumps are broken. Add cream, butter, salt, pepper, eggs and chives or onions. Whip until light and fluffy, using moderate mixer speed. Pile into potato shells or flute into shells using a pastry tube. Sprinkle with cheese. Bake at 425° for 10 minutes until tops are lightly browned. Be careful not to overbake. Can be prepared in advance up to the point of baking.

Serves 6 to 8

crunch-topped sweet potato casserole

2 cans (16 oz. each) sweet potatoes, undrained
¼ cup melted butter
1 cup sugar
½ tsp. salt
2 eggs, well beaten
½ cup milk
½ tsp. vanilla

Topping:
1 cup firmly packed brown sugar
¼ cup butter
⅓ cup flour
2 tsp. cinnamon
1 cup chopped nuts

In a saucepan, heat undrained potatoes to the boiling point. Drain. Mash potatoes with butter. Add remaining ingredients and blend well. Turn into a 9-inch square glass baking dish. For Topping: In a saucepan, combine brown sugar, butter, flour and cinnamon. Heat gently over medium heat. Remove from stove and stir in nuts. Spread over sweet potatoes. Bake at 350° for 40 minutes. Can be made ahead.

Serves 10 to 12

alice's hot potato salad

15 red potatoes, unpeeled
1 lb. bacon, cut in small pieces
4 bunches green onions, chopped
salt and pepper
celery salt and celery seed to taste
¾ cup each: sugar, vinegar, water
3 eggs, well beaten
¾ cup bacon drippings

Boil potatoes in skins, but do not let them become mushy. Cool. Dice potatoes (with skins on) and place in large bowl. Fry bacon, reserving ¾ cup bacon drippings. To potatoes, add bacon, onions, salt, pepper, celery salt and celery seed. When ready to serve, combine sugar, vinegar, water and eggs in saucepan; bring to a boil. Heat reserved bacon drippings in separate pan. Pour both over potatoes and stir gently. Serve warm. If desired, prepare potatoes ahead and add dressing just before serving.

Serves 16

fettucine with zucchini and mushrooms

½ lb. mushrooms, thinly sliced
¾ cup butter, divided
1¼ lbs. zucchini, scrubbed, cut into julienne strips
¾ cup whipping cream
12 oz. fettucine
¾ cup *freshly grated* Parmesan cheese
½ cup chopped parsley

In large skillet, saute mushrooms in ¼ cup of the butter for 2 minutes. Add zucchini, cream and remaining butter. Bring to boil; simmer mixture for 3 minutes. In a large saucepan, cook fettucine in boiling water for 7 minutes, or until done. Drain in colander. Add pasta to skillet with Parmesan cheese and parsley. Toss with wooden fork. Transfer to heated platter and serve with additional Parmesan cheese.

Serves 6

wild rice au vin

This may also be used as a stuffing for poultry or wild fowl.

1 cup wild rice
1 cup grated Cheddar cheese, divided
1 cup chopped ripe olives
1 cup canned tomatoes
1 cup sliced fresh or canned mushrooms
½ cup chopped onion
salt and pepper
½ cup melted butter
1 cup claret wine

Rinse wild rice; soak in water overnight. Drain. When ready to prepare casserole, combine drained rice with ½ cup of the grated cheese and remaining ingredients. Place mixture in a 2½-quart casserole. Top with remaining grated cheese. Cover and bake at 350° for 1 hour.

Serves 8

cashew rice ring

Impressive, gourmet accompaniment to shish-kabob or buffet menu.

¾ cup plus 2 T. butter
1 onion, finely chopped
1 lb. mushrooms, ground or minced
1 lb. chicken livers
2 cups *uncooked* white rice
2 cans (10 oz. each) chicken broth
2½ cups water
1 cup medium size raw cashews
2 tsp. salt
½ tsp. pepper
⅓ cup chopped parsley

Melt ¾ cup of the butter in a heavy skillet and saute onions and mushrooms for 5 minutes. Remove with slotted spoon and set aside. In same butter, saute livers until brown. (Livers should be slightly pink inside; do not overcook.) Coarsely chop livers. Place remaining 2 tablespoons of butter in another skillet and saute rice until golden. Add broth, water, sauteed onions and mushrooms. Bring to a boil. Cover and cook over low heat 20 minutes, or until liquid is nearly evaporated. Add livers, cashews, salt and pepper. Turn into a greased 2-quart ring or bundt mold. Bake at 350° for 30 minutes. When ready to serve, unmold on platter and garnish with parsley. Can prepare late in the afternoon and allow to remain covered in warm place in mold.

Serves 8 to 10

baked spaghetti with spinach and mushrooms

May be served as a side dish or for a light supper.

8 oz. spaghetti
2 pkgs. (10 oz. each) frozen, chopped spinach
½ cup chopped onion
½ cup grated Parmesan cheese
½ cup softened butter, divided
2 eggs, slightly beaten
3 cups fresh mushrooms, sliced
2 jars (16 oz. each) meatless spaghetti sauce

Cook spaghetti according to directions; drain. Meanwhile, cook spinach according to directions, adding onion. Drain. Combine spaghetti, spinach, cheese, ¼ cup of the butter and the eggs. Mix well. Turn into a greased and wax paper-lined 1½-quart ring mold. Cover and bake at 375° for 25 minutes. In a saucepan, cook mushrooms in remaining ¼ cup butter until tender. Add spaghetti sauce and heat through. Cool ring mold 5 minutes. Unmold. Serve with sauce. Can be made ahead and heated in microwave.

Serves 8

mushroom and noodle casserole

½ cup butter, divided
3 T. finely chopped onion
1 lb. mushrooms, sliced
salt and freshly ground pepper
½ cup dry white wine
1½ cups whipping cream
2 T. flour
2 eggs
¼ cup milk
¾ lb. medium noodles
¼ cup grated Parmesan cheese

Melt 2 tablespoons of the butter in a saucepan. Add onion and cook until tender. Add mushrooms, salt and pepper to taste. Cook 5 minutes. Add wine; cover and simmer 5 minutes. Add cream and cook 5 minutes. Make a roux by blending 2 tablespoons flour with 2 tablespoons of butter. Gradually add to cream sauce, stirring rapidly. Beat eggs with milk and add to creamed mushroom mixture. Cook the noodles until almost tender. Drain. Stir in remaining 4 tablespoons butter and toss well. Pour noodles into a 2½-quart baking dish; spread mushroom-cream sauce over all. Stir gently until lightly blended. Sprinkle with grated cheese. Bake at 375° for 30 minutes.

Serves 8 to 10

hot fruit compote

Delicious as a dessert, as a side dish for brunch or with roast pork or ham.

2 cups mixed, dried fruits
1 cup raisins
sugar
curry powder to taste, optional
whipping cream

Rinse fruits and raisins. In large saucepan, place fruits, raisins and enough water to cover; soak, covered, for 6 to 12 hours. Simmer fruit in same water until fruits are plump and syrup has cooked down to a medium consistency. Add sugar to taste while fruit is still hot. Add curry, if desired. Serve warm or hot in individual fruit dishes with a pitcher of cream. May be reheated in microwave oven for 2 to 4 minutes. This dish keeps 5 to 6 days in refrigerator.

Serves 4

scalloped pineapple

Warm, fragrant fruit dish to serve with ham or pork.

½ cup softened butter
1 cup sugar
2 eggs, well beaten
1 can (20 oz.) crushed pineapple, undrained
3 cups firmly packed bread cubes
1 cup miniature marshmallows

Mix butter and sugar, beating until well blended. Add eggs; mix. Add *undrained* pineapple, bread cubes and marshmallows. Bake, uncovered, at 350° for 45 minutes in a greased 1½-quart casserole.

Serves 6 to 8

hot mincemeat-filled peaches

8 canned peach halves, drained
¾-1 cup mincemeat
lettuce leaves

Fill each peach half with 1 to 2 tablespoons mincemeat. Place in a buttered 10-inch baking dish. Bake at 350° for 10 minutes or until mincemeat is warm. Serve individually on a lettuce leaf or in a decorative casserole as a side dish.

Serves 8

pumpkin shell casserole

Unusual and easy!

1 small pumpkin, 7 inches in diameter
2 cups peeled, chopped apples
1 cup raisins
1 cup chopped pecans
⅓ cup sugar
1 tsp. lemon juice
¼ tsp. each: nutmeg and cinnamon

Wash pumpkin; cut a lid and scrape out seeds. Combine remaining ingredients in a mixing bowl; toss gently. Spoon mixture into pumpkin shell. Replace lid and place pumpkin on lightly greased cookie sheet. Bake at 350° for 1 hour and 15 minutes. Remove from oven. Top with sour cream, if desired. May be served hot or cold.

Serves 4 to 6

persian baked apricots

1 lb. dried apricots
1 lb. light brown sugar (or less, to taste)
2 cups Ritz cracker crumbs
⅓ cup butter

Cook apricots in simmering water to cover until tender. Drain. In a 13 x 9 x 2-inch baking dish, arrange half the apricots. Sprinkle with half the brown sugar and half the crumbs. Dot with half the butter. Repeat. Bake at 300° for 1 hour. Mixture should be thick with a crusty top. Serve warm with a roast leg of lamb and rice pilaf for a Middle Eastern-flavored dinner.

Serves 10 to 12

far east celery

4 cups celery, cut into 1-inch pieces
1 can (5 oz.) water chestnuts, drained and sliced
1 can (10¾ oz.) condensed cream of chicken soup
¼ cup diced pimento
½ cup breadcrumbs
¼ cup toasted, slivered almonds
2 T. melted butter

Cook celery in small amount of salted, boiling water until tender-crisp, about 8 minutes. Drain. Combine celery, water chestnuts, soup and pimento in 1-quart casserole. Toss breadcrumbs with almonds and butter; sprinkle over casserole. Bake at 350° for 35 minutes or until bubbly.

Serves 6

chinese fried rice

2 T. vegetable oil
2 cups chopped onion
1 T. soy sauce
2 cups cooked rice, chilled
2 eggs, beaten
salt to taste
optional: 2 cups chopped shrimp, cooked ham, fried bacon, green pepper or peanuts

Heat wok or skillet over medium heat. Add oil and fry onion until browned. Add soy sauce, rice, eggs and salt. Saute quickly until eggs are set. Add one of the optional ingredients, if desired.

Serves 4 to 6

desserts

"Finger bowls are quite as needful as napkins,
for the fingers are also liable to become a little soiled in eating.
The fingers are slightly dipped into the bowl,
the juice from a small slice of lemon is squeezed upon them,
and then they are dried softly upon the napkin.
At dinner parties and luncheons they are indispensable."

chocolate-mint torte

An elegant dessert that must be prepared a day ahead.

2 pkgs. (4 oz. each) German sweet chocolate
½ cup sugar
½ cup water
2 tsp. peppermint flavoring
1 pkg. (10 oz.) pie crust mix
2 cups whipping cream, whipped

In top of double boiler, combine first 3 ingredients. Cook over low heat, stirring constantly, until smooth. Stir in peppermint; cool to room temperature. In a mixing bowl, combine ¾ cup of chocolate mixture with crumbled pie crust mix. Blend thoroughly. Divide pastry into 6 equal portions. Press each portion over the bottom of inverted 8-inch round cake pan to within ½-inch of edge. Bake at 425° for 5 minutes or until done. Do not let edges burn. Trim crusts to even edges. Cool slightly before removing from pans. Insert tip of knife under edges to loosen from pan. Lift off carefully. Place on sheets of paper toweling. Whip cream until it begins to hold soft peaks. Fold in remaining chocolate sauce. Stack baked pastry on a serving plate spreading chocolate cream between each layer and over top. Chill at least 8 hours or overnight.

Serves 8 to 10

rum chocolate cake

A rich, whipped-cream-topped dessert similar to a chilled mousse.

4½ squares semi-sweet chocolate
2 T. very strong coffee
¾ cup sugar
¼ tsp. salt
4½ T. flour
¾ cup melted butter
¼ cup rum
6 eggs, separated
1 cup whipping cream, whipped

Line the bottom of a greased 3-quart souffle dish or 8-inch spring form pan with greased wax paper. In top of double boiler, melt chocolate with coffee. Add the sugar, salt, flour, butter and rum; mix well. Remove from heat. In a large bowl, beat egg yolks lightly. Gradually add chocolate mixture, stirring well to mix. Beat egg whites until stiff, but not dry. Gently fold into chocolate mixture until no white is visible. Do not over mix. Pour into prepared dish. Set in a shallow pan of hot water. Bake 1 hour at 350° or until set. Cool to room temperature. Chill. The dessert will shrink as it cools. Unmold onto a serving platter and peel off paper. Frost with whipped cream. Decorate with candied violets, if desired. Chill until served.

Serves 10

mocha charlotte

For a variation, brush lady fingers with white creme de menthe.

2 dozen lady fingers
1 cup softened butter
2 cups sifted confectioners' sugar
¼ tsp. salt
½ tsp. vanilla
2 eggs, well beaten
3 oz. unsweetened chocolate, melted
4 T. strong coffee
1 cup whipping cream, whipped

Line sides and bottom of a spring-form mold with lady fingers. In a large bowl, cream together butter, sugar, salt and vanilla. In a small bowl, blend beaten eggs, melted chocolate and coffee. Add to butter mixture and beat well. Pour into mold. Top with remaining lady fingers. Refrigerate overnight. Just before serving, unmold and garnish with whipped cream.

Serves 12

toffee pecan ice cream torte

1 cup crushed saltine crackers
1 cup crushed graham crackers
½ cup melted butter
½ gallon butter pecan ice cream
2 pkgs. (3 oz. each) instant vanilla pudding mix
1½ cups milk
1 cup whipping cream, whipped
3 crumbled toffee candy bars

In a bowl, combine cracker crumbs with melted butter. Press into bottom of 9 x 13-inch pan. Bake at 350° for 10 minutes. Allow crust to cool before filling. Meanwhile, thaw ice cream until almost liquid. Prepare pudding mix using the amount of milk called for above. Add melted ice cream to pudding and beat until blended. Pour mixture into baked crust. Chill until firm. Before serving, top with whipped cream and crumbled candy bars.

Serves 12

rum pecan dessert

Rich and unusual.

Crust:
5 T. melted butter
2 cups graham cracker crumbs

Filling:
1 cup softened butter
5 cups sifted confectioners' sugar
6 eggs, well beaten
3 T. rum
1 tsp. vanilla
¼ tsp. salt
1½ cups chopped pecans

Topping:
2 cups whipping cream, whipped
1½ tsp. vanilla
⅓ cup sugar
chopped pecans

For Crust: Combine butter and graham cracker crumbs. Press into 9 x 13-inch pan. Set aside.

For Filling: In a large bowl, cream butter until light and fluffy. Add sugar and eggs, alternating for easier mixing. Cream thoroughly. Add rum, vanilla and salt. Mix well. Stir in chopped pecans. Pour mixture over crust.

For Topping: In another bowl, whip cream; add the vanilla and sugar. Spread whipped cream over filling. Garnish with chopped pecans. Chill overnight.

Serves 12

chocolate-cointreau mousse

Quick and easy!

2 eggs
1 cup (8 oz.) semi-sweetened chocolate chips
½ tsp. instant coffee
2 T. Cointreau
1 cup milk, scalded
1 cup whipping cream, whipped

Place the first 4 ingredients in a blender. Blend until creamy. Add scalded milk; cover tightly and blend for 2 more minutes. Pour mixture into four parfait glasses and chill. Before serving, garnish with whipped cream.

Serves 4

daiquiri chiffon with spirited custard sauce

Elegant . . .

1 T. plus 1 tsp. unflavored gelatin
¼ cup light rum, chilled
2 egg yolks (reserve whites)
1 cup sugar
½ tsp. salt
½ cup lime juice
1 tsp. grated lime rind
⅓ cup light rum
3 egg whites
18 lady fingers, halved
frosted seedless green grapes

Daiquiri Custard Sauce:
5 egg yolks
⅔ cup sugar
½ cup light rum
1 T. grenadine syrup
1 cup whipping cream, whipped

Soften gelatin in ¼ cup chilled rum. In top of double boiler, beat egg yolks and add sugar, salt and lime juice, blending well. Cook over hot water, stirring until mixture coats spoon. Remove from heat and add gelatin, stirring until dissolved. Add lime rind. Cool. Stir in ⅓ cup rum. Chill until partially set. In a separate bowl, beat egg whites until stiff. Fold into lime mixture. Line sherbet glasses with lady fingers, rounded ends up. Pour lime mixture into sherbets and chill for about 3 hours. Serve with Daiquiri Custard Sauce. Garnish with frosted seedless green grapes.

For Daiquiri Custard Sauce: In top of double boiler, beat egg yolks with rotary beater. Add sugar. Continue beating until mixture is thick and light in color. Blend in rum. Cook over hot water, stirring constantly, until mixture thickens. Remove from heat and add grenadine syrup. Chill. Before serving, fold in whipped cream.

Serves 6 to 8

blueberries in lemon mousse

4 egg yolks
½ cup sugar
3 T. lemon juice
1 tsp. grated lemon rind
2 egg whites, beaten until stiff
½ cup whipping cream, whipped
1 cup fresh blueberries, rinsed and dried

In top of double boiler, beat the egg yolks until thick and pale. Add sugar, lemon juice and lemon rind; continue beating. Place mixture over heat. Cook, stirring constantly, until thick. Cool. Fold in egg whites, whipped cream and blueberries. Pour into 4 serving dishes. Refrigerate until ready to serve. Garnish with a few blueberries. Do not prepare more than a day ahead.

Serves 4

fruit ice

Cool and refreshing.

3 medium, ripe bananas, mashed
3 eggs, well beaten
juice and pulp of 3 oranges
juice and pulp of 3 lemons
1 can (15 oz.) crushed pineapple
3 cups sugar
3 cups water
fresh mint sprigs (optional)

In a large bowl, combine the bananas, eggs, pulp and juice of the fruits and undrained pineapple. Add the sugar and water; mix well. Pour mixture into a 2-quart container and freeze. Remove from freezer 30 minutes before serving. Stir and spoon into stemmed sherbets. Garnish with fresh mint, if desired.

Serves 12

fresh fruit with honey-yogurt sauce

A natural dessert.

3 cups plain yogurt
½ cup honey
6 cups diced cantaloupe
4 cups sliced fresh peaches
4 ripe bananas, sliced
1 cup sliced pitted dates
1 cup shelled whole almonds

In a large bowl, mix yogurt and honey. Add the remaining ingredients and toss gently. Cover and refrigerate for 3 hours or longer to blend flavors.

Serves 12 to 16 (14 cups)

bananas flambe

A dessert especially for the microwave.

2 T. butter
2 large, ripe but firm bananas, cut into 1-inch chunks
2 T. brown sugar
1 tsp. cinnamon
3 T. dark rum
coffee or vanilla ice cream for 4 servings

Place butter in baking dish, one that can be brought to table for flaming. Put into microwave oven for 20 seconds to melt butter. Add bananas; roll in butter until well coated. Distribute bananas evenly in dish. Sprinkle with brown sugar and cinnamon. Microcook at high setting 3 to 4 minutes. (Bananas should retain shape. They should not be mushy). After 2 minutes, give dish a half turn and continue cooking. In a separate saucepan, warm rum. (Do not allow rum to boil or it will not flame). Pour rum over bananas and ignite. When flame dies, serve over ice cream.

Serves 4

frozen lime cream dessert

¼ cup plus 3 T. softened butter
⅓ cup ground pecans
½ cup flour
¼ cup confectioners' sugar
4 oz. softened cream cheese
½ cup sour cream
1 cup sugar
4 T. cornstarch
4 egg yolks
1½ cups milk
dash of salt
⅓ cup lime juice
2 cups frozen dessert topping, thawed
1 cup whipping cream, whipped with 2 T. sugar

Mix ¼ cup of the butter with the pecans, flour and confectioners' sugar to a granular consistency. Press into the bottom of a 11 x 7 x 1½-inch pan. Bake at 350° for 20 minutes or until lightly browned; cool. Mix together cream cheese and sour cream. Spread over cooled crust. Refrigerate for 1 hour. In top of double boiler, combine sugar, cornstarch, egg yolks, milk and salt. Cook until thickened. Remove from heat. Add remaining 3 tablespoons of butter and lime juice; cool. Fold dessert topping into custard mixture. Pour over cheese layer. Cover and freeze for at least 4 hours. Before serving, remove from freezer to refrigerator for 1 to 2 hours and cover with the sweetened whipped cream.

Serves 10 to 12

apple crisp

7 medium-size tart apples (Jonathan), peeled and diced
1 cup sugar
1 cup flour
1 tsp. baking powder
¾ tsp. salt
1 egg, well beaten
⅓ cup melted butter
cinnamon

Place apples in a greased 8-inch square baking dish. In a large bowl, mix dry ingredients together with a spoon. Add beaten egg and mix well. Spread crumbly mixture over apples. Pour melted butter over top. Sprinkle with cinnamon. Bake at 375° for 45 minutes. Serve with vanilla ice cream.

Serves 6

strawberry bavarian

No need to wait for the strawberry season.

1 pkg. (10 oz.) frozen strawberries, thawed
1 pkg. (3 oz.) strawberry gelatin
1 cup boiling water
¼ cup sugar
1 cup whipping cream, whipped

Drain strawberries, reserving juice. Set aside. In a bowl, dissolve gelatin in boiling water. Add reserved strawberry juice and sugar to the dissolved gelatin. Stir well. Chill until partially thickened. Fold the whipped cream and strawberries into gelatin. Pour the mixture into a 1-quart mold or into 6 to 8 individual molds or serving dishes. Refrigerate until ready to serve.

Serves 6 to 8

peach pudding

An old-fashioned touch.

1 cup firmly packed light brown sugar
⅓ cup butter or margarine, cut into slices
1 can (15 oz.) sliced peaches, drained
1 cup sugar
2 eggs
½ cup water
1½ cups flour, sifted
2 tsp. baking powder
¼ tsp. salt
1 tsp. vanilla
1 cup whipping cream, whipped (optional)

In the bottom of a greased 9 x 13-inch pan, sprinkle brown sugar. Cover with butter. Top with peaches. In a mixing bowl, combine sugar, eggs, water, flour sifted with baking powder, salt and vanilla; mix well. Pour batter over peaches. Bake, uncovered, at 350° for 30 minutes or until done. (Pudding is done when inserted toothpick comes out clean.) Serve with whipped cream, if desired.

Serves 12

peach cobbler

2 cups sliced, fresh peaches
2 cups sugar, divided
½ cup butter
¾ cup flour
2 tsp. baking powder
pinch of salt
¾ cup milk
sweet cream

Preheat oven to 350°. Mix peaches with 1 cup of the sugar; set aside. Put butter into a 9-inch square cake pan. Place in oven to melt. In a mixing bowl, combine remaining sugar, flour, baking powder, salt and milk. Blend until smooth. Pour over melted butter; do not stir. Top with peaches; do not stir. Bake at 350° for 1 hour or until golden brown. Batter will rise to top during baking. Serve with a pitcher of sweet cream.

Serves 9

kiwi fruit with sabayon sauce

4 kiwi fruits, peeled and sliced

Sabayon Sauce:
4 egg yolks
¼ cup sugar
½ cup Marsala or dry white wine
dash of vanilla

Place sliced kiwi fruit in 4 individual dessert dishes. Set aside. In top of double boiler, place egg yolks, sugar and wine, beating until thoroughly blended. Continue beating over simmering water until the Sabayon is thick and fluffy. Be careful not to let the water touch the bottom of the pan. Add vanilla and mix. Serve either warm or chilled over kiwi fruit or fresh strawberries.

Serves 4

strawberries jubilee

Flaming and festive.

1 T. butter
2 cups sliced fresh strawberries
¼ cup sugar
6 T. kirsch
3 T. strawberry liqueur
1 pint vanilla ice cream

In a chafing dish, melt butter. Add strawberries and sugar. Simmer a few minutes. In separate saucepan, warm the kirsch and strawberry liqueur. Ignite and pour over strawberries. Spoon over ice cream in individual dishes.

Serves 4

fresh strawberries with grand marnier sauce

Light and elegant.

5 egg yolks
½ cup plus 2 T. sugar
¼ cup Grand Marnier, divided
1 cup whipping cream, whipped
3 quarts fresh strawberries, washed and hulled

Put the egg yolks and ½ cup sugar into a 2-quart glass or ceramic mixing bowl that fits snugly on top of a slightly larger saucepan. Add about 2 inches of water to the pan. Heat water to boil; remove from heat. Beat egg yolks and sugar well. Place bowl over the barely simmering water. Continue beating for 10 minutes until the mixture is thick and pale yellow. Remove bowl from saucepan. Stir in half the Grand Marnier. Cool. Refrigerate until thoroughly chilled or overnight. Beat whipping cream with the remaining 2 tablespoons of sugar until almost stiff. Fold chilled egg mixture into cream. Stir in remaining Grand Marnier. Spoon sauce over fresh strawberries or a combination of strawberries and papaya slices.

Serves 10

luchow's lingonberry pancakes

6 large eggs
1½ cups sifted flour
¼ tsp. salt
1 T. sugar
2 cups milk
½ cup butter
1 jar (15 oz.) lingonberries
confectioners' sugar
cinnamon
juice of ½ lemon
¼ cup kirsch or rum, warmed

Beat eggs until foamy. Beat in flour, salt and sugar. Gradually add milk, beating several minutes. Cover batter and let stand 30 minutes. For each pancake, melt 1 tablespoon butter in an 8-inch crepe pan. When hot, pour in about ½ cup batter swinging pan around quickly to coat bottom of pan. When lightly brown, turn and quickly brown other side. Slide onto a hot platter. Repeat. Heat lingonberries. Sprinkle each pancake with confectioners' sugar, cinnamon and lemon juice. Spread with hot lingonberries. Roll up jelly roll fashion. Sprinkle with additional sugar and cinnamon. Bring to the table. Pour over the warmed kirsch or rum and ignite. If you have plain pancakes leftover, wrap them tightly and freeze. Reheat in a double boiler or microwave oven.

Serves 8

frozen peanut butter delight

For those with a sweet tooth.

Peanut Butter Crust:
½ cup firmly packed brown sugar
¼ cup margarine
½ cup smooth peanut butter
1 cup flour

Filling:
1 pkg. (8 oz.) softened cream cheese
¼ cup peanut butter
1 tsp. vanilla
½ cup sugar
2 eggs
2 cups (4½ oz.) frozen dessert topping, thawed
1 cup (8 oz.) semi-sweet chocolate chips

For Peanut Butter Crust: In a large bowl, cream brown sugar, margarine and peanut butter. Add flour until mixture is crumbly. Sprinkle into a 9 x 13-inch pan and bake at 350° for 10 minutes, stirring occasionally. Reserve one-third of mixture for top and press remaining in bottom of pan.

For Filling: Combine first four ingredients and beat until smooth. Add eggs, one at a time. Fold in thawed dessert topping. Pour over crust. Melt chocolate chips and drizzle over filling. Marble with knife blade. Sprinkle with reserved crumbs and freeze. Will keep 1 to 2 weeks in freezer. Before serving, take out of freezer for 15 to 20 minutes.

Serves 12 to 15

grapes florentine

Light dessert after a heavy meal.

1½ lbs. seedless grapes
3 egg yolks
⅔ cup sugar
⅔ cup sherry
1 cup whipping cream, whipped

Rinse, drain and halve the grapes. Set aside. In top of double boiler, beat the egg yolks until thick and pale. Gradually beat in sugar. Stir in sherry. Cook mixture, stirring constantly, until thickened. Add grapes to mixture. Chill overnight. Before serving, fold in whipped cream. Serve in parfait glasses.

Serves 6 to 8

toblerone chocolate fondue

Especially fun for a teenage party.

2 bars (3 oz. each) Toblerone bars (chocolate with nougat)
¼ cup whipping cream
¼ cup kirsch
angel food cake pieces
apple slices
orange sections
banana slices

In top of double boiler, place chocolate, broken into pieces, cream and kirsch. Stir until chocolate is melted. Transfer to a fondue pot and place over low heat. Serve with angel food cake pieces and fruit for dipping with fondue forks.

Serves 4

snowballs

A festive holiday dessert.

½ cup softened butter or margarine
1 cup sugar
1 cup crushed pineapple, drained
1 cup chopped pecans
2 egg yolks, beaten
1 box vanilla wafers or brown edge wafers, crushed
1½-2 cups whipping cream, whipped
2-4 T. sugar
1½-3 tsp. vanilla
shredded coconut

In a large bowl, cream butter and sugar. Stir in pineapple, pecans and egg yolks. Crush the wafers. In a 9 x 13-inch pan, layer half the wafers, filling and remaining wafers. Chill in freezer for 1 hour or in refrigerator overnight. Remove and form into balls the size of a lemon. Return to freezer. Before serving, whip cream, adding the sugar and vanilla. Remove balls from freezer and spread with or roll in whipped cream mixture. Sprinkle with coconut. Can be made ahead and frozen. At holiday time, decorate each with a sprig of fresh holly.

Serves 12

caramel sauce

2 cups sugar
¼ cup butter
1 cup whipping cream
1 tsp. vanilla

Heat a heavy cast aluminum or black iron skillet over medium heat until heat penetrates through bottom of pan. Pan should be no larger than burner. When pan is hot, add sugar. Stir with wooden spoon. Cook until sugar melts to a golden-colored syrup. Do not overcook as sugar scorches easily. Remove from burner. Stir in butter. When butter has melted, add cream a little at a time, stirring constantly. Stir in vanilla. Cool. Store in a covered glass container and refrigerate. Will keep in refrigerator for several weeks.

Makes 1½ cups sauce

plum sundae

This sauce also is delicious served on pancakes.

1 lb. well-ripened plums, sliced
1 T. cornstarch
¾ cup sugar
1 T. lemon juice
dash of salt
dash of cinnamon
vanilla ice cream

Combine all ingredients, except ice cream, in a saucepan and bring to a boil. Simmer 8 to 10 minutes. Cool. After sauce has cooled, layer with vanilla ice cream in parfait glasses. Freeze. Remove from freezer 10 to 15 minutes before serving.

Makes 1 pint sauce

hot fudge sauce

1 cup sugar
2 T. cocoa
2 T. butter or margarine
1 small can (6 oz.) evaporated milk
½ tsp. vanilla

In a saucepan, combine sugar and cocoa. Stir over low heat until warm. Add butter and blend. Add milk and bring to boil. Continue boiling until sauce has thickened to a pudding consistency. Cool and add vanilla. Can be refrigerated for several days.

Makes 1 to 1½ cups

cakes

"The plainest room may be made beautiful by taste,
and the homeliest fare appetizing by neatness and skill.
Little attentions to the decoration or pretty arrangement of the table
charm the eye and whet the appetite,
and make the home table powerfully attractive."

PHOTOGRAPHIC ARCHIVES, UNIVERSITY OF LOUISVILLE

applesauce cake with warm rum sauce

2 cups sifted flour
1 tsp. baking powder
½ tsp. baking soda
½ tsp. salt
½ tsp. ground cloves
1 tsp. cinnamon
½ cup butter or margarine
1½ cups sugar
2 eggs, beaten
1 cup applesauce
½-1 cup chopped pecans
½ cup raisins (optional)

Warm Rum Sauce:
1 cup half-and-half cream
1 cup sugar
¼ cup butter
1 T. rum or 1 tsp. vanilla

Sift together the first 6 ingredients. In a separate bowl, cream butter or margarine and sugar. Add eggs and beat well. Add applesauce and sifted dry ingredients. Beat well. Add pecans and raisins, if desired. Pour into a greased bundt pan and bake at 350° for 50 to 60 minutes. Cool for several minutes in pan before removing to rack or serving plate.

For Warm Rum Sauce: Combine all ingredients in a small saucepan. Boil slowly until thickened. Pour hot sauce over cake slices. Serve immediately.

Serves 10 to 12

orange custard angel cake

Custard:
1 envelope unflavored gelatin
¾ cup orange juice
2 cups milk
¼ cup flour
1 cup sugar
3 egg yolks, slightly beaten
1 tsp. grated orange peel
½ tsp. salt
3 egg whites
3 T. sugar

Cake:
1 angel food cake
1 cup whipping cream, whipped
½ tsp. orange flavoring
sugar to taste

For Custard: Soak gelatin in orange juice. Set aside. In top of double boiler, combine milk, flour, sugar, egg yolks, orange peel and salt. Cook until thickened, stirring constantly. Add gelatin mixture to hot custard, stirring until gelatin is dissolved. Cool. Beat egg whites until stiff. Add sugar; fold into custard.

For Cake: Trim brown crust, if any, from cake. Tear cake into bite-size pieces. Place half the cake pieces into bottom of a 9-inch springform pan. Cover with half the custard. Repeat the layers. Refrigerate overnight. Whip cream; add orange flavoring and sugar to taste. Remove cake from pan. Frost with whipped cream at least one hour before serving. Refrigerate.

Serves 10 to 12

pineapple cake

Cake:
2 cups sugar
2 cups flour
2 tsp. baking soda
2 eggs, beaten
1 can (20 oz.) crushed pineapple with juice

Cream Cheese Frosting:
1 pkg. (8 oz.) cream cheese
¼ cup margarine
1 cup confectioners' sugar
1 tsp. vanilla

For Cake: In a large bowl, sift together dry ingredients. Stir in eggs and pineapple. Blend well. Pour into an *ungreased* 9 x 13-inch pan. Bake at 350° for 35 minutes.

For Cream Cheese Frosting: Combine ingredients. Beat until smooth and creamy. Frost the cake while still warm.

Serves 15

carrot-pineapple cake with creamy frosting

Cake:
3 eggs
1¼ cups vegetable oil
1 can (8 oz.) crushed pineapple, undrained
1 cup chopped nuts
2 cups grated carrots
1½ tsp. vanilla
2 cups sugar
2 cups flour
2 tsp. baking powder
2 tsp. baking soda
2 tsp. cinnamon
1 tsp. salt

Creamy Frosting:
3 T. flour
1 cup milk
½ cup butter
½ cup margarine
1 cup sugar
2 tsp. vanilla

For Cake: Beat eggs until fluffy. Add vegetable oil, pineapple, nuts, carrots and vanilla. Blend well. Sift together dry ingredients. Gradually add to above mixture, mixing thoroughly. Grease and lightly flour a 10-inch bundt pan. Pour in the batter and bake at 325° for 1 hour. Cool.

For Creamy Frosting: In a saucepan, combine the flour and milk. Heat until thick and bubbly, stirring constantly; set aside to cool. In a mixing bowl, cream together the butter, margarine, sugar and vanilla. Gradually add the flour and milk mixture; blend thoroughly. Frost the cake when completely cooled.

Serves 10 to 15

fresh apple cake with caramel frosting

Cake:
4½ cups peeled and chopped raw apples
lemon juice
1½ cups vegetable oil
2 cups sugar
2 eggs, beaten
2½ cups sifted flour
1 tsp. salt
1 tsp. baking soda
2 tsp. baking powder
2 tsp. vanilla
1½ cups chopped pecans

Caramel Frosting:
½ cup butter
⅛ tsp. salt
2 T. milk
1 cup firmly packed brown sugar
¾-1 cup confectioners' sugar

For Cake: Sprinkle apples with lemon juice. Cover and set aside. In a large bowl, combine oil, sugar and eggs. Mix until smooth and creamy. In a separate bowl, sift together dry ingredients. Gradually add to creamed mixture. Add vanilla. The batter will be stiff at this point. Fold in apples and nuts with a wooden spoon. Grease and lightly flour a 9 x 13-inch pan. Pour in batter and bake at 350° for 50 to 55 minutes. Cool.

For Caramel Frosting: In a heavy saucepan, combine butter, salt, milk and brown sugar. Heat and stir until smooth. Remove from heat. Add confectioners' sugar to desired spreading consistency.

Serves 12 to 14

bundt pound cake

For variation, substitute a change of flavoring.

Cake:
1 cup vegetable shortening
2 cups sugar
4 tsp. vanilla
4 eggs, separated
3½ cups sifted cake flour
2½ tsp. baking powder
¾ tsp. salt
1 cup milk

Glaze:
1⅓ cups sifted confectioners' sugar
2 T. milk
¼ tsp. vanilla
dash salt

For Cake: In a large bowl, cream vegetable shortening with the sugar and vanilla. Blend in egg yolks, one at a time. Combine thoroughly. In a separate mixing bowl, sift together the flour, baking powder and salt. Add the milk and dry ingredients alternately to the above mixture, blending well. Beat egg whites until stiff and gently fold into batter. Pour the batter into a greased and lightly floured bundt or tube pan. Bake at 350° for 1 hour. Cool ten minutes. Turn out of pan and glaze.

For Glaze: Mix ingredients until well blended. Drizzle over cake.

Variation: Substitute lemon, orange, rum or almond extract for the vanilla for a change of flavor.

Serves 15 to 20

tiny cheesecakes

Filling:
3 eggs, separated
2 pkgs. (8 oz. each) softened cream cheese
¾ cup sugar
½ cup graham cracker crumbs mixed with 2 T. sugar

Topping:
¾ cup sour cream
2 T. sugar
½ tsp. vanilla

For Filling: Beat egg whites until stiff. Set aside. In a separate bowl, combine the cream cheese, egg yolks and sugar. Beat until light and fluffy. Fold in egg whites. Generously butter mini-muffin tins (approximately 1½-inches in diameter). Coat tins well with graham cracker crumb mixture. Fill with cream cheese mixture. Bake at 350° for 15 to 20 minutes. Remove from oven to cool. A small depression will occur on the top. For Topping: In a small bowl, combine the sour cream, sugar and vanilla. Place ½ teaspoon of this mixture in the depression of each mini-cake. Bake again at 400° for 5 minutes. Remove from pans while still warm.

Makes 3 dozen

rhubarb cheesecake

2 cups sugar, divided
3 cups diced rhubarb
2 T. cornstarch
2 eggs
1 T. flour
1 pkg. (8 oz.) softened cream cheese
⅔ cup whipping cream or half-and-half cream
1 T. lemon juice
½ tsp. grated lemon peel
1 unbaked 9-inch pie shell

In a saucepan, combine 1½ cups of the sugar, rhubarb and cornstarch. Cook over medium heat until mixture boils and thickens. Pour fruit mixture into a pastry shell and bake for 10 minutes at 325°. In a small bowl, beat eggs thoroughly. Stir in remaining ½ cup of sugar and flour. Set aside. In a large mixing bowl, blend cream cheese and whipping cream until smooth. Add the lemon juice and lemon peel. Add egg mixture to cream cheese mixture. Blend well. Pour over the rhubarb in pastry shell. Bake at 325° for 30 minutes. Cool and chill.

Serves 6 to 8

grandmother's graham cracker cake

A delicious and moist cake that has been a favorite for three generations.

Cake:
2 cups finely crushed graham cracker crumbs
1 cup cake flour (do not sift before measuring)
2 heaping tsp. baking powder
1 cup butter
1 cup firmly packed dark brown sugar
2 eggs
1 cup milk
1-2 bananas, sliced

Vanilla Cream Frosting:
⅓ cup softened butter
1 tsp. vanilla
1 lb. confectioners' sugar
¼ tsp. salt
3-4 T. milk

For Cake: Sift crumbs with cake flour and baking powder. Set aside. In a large bowl, cream butter and sugar until fluffy. Stir in eggs. Add the milk and dry ingredients alternately to the creamed mixture. Blend thoroughly. Pour into two wax paper-lined 8 or 9-inch round layer cake pans. Line bottom of pan only. Bake at 350° for 22 to 25 minutes. Cool

For Vanilla Cream Frosting: Combine butter and vanilla. Gradually add sugar and salt. Stir in milk, beating until mixture is smooth and of spreading consistency. Frost bottom layer. Cover with banana slices. Top with second cake layer. Frost sides and top of cake. Store cake in a covered container to keep moist. The cake becomes better and more moist daily.

Serves 10

amish oatmeal cake

1 cup rolled oats
1¼ cups boiling water
½ cup softened margarine
1 cup sugar
1 cup firmly packed brown sugar
1 tsp. vanilla
2 eggs, beaten
1½ cups sifted flour
1 tsp. baking soda
½ tsp. salt
2 tsp. cinnamon
whipped cream

In a saucepan, pour boiling water over oats. Cover and let stand 20 minutes. In a large bowl, cream together margarine, sugars, vanilla and eggs. Add oats and mix well. Sift together remaining dry ingredients and add to the above mixture. Grease and lightly flour an 8 x 12-inch pan. Pour in batter and bake at 350° for 50 minutes. Cool and cut into squares. Top with whipped cream.

Serves 12

old-fashioned gingerbread with hot lemon sauce

Find a good hiding place! It will disappear like magic!

Cake:
½ cup molasses
½ cup sugar
1½ cups sifted flour
1 tsp. ginger
1 tsp. baking soda
1 egg, slightly beaten
½ cup butter
½ cup boiling water

Hot Lemon Sauce:
½ cup sugar
1 T. cornstarch
1 cup boiling water
3 T. butter
juice and grated rind of 1 lemon

For Cake: Place molasses and sugar in a large bowl. Sift dry ingredients together. Add to molasses mixture. Stir in egg. In a small bowl, stir butter and boiling water together until butter is melted. Add to other ingredients. Mix thoroughly by hand. Turn into a buttered 9-inch square baking pan. Bake at 350° for 30 minutes or until toothpick comes out clean. Cool. Cut into squares. Serve with Hot Lemon Sauce.

For Hot Lemon Sauce: Combine sugar and cornstarch in a saucepan. Add boiling water and cook over hot water or very low heat, stirring constantly, until mixture is fairly thick and clear—about 10 minutes. Remove from heat. Stir in the butter, lemon juice and rind. Pour over cake and serve immediately.

Serves 8

fudge cupcakes

Moist and perfectly delicious without frosting.

4 squares semi-sweet chocolate
1 cup butter or margarine
1 cup flour
1¾ cups sugar
4 eggs, beaten
1 tsp. vanilla
1½ cups chopped nuts

In top of a double boiler, melt chocolate and butter or margarine. Pour into a large mixing bowl. Add flour, sugar, eggs, vanilla and chopped nuts. Blend well, but do not beat. Pour batter into well-greased cupcake tins. Fill almost to the top. Bake at 350° for 35 minutes. Sprinkle with confectioners' sugar, if desired.

Makes 18 large cupcakes

dutch chocolate cake

1 cup softened butter
1½ cups sugar
2 eggs
2 T. water
2½ cups sifted flour
1 tsp. salt
¼ cup Dutch cocoa
1 cup buttermilk
1 tsp. vanilla
1 tsp. vinegar
1 tsp. baking soda

Dutch Chocolate Frosting:
¼ cup softened butter
3 cups confectioners' sugar, divided
1 egg yolk
3 T. Dutch cocoa
3-4 T. milk or cream
1 tsp. vanilla

Cream butter and sugar together in a large mixing bowl. Add eggs and water; beat well. Sift flour, salt and cocoa together. Add to the creamed mixture alternately with buttermilk and vanilla. Combine the vinegar and soda; fold into batter. Bake in three 9-inch round cake pans which have been greased and floured. Bake 25 to 30 minutes at 350°. Cool and frost.

For Dutch Chocolate Frosting: In a small mixing bowl, cream butter and 1 cup of the sugar until well mixed. Add egg yolk. Combine cocoa with remaining sugar. Add to creamed mixture alternately with milk or cream to desired spreading consistency. Stir in vanilla. Frost tops and sides of cake.

Serves 10 to 12

mocha cake

Cake:
2 T. sifted flour
2½ tsp. baking powder
4 eggs
¾ cup sugar
1 cup hazelnuts, black walnuts or walnuts

Mocha Whipped Cream Frosting:
½ cup sugar
⅓ cup cocoa
1 T. powdered instant coffee
¼ tsp. salt
1½ cups whipping cream
2 tsp. vanilla

For Cake: Prepare two 8-inch round pans. Grease and line with wax paper. Then grease the wax paper. Sift flour and baking powder together; set aside. In a blender, mix eggs and sugar. Add nuts, blending until fine. Add flour and mix thoroughly. Pour batter into pans. Bake at 350° for 20 minutes. Remove from pans; cool.

For Mocha Whipped Cream Frosting: Mix together sugar, cocoa, coffee and salt. Set aside. Whip the cream with vanilla until stiff. Fold in dry ingredients. Frost. Refrigerate until serving time.

Serves 8 to 10

pumpkin and spice roll

Perfect for a coffee or bridge club.

Cake:
3 eggs
1 cup sugar
⅔ cup canned pumpkin
1 tsp. lemon juice
¾ cup sifted flour
2 tsp. cinnamon
1 tsp. baking soda
1 tsp. ginger
½ tsp. nutmeg
½ tsp. salt
1 cup finely chopped walnuts
½ cup confectioners' sugar

Filling:
1 cup confectioners' sugar
2 pkgs. (3 oz. each) softened cream cheese
¼ cup softened butter
½ tsp. vanilla

For Cake: In a large bowl, beat eggs for 5 minutes at high speed. Gradually add sugar, mixing well. Stir in pumpkin and lemon juice. In a separate bowl, combine flour, cinnamon, baking soda, ginger, nutmeg and salt. Fold into the pumpkin mixture. Grease and lightly flour a 15 x 10 x 1-inch jelly roll pan. Spread mixture into pan and top with walnuts. Bake at 375° for 15 minutes. Turn cake onto a terry cloth towel that has been sprinkled with confectioners' sugar. Roll the towel and cake together. Cool.

For Filling: Combine all the ingredients and blend until smooth. Unroll cake; spread with filling. Roll up and chill well. Slice and serve. May be frozen.

Serves 16

cheese ripple fudge cake

Cake and Filling:
1 pkg. fudge cake mix
1½ cups water
½ cup sour cream
4 eggs, divided
1 pkg. (8 oz.) softened cream cheese
⅓ cup sugar

Fudge Frosting:
1 pkg. fudge frosting mix
1 pkg. (3 oz.) softened cream cheese
¼ cup softened butter
⅓ cup lukewarm water
1 pkg. (6 oz.) slivered almonds for garnish

For Cake and Filling: In a large bowl, mix together the fudge cake mix, water, sour cream and 2 eggs. Pour ⅔ of this batter into a greased and lightly floured 9 x 13-inch pan. Set aside. Mix together cream cheese, 2 eggs and sugar. Whip until smooth. Spoon evenly over the batter. Pour remaining batter over filling. Bake at 350° for 35 to 45 minutes. Test for doneness. Cool completely.

For Fudge Frosting: Combine fudge frosting mix, cream cheese, butter and water. Blend thoroughly. Frost cake and garnish with slivered almonds.

Serves 12

pies

"In all well-regulated families, the dinner is a formal repast,
even if there are but two persons present.
It should be the time for family visiting, for cheerful conversation,
and never less than an hour should be spent at the table.
It is the family reunion and all business, care and worry should be laid aside,
and only sunshine flood the room."

LIBRARY OF CONGRESS

chocolate angel strata pie

2 eggs, separated
½ tsp. vinegar
¼ tsp. salt
2 dashes cinnamon
¾ cup sugar, divided
¼ cup water
1 pkg. (6 oz.) semi-sweet chocolate pieces, melted
1 cup whipping cream, whipped
1 baked 9-inch pie shell

In a mixing bowl, beat egg whites with vinegar, salt and 1 dash of cinnamon. Gradually add ½ cup of the sugar beating until the meringue stands in stiff glossy peaks. Spread on bottom and sides of pie shell. Bake at 325° for 15 to 18 minutes until lightly browned. Cool. Beat the egg yolks slightly. Combine with the water and melted chocolate. Spread 3 tablespoons of the chocolate mixture over the meringue; chill the remainder. Combine the remaining ¼ cup sugar, dash of cinnamon and whipping cream. Beat until thick. Spread half of the whipped cream over the chocolate in pie shell. Combine the remaining whipped cream with the remaining chocolate mixture. Spread as the top layer of pie. Chill 4 hours.

Serves 6 to 8

chocolate almond pie

Yummmm!

Crust:
1¼ cups (scant) chocolate wafer crumbs
¼ cup butter, melted

Filling:
1 cup cream
1 cup milk
1 pkg. (4½ oz.) instant dark-chocolate pudding mix
⅓ cup chopped slivered almonds, toasted
1 cup whipping cream, whipped
2 tsp. kahlua

For Crust: Combine wafer crumbs and butter. Press firmly into an 8-inch pie pan. Refrigerate at least 15 minutes.

For Filling: In small, deep mixing bowl, beat cream and milk with pudding mix at low speed for 2 minutes. Fold in almonds. Pour into prepared pie shell. Chill until firm, about 1 hour. Garnish with whipped cream flavored with kahlua.

Serves 6 to 8

black bottom pie

Simply superb!

2 tsp. unflavored gelatin
3 T. cold water
½ cup sugar
2 T. cornstarch
½ tsp. salt
2 cups milk
2 egg yolks, slightly beaten
1 square (1 oz.) melted unsweetened chocolate
2 tsp. pure rum flavoring or 1 tsp. imitation rum flavoring
2 egg whites
¼ tsp. cream of tartar
⅓ cup sugar
whipped cream
chocolate curls
1 baked 9-inch pie shell

Soften gelatin in water. Place sugar, cornstarch and salt into a 2-quart saucepan and slowly stir in milk. Boil 1 minute, stirring constantly, over medium heat. Remove pan from heat. Stir half of the hot mixture into egg yolks. Return to hot mixture in saucepan and blend. Boil 1 minute, stirring constantly. Remove from heat. Pour 1 cup of mixture into bowl; add the melted chocolate. Blend well and pour into shell. Stir softened gelatin into mixture remaining in saucepan. Place pan in cold water. When custard cools and mounds slightly, blend in flavoring. Meanwhile, beat egg whites and cream of tartar until soft peaks form. Gradually add sugar, beating until stiff. Fold reserved, cooled custard into egg whites. Spread over chocolate layer. Chill until firm. Top with whipped cream and chocolate curls.

Serves 8

"blizzard blues" ice cream pie

A perfect cheer-up when you're snowed-in!

Crust:
1½ cups graham cracker crumbs
3 T. sugar
⅓ cup melted butter

Filling:
1 (8 oz.) chocolate bar with almonds
½ cup strong brewed coffee
1½ quarts coffee ice cream
½ cup chopped toasted almonds
chocolate curls or grated chocolate, for garnish

For Crust: In a medium bowl, combine crumbs and sugar. Stir in butter and blend thoroughly. Press into the sides and bottom of a 9-inch pie plate. Bake at 350° for 8 minutes. Cool.

For Filling: Melt chocolate with coffee in top of double boiler over simmering water. Pour into pie shell. Place in freezer until completely chilled. Turn ice cream into large bowl of electric mixer. Allow to soften just slightly. Add almonds. Beat until smooth but not melted. Spoon over chilled chocolate layer in pie shell. Garnish top with chocolate curls or grated chocolate. Freeze several hours. Remove from freezer about 15 minutes before serving time. Cut and serve.

Variation: If coffee ice cream is not available, stir powdered coffee, to taste, into vanilla ice cream.

Serves 6

frozen mocha mousse pie

Crust:
4 egg whites, at room temperature
⅔ cup sugar
1 cup finely ground hazelnuts or walnuts

Mocha Mousse Filling:
½ cup chocolate chips
1 T. instant coffee
⅔ cup sweetened condensed milk
¼ cup light corn syrup
1 tsp. vanilla
1 cup whipping cream, whipped

For Crust: Beat egg whites until frothy. Gradually add sugar, 1 tablespoon at a time, beating at high speed. Continue beating until stiff. Gently fold in ground nuts by hand. Turn into a buttered and floured 9-inch pie pan. Spread evenly over bottom and up the sides. Bake at 275° for 1 hour. Leave in a turned-off oven for 2 hours. Chill well before filling.

For Mocha Mousse Filling: In top of double boiler, place chocolate chips, coffee, condensed milk and corn syrup. Stir until chocolate is melted. Add vanilla. Cool and chill in refrigerator. Fold in whipped cream. Turn into pie shell and freeze.

Serves 6 to 8

coffee sundae pie

Incredibly delicious!

22-25 chocolate wafer cookies (1½ cups when crushed)
6 T. melted butter
1 quart coffee ice cream
1 pkg. (6 oz.) semi-sweet chocolate chips
1 can (6 oz.) evaporated milk

Crush cookies. Mix with melted butter and press into bottom and sides of a 10-inch pie pan. Refrigerate until firm. Soften ice cream slightly. Turn into pie shell and freeze until firm. Melt chocolate chips over hot water. Slowly add milk, stirring constantly. Simmer a few minutes; let cool. When ice cream is firm, spread chocolate over ice cream and return to freezer.

Serves 8 to 10

pie au liqueur

Add a favorite after-dinner liqueur for a perfect pie when guests come for dinner.

Crust:
18 chocolate wafer cookies, crushed
3 T. melted butter

Filling:
28 large marshmallows
½ cup milk
liqueur (see below for variations)
1 cup whipping cream, whipped
whipped cream (optional)
shaved chocolate (optional)

For Crust: Mix cookie crumbs with butter and press into a 9-inch pie pan. Chill.

For Filling: In top of double boiler, melt marshmallows with milk. Cool. Add liqueur and mix well. Chill. Fold in whipped cream. Pour into pie shell and freeze. If desired, garnish with whipped cream or shaved chocolate.

Variations: For Grasshopper Pie, add 3 tablespoons each green creme de menthe and white creme de cacao. For Kahlua Pie, add 6 tablespoons kahlua. For Brandy Alexander Pie, add 3 tablespoons each brandy and white creme de cacao. For Stinger Pie, add 4 tablespoons brandy and 1 tablespoon white creme de cacao.

Serves 6 to 8

rum cream pie

Crumb Crust:
2¼ cups crushed graham crackers
½ cup melted butter
2 T. sugar
½ tsp. cinnamon

Filling:
1 pkg. unflavored gelatin
½ cup cold water
5 egg yolks
1 cup sugar
⅓ cup rum
1½ cups whipping cream, whipped
unsweetened chocolate, grated

For Crumb Crust: Combine all ingredients in a medium bowl. Press into bottom and sides of 2 9-inch pie plates. Chill.

For Filling: In a saucepan, soften gelatin in water. Place over low heat until dissolved. In a separate bowl, beat egg yolks and sugar until light. Stir gelatin into egg mixture. Cool 5 minutes. Gradually add rum, beating constantly. Cool and chill. Fold whipped cream into gelatin mixture. Cool until partially thickened. Spoon into crusts and chill. Top with grated chocolate.

Serves 12 to 16

ice box pie

A light and airy dessert.

1 T. unflavored gelatin
1 cup milk
4 egg yolks, beaten
1 cup sugar
1 tsp. vanilla
pinch of salt
4 egg whites
2 cups whipping cream, whipped
2 10-inch graham cracker pie crusts

Soften gelatin in milk. Combine egg yolks, sugar, vanilla, salt and gelatin-milk mixture in top of double boiler. Cook over boiling water until partially thickened. Cool. Beat egg whites until fluffy. Fold into cooled mixture. Fold in whipped cream. Pour into pie shells. Sprinkle with additional graham cracker crumbs. Refrigerate a minimum of three hours.

Variation: Add lemon or lime juice and rind for flavoring.

Serves 12

island coconut cream pie

1 T. plus 1½ tsp. unflavored gelatin
¼ cup cold water
2 cups scalded milk
3 egg yolks, beaten
⅔ cup plus 3 T. sugar
⅛ tsp. salt
½ tsp. vanilla
1½ cups grated coconut, divided
3 egg whites
½ cup whipping cream, whipped
1 baked 9-inch pie shell

Sprinkle gelatin in water; let stand for 5 minutes. Scald milk in top of double boiler. Combine egg yolks, ⅔ cup of the sugar, and salt; beat well. Stir small amount of scalded milk into egg mixture. Gradually stir this mixture into remaining milk. Cook until mixture coats spoon. Do not boil. Remove from heat; add softened gelatin. Stir until dissolved. Cool. When cool, add vanilla and 1¼ cups of the coconut. Chill until mixture begins to thicken. Beat egg whites until stiff. Gradually add remaining 3 tablespoons sugar. Fold into thickened gelatin mixture. Chill until firm, 3 to 4 hours. When firm, spread with whipped cream. Sprinkle top with remaining coconut.

Serves 6 to 8

lemon-sour cream pie

The best!

1 cup sugar
3 T. cornstarch
dash salt
1 cup milk
3 eggs, separated
4 T. softened butter
1 tsp. grated lemon peel
¼ cup lemon juice
1 cup sour cream
¼ tsp. cream of tartar
½ tsp. vanilla
6 T. sugar
1 baked 9-inch pie shell

In a saucepan, combine sugar, cornstarch and salt. Stir in milk. Bring to boil and cook until thick. Blend small amount of hot mixture into slightly beaten egg yolks. Return to hot mixture. Add butter, lemon peel and juice. Stir to melt butter. Cover and cool. Fold in sour cream. Spoon into pie shell. Beat egg whites, cream of tartar and vanilla until soft peaks form. Gradually add sugar, beating until stiff. Spread on top of pie, sealing edges. Bake at 350° for 12 to 15 minutes or until golden. Cool before serving.

Serves 8

sunny silver pie

Especially good after a fish or ham dinner.

1 pkg. unflavored gelatin
¼ cup cold water
6 eggs, separated
2 cups sugar, divided
juice of 2 lemons (6 T.) and grated peel
sweetened whipped cream
2 baked 9-inch pie shells

Dissolve gelatin in water. Set aside. In top of double boiler, combine egg yolks, 1½ cups of the sugar, lemon juice and peel. Heat over boiling water until light yellow, thick and fluffy. Remove from heat. Stir in gelatin while hot. In a large bowl, beat egg whites until stiff. Beat in remaining ½ cup sugar until well mixed. Add a small amount of the beaten egg whites to egg yolk mixture, stirring to lighten. Fold egg yolk mixture into remaining beaten egg whites. Pour into pie shells. Refrigerate several hours. Garnish with sweetened whipped cream.

Serves 12

crumb-topped apple pie en papillote

6 large tart cooking apples, peeled and sliced
½ cup sugar
2 tsp. flour
1 tsp. lemon juice
dash of cinnamon
1 unbaked 10-inch pie shell

Topping:
½ cup sugar
½ cup flour
½ cup margarine

In a large mixing bowl, combine apples, sugar, flour, lemon juice and cinnamon. Mix until apples are well coated. Place mixture in pie shell. Combine and mix ingredients for Topping until it resembles coarse crumbs. Put mixture on top of apples. Place in a brown paper bag. Tuck ends of bag under pie. Bake at 425° for 50 minutes. Take out of bag and brown for another 5 minutes. Serve with ice cream or slices of Cheddar cheese.

Note: Be sure to preheat oven. The bag will not burn, though it may smell hot.

Serves 6 to 8

glazed fresh fruit pie

6 cups fresh fruit (see below)
1 cup sugar
3 T. cornstarch
½ cup fruit juice (see below)
2 T. lemon juice (omit if using strawberries or raspberries)
food color (see below)
whipped cream for garnish
1 baked 9-inch pie shell

Mash enough fruit to measure 1 cup. Blend sugar and cornstarch in saucepan. Stir in fruit juice and mashed fruit. Cook over medium heat, stirring constantly until mixture thickens, about 8 minutes. Boil and stir 1 minute. Remove from heat. Stir in lemon juice and food color. Cool. Pour half of mixture into pie shell; spread over bottom and up sides completely covering shell. Fill with remaining fruit. Pour remaining glaze over top, completely covering fruit. Refrigerate at least 3 hours before serving. Garnish with whipped cream before serving.

Note: Sliced peaches, nectarines, Bartlett pears, whole strawberries, raspberries, blueberries or grapes can be used. Use pear nectar with pears, orange juice with peaches, nectarines, strawberries, raspberries or blueberries and white grape juice with grapes. Do not use food color with peaches, nectarines, blueberries or pears. Use 1 or 2 drops of red food color with strawberries or raspberries. Use 4 drops of yellow food color with grapes.

Serves 6 to 8

peach custard pie

⅔ cup sugar
¼ cup melted butter
2 T. flour
1 egg
¼ tsp. almond extract
5 cups peeled, sliced, fresh peaches
1 unbaked 9-inch pie shell

Sour Cream Topping: (optional)
1 cup sour cream
2 tsp. brown sugar
½ tsp. nutmeg
1 tsp. cinnamon

In a mixing bowl, mix together sugar, butter, flour, egg and almond extract. Place sliced peaches in pie shell. Pour egg mixture over top. Bake at 350° for 60 to 70 minutes or until peaches are tender.

For Sour Cream Topping: Combine ingredients. Pour over pie while still warm. Serve immediately or refrigerate until serving time.

Serves 6

peach parfait pie

Cool and delightful when fresh peaches are in season!

Crust:
1 cup quick rolled oats
½ cup sliced almonds
½ cup firmly packed brown sugar
⅓ cup melted butter

Filling:
1 cup boiling water
1 pkg. (3 oz.) orange gelatin
1 pint softened peach ice cream
2½ cups fresh, sliced peaches

For Crust: In a 9-inch glass pie dish, place the oats and toast in a 350° oven for 7 minutes. Add almonds and toast for 7 more minutes. Combine all the ingredients for the crust and press into bottom and sides of pie pan, reserving ½ cup. Chill.

For Filling: In large bowl, pour hot water over gelatin. Stir until dissolved. Add softened ice cream. Stir until melted and smooth. Place in refrigerator until thickened but not set. Fold in prepared peaches. Pile and mound filling into crust. Sprinkle reserved crumbs on outer edge of pie.

Serves 6 to 8

fresh pear pie

Tantalizing taste!

⅔ cups sugar
3 T. flour
½ tsp. nutmeg
¾ tsp. cinnamon
⅛ tsp. salt
6-7 cups fresh pears, peeled and sliced (not overripe)
1 T. butter or margarine
1 unbaked 9-inch pie shell and top

Combine sugar, flour, nutmeg, cinnamon and salt. Mix gently with pears. Place mixture into pie shell. Dot with butter. Put top pie crust on, seal edges and cut slits in top to allow steam to escape. Bake at 425° about 45 minutes.

Serves 8

sour cream rhubarb pie with crumb topping

1½ cups sugar
2 T. flour
¼ tsp. salt
1 cup sour cream
1 egg
1½ tsp. vanilla
3½ cups diced rhubarb
1 unbaked 9-inch pie shell

Crumb Topping:
⅓ cup flour
⅓ cup sugar
¼ cup butter

In a large mixing bowl, combine sugar, flour and salt. Beat in sour cream, egg and vanilla until smooth. Stir in rhubarb. Pour mixture into pie shell. Bake at 425° for 15 minutes. Reduce temperature to 350° and bake 30 minutes longer. Remove from oven. Sprinkle top with Crumb Topping. Increase temperature to 400° and bake for 10 minutes.

For Crumb Topping: Blend ingredients and set aside.

Serves 6 to 8

pineapple-sour cream pie

Tropical treat.

1 pkg. (3¾ oz.) instant vanilla pudding and pie filling
1 can (8 oz.) crushed pineapple, undrained
2 cups sour cream
1 T. sugar
whipped cream
fresh pineapple or cherries for garnish
1 9-inch graham cracker crust

Combine pie filling, undrained pineapple, sour cream and sugar. Beat slowly at lowest speed for 1 minute. Pour into pie shell. Chill for at least three hours. Garnish with whipped cream and fresh pineapple or cherries.

Serves 6 to 8

creamy pumpkin-praline pie

¼ cup butter
½ cup sugar
1 cup chopped pecans
1 pkg. (3¾ oz.) instant vanilla pudding mix
½ cup brown sugar
1 cup canned pumpkin
⅔ cup milk
¼ tsp. each: nutmeg, ginger, cinnamon
1 cup prepared whipped topping mix
1 cup whipping cream, whipped
1 baked 9-inch pie shell, cooled

In a saucepan, melt butter. Add sugar and chopped pecans. Cook over medium heat until golden brown, stirring constantly. Cool and crumble. Place half the praline mixture in shell. Beat together the pudding mix, brown sugar, canned pumpkin, milk and spices. Blend well. Fold in prepared whipped topping mix. Pour into pie shell. Refrigerate several hours. Spread whipped cream on top of pie and garnish with remaining nut mixture. Keeps in refrigerator for at least 2 days. Can also be made with graham cracker crust.

Serves 8

southern-style rhubarb pie

3½ cups rhubarb
1½ cups sugar
2 eggs, slightly beaten
3 T. flour
1 tsp. vanilla
1 unbaked 9-inch pie shell and top

Place rhubarb in pie shell. In a large bowl, mix sugar, eggs, flour and vanilla. Pour mixture over rhubarb and cover with top crust. Pinch edges to seal. Cut slits in top to allow steam to escape. Bake at 425° for 45 minutes.

Serves 6 to 8

grandmother's mincemeat

A holiday tradition after roast goose dinner.

4 lbs. lean boiling beef
1 lb. chopped suet
8 lbs. tart apples, peeled, cored and chopped
3 lbs. seedless raisins
2 lbs. currants
1 lb. brown sugar
2 quarts cider
1 T. each: salt, pepper, nutmeg, allspice, cinnamon, ground cloves
2 cups sweet pickle juice
brandy to taste (optional)

Grind the meat or have the butcher do it for you. Place in a large kettle with remaining ingredients except optional brandy. Cook together slowly for 2 or 3 hours, covered. Add brandy, if desired, and pour into 12 1-quart sterilized jars. Seal and process for canning. In preparing mincemeat pie, use 2 to 2½ cups mincemeat for a 9-inch pie.

Makes enough for 24 pies or 12 quarts

mrs. adams' special pie crust

A single, no-roll flaky crust.

1½ cups flour
1 tsp. sugar
½ tsp. salt
½ cup oil
2 T. milk

In a large bowl, sift together flour, sugar and salt. In a separate small bowl, mix oil and milk together; add to flour. Mix well. Press or pat into a 9-inch pie pan. An all-purpose crust that freezes well.

Makes 1 crust

sour cream pastry

2 cups flour
1 T. sugar
1 tsp. salt
½ cup shortening
1 egg yolk
1 cup sour cream

In a large bowl, sift flour, sugar and salt together. Cut in shortening. Add egg yolk and sour cream. Mix until dough is smooth. Cover bowl and chill 2 hours or until firm enough to roll out on a floured board.

Makes 2 9-inch pie crusts

cookies, candies and condiments

"What a rare gift is that of manners.
Better for one to possess them than wealth, beauty or talent;
they will more than supply all."

bev's creamy chocolate wafers

Wickedly rich and delicious!

Brownie Layer:
4 oz. unsweetened chocolate
1 cup butter
4 eggs
2 cups sugar
1 cup flour

Vanilla Buttercream Layer:
½ cup softened butter
4 cups confectioners' sugar
¼ cup cream
1 tsp. vanilla

Chocolate Glaze:
4 oz. semi-sweet chocolate
4 T. butter

For Brownie Layer: Melt chocolate and butter in top of double boiler. Cool slightly. In a separate bowl, beat eggs until light and lemon-colored. Gradually add sugar to egg mixture. Add butter and chocolate; stir in flour. Pour into a greased and floured 15½ x 10½-inch jelly roll pan. Bake at 350° for 15 to 20 minutes or until toothpick poked in the center comes out clean. Cool and chill in refrigerator.

For Vanilla Buttercream Layer: Cream butter thoroughly with electric mixer. Gradually add confectioners' sugar alternately with cream. Add vanilla and beat until very light and fluffy. Spread evenly over cooled Brownie Layer. Chill in refrigerator at least 10 minutes.

For Chocolate Glaze: Melt chocolate and butter together in top of double boiler. Beat well. Drizzle over the chilled buttercream in a lacy pattern. Chill one hour or longer. Cut into squares and serve.

Makes 2 dozen

spicy coffee squares

1 cup light raisins
⅔ cup strong coffee
1½ cups sifted flour
½ tsp. each: baking powder, baking soda, allspice, cinnamon
¼ tsp. salt
⅔ cup butter or margarine
1 cup sugar
2 eggs

Frosting:
2 cups sifted confectioners' sugar
¼ cup cold, strong coffee

Combine raisins and hot coffee. Let stand 10 minutes. Sift together flour and seasonings. In a mixing bowl, cream butter and sugar. Beat in eggs, one at a time. Add dry ingredients alternately with raisin mixture; begin and end with flour mixture. Spread batter into a greased 10 x 15 x 1-inch baking sheet. Bake at 350° for 25 minutes. While warm, but not hot, spread with Frosting. Cool and cut into squares.

For Frosting: Combine sugar and coffee in a mixing bowl; beat until smooth.

Makes 35 squares

fudge brownies with fudge frosting

Brownies:
1 cup margarine
4 squares unsweetened chocolate
1½ cups plus 2 T. sifted flour
½ tsp. baking powder
1 tsp. salt
4 eggs, beaten
2 cups sugar
1 tsp. vanilla
¾ cup chopped nuts

Fudge Frosting:
2 squares unsweetened chocolate
3 T. butter
5 T. milk

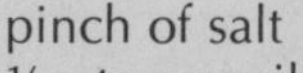

pinch of salt
½ tsp. vanilla
2 cups confectioners' sugar

For Brownies: In a saucepan, melt margarine and chocolate. Set aside and cool. In a bowl, sift together flour, baking powder and salt. In a separate bowl, beat eggs; add sugar and vanilla. Stir in chocolate mixture. Add dry ingredients and mix well. Add nuts. Turn into greased 9 x 13 x 1½-inch pan. Bake at 375° for 30 minutes. Cool before frosting.

For Fudge Frosting: Combine chocolate, butter and milk in top of double boiler; stir until blended. Add salt and vanilla. Stir in sugar; beat to spreading consistency. Spread on Brownies.

Makes 2 dozen

croatian pita

Meringue-topped apricot squares, perfect for all occasions. Especially nice to have for weekend guests.

1 cup butter
1 cup sugar
6 egg yolks
2½ cups sifted flour
1 tsp. baking powder
1 jar (12 oz.) apricot jam

Topping:
6 egg whites
1 cup sugar
½ cup ground walnuts
confectioners' sugar

In a large bowl, cream butter and sugar. Add egg yolks, one at a time; beat well. Sift flour and baking powder. Add to batter and mix by hand. Pat into a 10 x 15-inch jelly roll pan. (Dough is quite heavy.) Smooth and cover thinly with jam.

For Topping: Beat egg whites until foamy. Gradually add sugar; beat until stiff. Fold in walnuts. Spread mixture over jam. Do not seal over edges of pan as you may get a steam pocket while baking. Bake at 350° for 25 to 30 minutes. When cool, cut into 1½-inch squares. Sprinkle lightly with confectioners' sugar.

Makes 2 dozen

million dollar bars

Moist, delicious dessert bars that stay fresh for days.

Cookie Bars:
⅓ cup cocoa
2 cups sugar
1½ cups flour
¼ tsp. salt
1 cup melted butter or margarine
4 eggs, beaten
1 tsp. vanilla
1½ cups chopped walnuts
miniature marshmallows

Cocoa Frosting:
1 pkg. (1 lb.) confectioners' sugar
⅓ cup cocoa
½ cup melted margarine
⅓ cup milk
1 tsp. vanilla

For Cookie Bars: Mix together cocoa, sugar, flour and salt. Add melted margarine, beaten eggs, vanilla and walnuts. Mix well. Spread mixture in a greased and floured 15½ x 10½-inch jelly roll pan. Bake at 350° for 25 minutes. Remove from oven and place a layer of miniature marshmallows on top. Move rack to lowest setting in oven. Broil for 1 minute, *watching constantly.* Do not place too near heat as they should melt, not brown. Cool completely. Spread with Cocoa Frosting. Cut into bars.

For Cocoa Frosting: Combine all ingredients in a mixing bowl; beat until smooth.

Makes 2 dozen

caramel layer choco-squares

1 pkg. (16 oz.) light caramels
⅔ cup evaporated milk, divided
1 pkg. German chocolate cake mix
⅔ cup softened butter
½ cup chopped nuts
1 pkg. (12 oz.) chocolate chips

In a heavy saucepan, melt caramels in ⅓ cup of milk over low heat; set aside. In a large bowl, combine remaining ingredients, except chocolate chips. Mix until dough is crumbly but holds together. Press *half* the dough into a greased and floured 9 × 13-inch pan. Bake at 350° for 6 minutes. Remove from oven. Sprinkle chocolate chips over dough. Pour caramel mixture over chips. Top with remaining dough. Bake for 15 to 20 minutes. Chill.

Makes 2 dozen

butterscotch brownies with caramel frosting

¾ cup melted butter
2 cups firmly packed light brown sugar
3 eggs
2 cups flour
2 tsp. baking powder
¼ tsp. salt
1 tsp. vanilla
1 cup chopped pecans
1 pkg. (6 oz.) butterscotch chips

Caramel Frosting:
½ cup butter
½ cup firmly packed light brown sugar
¼ cup half-and-half cream
2 cups confectioners' sugar
1 tsp. vanilla

Combine butter and sugar in large bowl; beat until creamy smooth. Add eggs one at a time. Beat thoroughly after each addition. Sift together flour, baking powder and salt. Add to above mixture and beat until well blended. Stir in vanilla, nuts and butterscotch chips. Spread in greased and floured 9 x 13-inch pan. Bake at 350° for 20 to 25 minutes. May serve plain or sprinkled with confectioners' sugar or spread with Caramel Frosting.

For Caramel Frosting: In a medium-size saucepan, melt butter until brown. Add brown sugar. Stir constantly until melted. Pour in cream. Mix well. Cool. Add confectioners' sugar and vanilla. Beat until thick enough to spread.

Makes 32 bars

crisp danish lace cookies

Almond flavored with a hint of orange.

½ cup plus 1 T. sifted flour
½ cup sugar
¼ tsp. baking powder
½ cup uncooked quick rolled oats
⅓ cup melted butter
2 T. whipping cream
2 T. light corn syrup
2 tsp. vanilla
1 tsp. almond extract
1 tsp. finely grated orange peel

Sift flour, sugar and baking powder together into a large mixing bowl. Add rolled oats, butter, whipping cream, corn syrup, vanilla, almond extract and orange peel; mix well. Drop by ½ teaspoonfuls onto ungreased cookie sheet. Space 4 inches apart. Bake at 350° for 6 to 8 minutes. Cool for a few seconds. When slightly firm, remove quickly to wire rack with a flexible metal spatula.

Makes 6 dozen

grandmother gilmore's skillet cookies

A no-bake date-nut cookie.

½ cup butter or margarine
1 cup chopped dates
1 cup sugar
1 egg, slightly beaten
2 cups crisp rice cereal
1 cup chopped nuts
1 tsp. vanilla
3 oz. shredded coconut

In a large skillet, melt the butter or margarine. Add dates, sugar and egg. Stir constantly over low heat for 5 minutes. Remove from heat. Add cereal, nuts and vanilla. Mix thoroughly. Take a small amount on a teaspoon and dip in coconut. Roll in hands to form a ball. Place on a cookie sheet that has been lined with wax paper. Cool for 10 minutes. These cookies are a little sticky. They can be stored in the refrigerator, if desired.

Makes 4 dozen

dempse

A delicate almond-butter cookie of European origin.

2 cups softened butter
1 cup sugar
1½ cups finely ground almonds
4 cups flour
1 jar (10 oz.) currant jelly
confectioners' sugar

Combine the first 4 ingredients in a mixing bowl. Mix with pastry blender and hands until dough forms into a solid ball. Shape dough into 3 or 4 rolls, 1½-inch in diameter. Wrap in wax paper and refrigerate for several hours or overnight. Cut into ⅛-inch slices; place on ungreased baking sheets. Bake at 350° for 8 to 10 minutes or until cookies begin to brown. Remove from pan immediately. Cool. Put flat sides together with currant jelly. Cookies are delicate and must be handled carefully when spreading with jelly. Sprinkle both sides with confectioners' sugar. If possible, store in tin container. Before serving, sprinkle with additional sugar, if desired. Dough may be made ahead and frozen several weeks before baking.

Makes 7 to 8 dozen

monster cookies

Texas-size goodies . . . made *without* flour. Great for kids' parties or anytime.

6 eggs
2¼ cups light brown sugar
2 cups sugar
1½ tsp. vanilla
1½ tsp. light corn syrup
4 tsp. baking soda
1 cup butter (*not* margarine)
3 cups peanut butter
9 cups uncooked rolled oats
1 cup semi-sweet chocolate chips
1 cup M & M's candies

In a large bowl, mix all ingredients in order listed. Drop dough from well-rounded tablespoon (or use small ice cream scoop) onto ungreased cookie sheet. Flatten cookies. Place only 6 cookies on baking sheet. Bake at 350° for 12 minutes. Do not overbake. Allow to cool on sheet for 1 minute to avoid breaking cookies. These freeze well.

Makes 6 dozen

kieflies

A Hungarian cookie that is well worth the effort.

Cookie:
6 cups flour
1½ tsp. salt
1 lb. butter
12 egg yolks, whites reserved
1 cup sour cream
1 tsp. vanilla

Filling:
12 egg whites
3½ cups (1 lb.) confectioners' sugar
6 cups (1½ lbs.) chopped nuts

For Cookie: Mix flour and salt together. Cut butter into flour mixture until completely blended. In a separate bowl, mix egg yolks, sour cream and vanilla. Add to flour and butter mixture. Blend and knead until mixture is consistency of pie dough. Form into small walnut size balls. Refrigerate.

For Filling: Beat egg whites until stiff. Add sugar and beat well. Stir in nuts. Refrigerate.

To assemble: Take a few balls from the refrigerator. Roll each ball into a thin circle on well-floured surface. Place a heaping teaspoon of Filling on each circle. Roll up into crescent shape and pinch ends. Bake at 350° for 12 minutes. Cool and sprinkle with confectioners' sugar.

Makes 6 dozen

butterscotch refrigerator cookies

A good, rich cookie with a crunch.

1 pkg. (6 oz.) butterscotch chips
½ cup butter
⅔ cup light brown sugar
1 egg
1½ cups flour
¾ tsp. baking soda

Melt butterscotch chips in a saucepan over low heat; set aside. In a medium bowl, cream butter until soft. Add sugar gradually and blend until very light and creamy. Beat in egg and melted butterscotch. Sift together flour and baking soda; add gradually to other ingredients. Mix well. Shape dough into long roll, 2-inches in diameter. Place on piece of foil and wrap. Chill dough overnight. Slice thinly for baking. Bake at 375° on greased cookie sheet for 8 to 10 minutes.

Makes 4 dozen

rolled spice cookies

A delicious Halloween, Thanksgiving and Christmas cut-out.

1 cup sugar
¼ cup dark corn syrup
2 tsp. each: cinnamon, cloves, nutmeg
⅓ cup water
1 cup softened butter
4 cups sifted flour
1 tsp. baking soda
¼ tsp. salt

Combine sugar, syrup and spices with water in a large saucepan. Bring mixture to boil; remove from heat and add butter. Cool for 30 minutes. Combine dry ingredients; add to cooled mixture. Mix with wooden spoon until flour disappears. Form dough into ball. Wrap in wax paper and chill 2 hours or more. Roll ¼-inch thick on floured surface. Cut into shapes. Bake on greased baking sheets at 350° for 6 to 8 minutes. Cool and decorate as desired.

Makes 4 dozen

oatmeal cookies

Light, delicate and delicious.

1 cup butter
½ cup sugar
1 cup flour
1½ cups uncooked rolled oats
confectioners' sugar

Cream together butter and sugar. Add flour and rolled oats. Form into 1-inch balls and place on ungreased cookie sheet. Flatten balls with fork. Bake at 350° for 10 minutes. Sprinkle with confectioners' sugar.

Makes 4 dozen

the sugar cookie

1 cup margarine or butter
1 cup vegetable oil
1 cup sugar
1 cup confectioners' sugar
2 eggs
1½ tsp. vanilla
4 cups flour
1 tsp. salt
1 tsp. cream of tartar
1 tsp. baking powder
granulated sugar for sprinkling on top

In a large mixing bowl, cream margarine, oil and sugars. Blend in eggs and vanilla. Sift together dry ingredients; blend into creamed mixture. Drop by heaping teaspoonfuls onto ungreased cookie sheets. Press down with a spiral shaped whisk. Sprinkle with granulated sugar before and after baking. Bake at 350° for 12 to 15 minutes or until cookies begin to brown lightly.

Makes 7 dozen

molasses sugar cookies

1 cup sugar
¾ cup butter or margarine
½ cup molasses
1 egg
2 cups sifted flour
2 tsp. baking soda
1 tsp. each: cinnamon, cloves, ginger

With electric mixer, cream sugar and shortening until fluffy. Beat in molasses and egg. Sift together flour, baking soda and spices in a separate bowl. Gradually add flour mixture to creamed ingredients. Mix well. Refrigerate until firm. Lightly flour hands as dough will be sticky. Shape dough into 1-inch balls and roll in granulated sugar. Place on lightly greased cookie sheet. Bake 9 to 11 minutes at 375°. Allow cookies to cool for 1 minute before removing from cookie sheet.

Makes 4 dozen

candy coated pecan halves

Easy-to-make gift from the kitchen. It even travels well in the mail.

1 cup firmly packed brown sugar
½ cup sugar
½ cup sour cream
1 tsp. vanilla
dash cinnamon
2½ cups pecans

In a saucepan, combine the 2 sugars and sour cream. Stirring constantly, cook to soft ball stage (234°F.). Remove from heat. Add vanilla and cinnamon. Beat until mixture begins to thicken. Add nuts, stirring until well coated. Turn out on a well-buttered cookie sheet. When cool, break into bite-size pieces.

Variation: Can use walnut halves.

Makes 2 dozen pieces

mom's favorite fudge

Makes enough to last through the holidays!

1 (8 oz.) large, plain milk chocolate bar
2 squares (2 oz.) unsweetened chocolate
1 pkg. (12 oz.) chocolate chips
2 cups chopped nuts
1 jar (16 oz.) marshmallow creme
1 T. vanilla
1 can (13 oz.) evaporated milk
4½ cups sugar
½ cup butter
½ cup margarine

Break into pieces the chocolate bar and chocolate squares. Place in a large bowl with the chocolate chips, nuts, marshmallow creme and vanilla. In a large, heavy saucepan, place the evaporated milk, sugar, butter and margarine. Bring mixture to a *full, rolling* boil; boil for 6 minutes. Pour over mixture in bowl; stir until chocolate is well melted and ingredients are blended. Pour into 2 greased 9 x 12 x 2-inch pans to set. Cut into squares when cool.

Makes about 4 pounds

peanut butter bonbons

½ cup softened margarine
3½ cups confectioners' sugar
2 cups chunky peanut butter
3 cups slightly crushed Rice Krispies
1 pkg. (12 oz.) chocolate or butterscotch chips
½ bar parafin

In large bowl, combine margarine, sugar, peanut butter and Rice Krispies. Mix well. Form into balls and chill at least 2 hours. Melt chocolate or butterscotch chips and parafin in double boiler. Dip balls on toothpicks into melted mixture and lift out onto wax paper to cool and set. (May also lift balls out of mixture with a fork.) Store candy in a covered container in a cool place or refrigerate. May be frozen.

Makes about 75 balls

peanut clusters

½ cup peanut butter
1 cup chocolate chips
1½ cups peanuts

In top of double boiler, melt chocolate chips and peanut butter. Add peanuts and mix well. Drop by spoonfuls on wax paper and chill.

Makes 30 candies

holiday peppermint meringues

An easy and unusual candy-cookie.

4 egg whites
¼ tsp. cream of tartar
1¼ cups sugar
½ tsp. peppermint extract
red food color
green food color

In a small bowl, beat egg whites until foamy with cream of tartar. Add sugar in ¼-cup portions, beating well after each addition. Add peppermint and continue beating until mixture stands in stiff peaks; divide in half. Tint one-half with a few drops red food color; tint second half with a few drops green food color. Spoon heaping teaspoonfuls onto heavy brown paper on baking sheet. Bake at 250° for 30 to 40 minutes or until set but not brown. An excellent way to use leftover egg whites any time of the year. Can omit food color and substitute other flavorings.

Makes 5 dozen

crunchy cashew nuggets

1 cup softened butter or margarine
½ cup confectioners' sugar
1 tsp. vanilla
2 cups sifted flour
1 cup chopped cashews
confectioners' sugar

Combine butter or margarine, sugar and vanilla in a mixing bowl. Beat until light and fluffy. Add flour and cashews; mix until dough forms a solid ball. Shape dough into 1-inch balls. Place on ungreased baking sheet. Bake at 350° for 10 to 12 minutes or until set but not browned. Roll in or sprinkle with confectioners' sugar while warm. Sprinkle with additional sugar before serving, if necessary.

Makes 3 dozen

caramel popcorn

2 cups brown sugar
½ cup light corn syrup
1 cup butter or margarine
½ tsp. baking soda
pinch of salt
½ tsp. vanilla
8 quarts popped corn

In a small saucepan, combine the sugar, syrup and butter. Bring to boil and boil 5 minutes. Remove from heat. Stir in baking soda, salt and vanilla. Pour mixture over popcorn in a 10-quart pan. Mix well. Bake at 225° for 1 hour, stirring every 15 minutes.

Makes 8 quarts

english toffee

A delicious and not-extremely-hard-textured toffee.

1 cup sugar
½ lb. butter or margarine
3 T. water
1 tsp. vanilla
3 bars (1.2 oz. each) milk chocolate, at room temperature
¾ cup chopped pecans

Place sugar, butter or margarine and water in a saucepan. Cook over low heat for 10 minutes until syrup is golden, stirring constantly. Remove from heat; stir in vanilla. Pour into a buttered 9 x 13-inch pan. Lay chocolate bars over the hot mixture; spread evenly. While warm, sprinkle nuts over top. Cool for several hours. Break into pieces.

Makes about 1 pound

lee's original peanut brittle

Best if made on a cool, sunny day.

1 cup white sugar
1 cup light corn syrup
1-1½ cups raw Spanish peanuts
1 tsp. salt
1 tsp. baking soda

Grease an aluminum cookie sheet onto which cooked candy can be poured. In a heavy skillet, combine sugar, syrup and peanuts. Bring to boil over medium heat. Stir often to prevent mixture from burning. Test often by making a smear on top of the stove to test syrup for brittleness. It will pop like glass when picked up in fingers and broken. When mixture becomes brittle, continue stirring. Add salt and soda, stirring well after each addition. Remove from heat. Stir well. Pour onto cookie sheet. As candy cools, start at edges to pull off pieces. Cut it loose. Stretch as thinly as possible. Place on a cool table. Continue process until all is cut and pulled. Store in covered tin.

Makes 1½ pounds

pralines

2 cups sugar
¾ tsp. baking soda
1 cup half-and-half cream
1½ T. butter
2 cups pecan halves
1 T. hot water, if necessary

In a deep 3-quart saucepan, combine sugar and soda. Mix well. Add cream. Stir carefully over low heat to keep sugar crystals in lower part of pan. Put lid on pan 2 to 3 minutes to wash down any sugar crystals. All crystals should be dissolved when candy boils. Bring to boil over medium heat, stirring occasionally to prevent scorching. Cook candy until it forms a soft ball in cold water or registers 234° on candy thermometer. Remove pan from heat. Add butter immediately. Measure accurately, as too much butter will prevent pralines from firming. Add pecan halves. Beat 2 to 3 minutes until mixture is thick enough to drop from a spoon. Drop candy on wax paper or aluminum foil. If necessary, add 1 tablespoon or more hot water to keep candy at right stage for dropping from spoon. Wrap in foil. Store in tightly covered container.

Makes 2 to 2½ dozen 1½-inch patties.

taffy-pull taffy

Children love this!

1¼ cups granulated sugar
¼ cup water
2 T. mild vinegar
1½ tsp. butter
½ tsp. flavoring (orange, peppermint, etc.)

Combine all the ingredients *except the flavoring* in a saucepan. Cook without stirring to 268°-270° or between the very hard ball and light crack stage. Add choice of flavoring. Pour candy onto a large, buttered platter. Cool until finger imprint can be seen or until candy can be handled. Butter hands. Pull taffy; join ends held in hands and pull again. Repeat process until taffy has a satin-like sheen. Form into shapes, rolls or braids. Cut into bite-size pieces. If creamy candy is desired, store in an air-tight container.

Makes 2 dozen pieces

peanut-butterscotch drops

A candy-like cookie . . . simple enough for children to prepare.

2 pkgs. (6 oz. each) butterscotch chips
½ cup peanut butter
6 cups corn flake cereal

Melt butterscotch chips and peanut butter together in large saucepan over low heat. Remove from heat. Add cornflakes; mix well until the flakes are coated. Shape small amounts (1 heaping teaspoonful) into balls and place on wax paper. Refrigerate 1 hour or until mixture holds together.

Makes 3½ to 4 dozen

vanilla caramels

Rich and creamy.

2 cups sugar
¾ cup light corn syrup
½ cup butter or margarine
2 cups whipping cream, divided
1 tsp. vanilla
1 cup nuts (optional)

In a heavy pan or Dutch oven, combine sugar, corn syrup, butter and 1 cup of the whipping cream. Stir until ingredients come to a full boil. Gradually add remaining cream, stirring constantly. Do not stop the boiling. Heat to 242° F. on candy thermometer, about 20 minutes. Add vanilla and nuts. Pour into well-greased 8 x 8-inch pan. When completely cooled, cut into small squares and wrap in wax paper.

Makes 60 to 80 pieces

homemade apple butter

Delicious—the best apple butter in Indiana.

1 peck or 24 lbs. apples
1 pkg. (12 oz.) cinnamon candies
16 cups sugar
3 T. cinnamon
1 T. ground cloves

Pare apples and quarter. Cook until very tender with a little water in a Dutch oven. Puree the cooked apples through a food mill. Measure 30 cups of the puree into an enameled roaster pan. *Never use an aluminum pan.* While still warm, stir in cinnamon candies, sugar, cinnamon and cloves. Mix well. Bake mixture at 350° for 30 minutes. Reduce temperature to 325° and cook for 3½ to 5 hours depending on the type of apples and how fast the mixture thickens. Stir often as the apple butter has a tendency to cook faster around the edges of the pan. When the apple butter is of a medium-thick consistency, *put directly into hot sterilized glass jars.* Seal jars immediately. Store in a cool dry place.

Makes 20 to 24 pints

new orleans hot pepper jelly

A convenient, delicious hors d'oeuvre. Spread on top of cream cheese square and serve with crackers.

1½ cups chopped green pepper, seeded
¼ cup chopped *hot* pepper jalapeno
6½ cups sugar
1½ cups cider vinegar
1 bottle (6 oz.) liquid pectin
5 drops green or red food color

Put chopped peppers into blender; puree. Pour puree into Dutch oven or large pan. Add sugar and vinegar; boil for 3 minutes. Add pectin; boil for 1 minute, stirring constantly. Pour through strainer if clear jelly is desired. Add food color. Remove foam from top of jelly mixture with a metal spoon. Pour into jelly jars and seal.

Note: After opening, jelly keeps indefinitely in refrigerator. Nice to give for Christmas gifts, bazaar sale or as a thank you gesture to a dinner hostess.

Makes 6 cups

substitutions

Ingredient	*Amount*	*Substitution*
baking powder	1 teaspoon	¼ teaspoon baking soda plus ½ cup buttermilk Lessen liquid by ½ cup. ¼ teaspoon baking soda plus ½ teaspoon cream of tartar
butter	1 cup	1 cup margarine ⅞-1 cup hydrogenated fat plus ½ teaspoon salt ⅞-1 cup lard plus ½ teaspoon salt ⅞ cup rendered fat plus ½ teaspoon salt
chocolate, unsweetened	1 ounce square	3 tablespoons cocoa plus 1 tablespoon shortening
chocolate, semi-sweet	1 ounce square	3 tablespoons cocoa plus 1 tablespoon shortening plus 4 teaspoons sugar, or 1 ounce square unsweetened chocolate plus 4 teaspoons sugar
cornstarch	1½ teaspoons	1 tablespoon flour
cream, half-and-half	1 cup	3 tablespoons butter plus about ⅞ cup milk
cream, whipping	1 cup	⅓ cup butter plus about ¾ cup milk
cream, sour	1 cup	⅓ cup butter plus ⅔ cup milk
egg	1 whole	2 egg yolks plus 1 tablespoon water
flour, all-purpose (for thickening)	1 tablespoon	½ tablespoon cornstarch, potato-flour; or 2 teaspoons quick-cooking tapioca

flour, cake	1 cup sifted	1	cup sifted all-purpose flour, less 2 tablespoons
honey	1 cup	1¼	cups sugar plus ¼ cup liquid
milk, whole	1 cup	½	cup evaporated milk plus ½ cup water
		1	cup reconstituted nonfat dry milk plus 2 tablespoons butter
buttermilk or sour milk	1 cup	1	tablespoon vinegar or lemon juice plus enough whole milk to make one cup (let stand 5 minutes)
		1¾	teaspoons cream of tartar plus 1 cup whole milk
sugar	1 cup	1	cup molasses plus ¼-½ teaspoon baking soda. Omit baking powder.
		½	cup maple syrup plus ¼ cup corn syrup. Lessen liquid by 2 tablespoons.
tomatoes	1 cup canned	1⅓	cups cut-up fresh tomatoes, simmered 10 minutes
yogurt	1 cup	1	cup buttermilk

metrics and equivalents

Weight Equivalents in Grams

1 gram = 0.035 ounces
1 kilogram = 2.21 pounds
1 microgram = 0.001 milligrams
1 milligram =1000 micrograms
1 gram =1000 milligrams
1 ounce =28.35 grams
1 pound =453.59 grams

Metric Liquid-Measure Volume Equivalents

1 pint =.4732 liters
1 quart = .9464 liters
1 quart = 946.4 milliliters
1 liter = 1000 milliliters or 1.06 quarts
1 gallon = 3.785 liters
1 cup = 237 milliliters or ¼ liter, approximately
1 teaspoon = 5 milliliters
1 tablespoon = 14.8 milliliters
16⅔ tablespoons = 1 liter

Metric Dry-Measure Volume Equivalents

1 pint = .551 liters
1 quart = 1.101 liters
1 peck = 8.81 liters
1 bushel = 35.24 liters

Fahrenheit to Centigrade Conversions

To convert Fahrenheit to Centigrade:
subtract 32, multiply by 5, divide by 9.
To convert Centigrade to Fahrenheit:
multiply by 9, divide by 5, add 32.

1 teaspoon = ⅓ tablespoon
1 tablespoon = 3 teaspoons
2 tablespoons = 1 fluid ounce
4 tablespoons = ¼ cup
5⅓ tablespoons = ⅓ cup
8 tablespoons = ½ cup or 4 ounces
16 tablespoons = 1 cup or 8 ounces
1 cup = ½ pint or 8 ounces
2 cups = 1 pint
4 cups = 1 quart
1 pint, liquid = 16 fluid ounces
1 quart, liquid = 2 pints
1 gallon, liquid = 4 quarts
8 quarts, dry measure = 1 peck
4 pecks, dry measure = 1 bushel

acknowledgments

To the great photographers of an earlier era who captured the unique warmth and spirit of Americana, we owe our gratitude. Equal indebtedness is acknowledged to the individuals and institutions who made available to us photographs from their treasured collections. Page references in parentheses indicate where the pictures appear in the book.

The Alfrey Family, Syracuse, Indiana (24, 232)
The Bettmann Archive, New York, New York (156)
William A. Bradford, Goshen, Indiana (8)
Brown Brothers, Sterling, Pennsylvania (title page, 158, back cover)
Culver Pictures, New York, New York (108, 142)
Mr. and Mrs. Karl Freese, Nappanee, Indiana (154)
Mr. and Mrs. John C. Frieden, South Bend, Indiana (150)
Mr. and Mrs. Jerry Hubner, South Bend, Indiana (42, 160, 290)
The Mott Family, Warren, Indiana (front cover)
The Northern Indiana Historical Society, South Bend, Indiana (62, 270)
Library of Congress, Prints and Photographs Division, Washington, D. C. (128, 140, 146, 256)
Photographic Archives, University of Louisville, Louisville, Kentucky (152, 246)
Historical Room of the Nappanee Public Library, Nappanee, Indiana (30, 82, 186)
New Haven Colony Historical Society, New Haven, Connecticut (206)
Mrs. Edward A. Rodgers, South Bend, Indiana (144)
Syracuse Public Library, Syracuse, Indiana (148)

The sources for the section divider quotations are indicated below.
Manners and Customs of Today by Mrs. Sara B. Maxwell. Published by The Cline Publishing House, Des Moines, Iowa, 1890.
Our Home Cyclopedia published by The Merchantile Publishing Co., Detroit, Michigan, 1890.
Practical Housekeeping published by The Buckeye Publishing Co., 1886.

JELL-O
Five pure fruit flavors
5¢
OLD GOLD
DUTCH MASTERS
fine as any imported cigar
DUTCH MASTERS
fine as any imported cigar

index

BACK COVER: BROWN BROTHERS

nutbread and nostalgia

the junior league of south bend, inc.
p.o. box 305
south bend, indiana 46624

e send me ________ copies at $11.95 each (for Indiana
eries add $.60 sales tax) plus $1.75 per book for postage.
sed is my check or money order for ____________________.
checks payable to The Junior League of South Bend, Inc.

eck if gift wrapping at $.50 per book is desired.

____

ss ______________________________________

nd State ____________________ Zip __________

nutbread and nostalgia

the junior league of south bend, inc.
p.o. box 305
south bend, indiana 46624

Please send me ________ copies at $11.95 each (for Indiana deliveries add $.60 sales tax) plus $1.75 per book for postage. Enclosed is my check or money order for ____________________. Make checks payable to The Junior League of South Bend, Inc.

☐ Check if gift wrapping at $.50 per book is desired.

Name ____

Address ______________________________________

City and State ____________________ Zip __________

nutbread and nostalgia

the junior league of south bend, inc.
p.o. box 305
south bend, indiana 46624

e send me ________ copies at $11.95 each (for Indiana
eries add $.60 sales tax) plus $1.75 per book for postage.
sed is my check or money order for ____________________.
checks payable to The Junior League of South Bend, Inc.

eck if gift wrapping at $.50 per book is desired.

____

ss ______________________________________

nd State ____________________ Zip __________

nutbread and nostalgia

the junior league of south bend, inc.
p.o. box 305
south bend, indiana 46624

Please send me ________ copies at $11.95 each (for Indiana deliveries add $.60 sales tax) plus $1.75 per book for postage. Enclosed is my check or money order for ____________________. Make checks payable to The Junior League of South Bend, Inc.

☐ Check if gift wrapping at $.50 per book is desired.

Name ____

Address ______________________________________

City and State ____________________ Zip __________

nutbread and nostalgia

the junior league of south bend, inc.
p.o. box 305
south bend, indiana 46624

e send me ________ copies at $11.95 each (for Indiana
eries add $.60 sales tax) plus $1.75 per book for postage.
sed is my check or money order for ____________________.
checks payable to The Junior League of South Bend, Inc.

eck if gift wrapping at $.50 per book is desired.

e ____

ss ____

nd State ________________________ Zip ____________

nutbread and nostalgia

the junior league of south bend, inc.
p.o. box 305
south bend, indiana 46624

Please send me ________ copies at $11.95 each (for Indiana deliveries add $.60 sales tax) plus $1.75 per book for postage. Enclosed is my check or money order for ____________________. Make checks payable to The Junior League of South Bend, Inc.

☐ Check if gift wrapping at $.50 per book is desired.

Name ____

Address ____

City and State ________________________ Zip ____________

nutbread and nostalgia

the junior league of south bend, inc.
p.o. box 305
south bend, indiana 46624

e send me ________ copies at $11.95 each (for Indiana
eries add $.60 sales tax) plus $1.75 per book for postage.
sed is my check or money order for ____________________.
checks payable to The Junior League of South Bend, Inc.

eck if gift wrapping at $.50 per book is desired.

e ____

ss ____

nd State ________________________ Zip ____________

nutbread and nostalgia

the junior league of south bend, inc.
p.o. box 305
south bend, indiana 46624

Please send me ________ copies at $11.95 each (for Indiana deliveries add $.60 sales tax) plus $1.75 per book for postage. Enclosed is my check or money order for ____________________. Make checks payable to The Junior League of South Bend, Inc.

☐ Check if gift wrapping at $.50 per book is desired.

Name ____

Address ____

City and State ________________________ Zip ____________